KAZAKHSTAN

CAUCASUS

Caspian
Sea

GEORGIA
Tblisi ★

ARMENIA   AZERBAIJAN
Yerevan ★   ★ Baku   TURKMENISTAN

ELBURZ   MTS.
★ Tehran

Tigris

IRAN

Baghdad ★
IRAQ

kcomp, Inc.

Map of the Caucasus. Cartography by Bo

Culture and Customs
of the Caucasus

PETER L. ROUDIK

713703

Culture and Customs of Europe

GREENWOOD PRESS
Westport, Connecticut • London

Library of Congress Cataloging-in-Publication Data

Roudik, Peter L.
    Culture and customs of the Caucasus / Peter L. Roudik.
        p.   cm.—(Culture and customs of Europe)
    Includes bibliographical references and index.
    ISBN 978–0–313–34885–3 (alk. paper)
    1. Caucasus-Social life and customs.   2. Caucasus-Civilization.   I. Title.   II. Series.
    DK509.R68   2009
    947.5—dc22   2008033459

British Library Cataloguing in Publication Data is available.

Library of Congress Catalog Card Number: 2008033459
ISBN: 978–0–313–34885–3

First published in 2009

Greenwood Press, 88 Post Road West, Westport, CT 06881
An imprint of Greenwood Publishing Group, Inc.
www.greenwood.com

Printed in the United States of America

The paper used in this book complies with the
Permanent Paper Standard issued by the National
Information Standards Organization (Z39.48–1984).

10 9 8 7 6 5 4 3 2 1

Contents

Series Foreword

THE OLD WORLD and the New World have maintained a fluid exchange of people, ideas, innovations, and styles. Even though the United States became the de facto world leader and economic superpower in the wake of a devastated Europe in World War II, Europe has remained for many the standard bearer of Western culture.

Millions of Americans can trace their ancestors to Europe. The United States as we know it was built on waves of European immigration, starting with the English who braved the seas to found the Jamestown Colony in 1607. Bosnian and Albanian immigrants are some of the latest new Americans.

In the Gilded Age of one of our great expatriates, the novelist Henry James, the Grand Tour of Europe was de rigueur for young American men of means, to prepare them for a life of refinement and taste. In a more recent democratic age, scores of American college students have Eurailed their way across Great Britain and the Continent, sampling the fabled capitals and bergs in a mad, great adventure, or have benefited from a semester abroad. For other American vacationers and culture vultures, Europe is the prime destination.

What is the New Europe post–Cold War, post–Berlin Wall in a new millennium? Even with the different languages, rhythms, and rituals, Europeans have much in common: they are largely well educated, prosperous, and worldly. They also have similar goals and face common threats and form alliances. With the advent of the European Union, the open borders, and the Euro and considering globalization and the prospect of a homogenized Europe, an updated survey of the region is warranted.

Culture and Customs of Europe features individual volumes on the countries most studied and for which fresh information is in demand from students and other readers. The Series casts a wide net, inclusive of not only the expected countries, such as Spain, France, England, and Germany, but also countries such as Poland and Greece that lie outside Western Europe proper. Each volume is written by a country specialist, with intimate knowledge of the contemporary dynamics of a people and culture. Sustained narrative chapters cover the land, people, and brief history; religion; social customs; gender roles, family, and marriage; literature and media; performing arts and cinema; and art and architecture. The national character and ongoing popular traditions of each country are framed in an historical context and celebrated along with the latest trends and major cultural figures. A country map, chronology, glossary, and evocative photos enhance the text.

The historied and enlightened Europeans will continue to fascinate Americans. Our futures are strongly linked politically, economically, and culturally.

Preface

EVERYBODY KNOWS ABOUT Noah's ark, the Golden Fleece, the Nobel Prize, and Joseph Stalin, but not many realize what all of them have in common. Noah's ark finished its floating at the summit of Mount Ararat, Armenia's national symbol; the legend of the Golden Fleece brought the Greek Argonauts to Colchis, an ancient state on the easternmost shore of the Black Sea; Alfred Nobel made his money extracting oil in Azerbaijan; and Comrade Stalin was born and spent his formative years in Georgia, then a southern province of the Russian empire. Today, all these places are covered by one word, *Transcaucasus*, which has been the subject of numerous scholarly discussions and many controversial attempts to define it. For the purpose of this book, by the words *Transcaucasus*, *Transcaucasia*, or *South Caucasus*, I mean the three newly independent former Soviet republics of Armenia, Azerbaijan, and Georgia, tied together by geographic proximity, as well as political, cultural, and economic connections. However, these factors in no way are commonalities, and they have often led to almost irreconcilable differences.

A region slightly larger than New England, Transcaucasus is a unique model of economic and political reforms, religious tolerance, and active civil society. The countries are democratic and secular, but religion is an important factor in all three states, and should be taken into account by all political and social forces. Although geographically the region is the easternmost outpost of Europe, for many the question of where Transcaucasus really belongs is still unanswered, though the region's future substantially depends on the answer. Most of the people in the Transcaucasus see themselves as closer to the

Western world in culture, lifestyle, political aspirations, and values, although historically they have much in common with their immediate neighbors in the Middle East. Relatively peaceful coexistence (in many ongoing conflicts in the region, religion is not the major factor) of three world faiths—Judaism, Christianity, and Islam—and their constant and sometimes close interaction transform this territory into a unique zone where different cultural traditions are preserved and continue to develop.

Hidden high in the mountains between two seas, the region was always of interest to the great powers. Alexander the Great, Genghis Khan, Turkish sultans, Persian shahs, and British and Russian crowns were among those who attempted to establish control over the territory. Today, the region remains the focus of world attention because of its proximity to the area of major antiterrorist operations and vital American interests. An active Armenian diaspora, efforts of the world community to resolve the territorial dispute between Armenia and Azerbaijan, business interests of major oil companies in Azerbaijan, and the political activity of the Georgians contribute to the interest of the world media in the region.

Hundreds of volumes have been written on the history of these states and their contemporary developments. Some aspects of their social and cultural lives were analyzed in books published in the Soviet Union. However, this part of the world, squeezed between Russia, Iran, and Turkey, remains largely unknown to the general public, especially the cultural traditions, scholarly achievements, and developments in art. As its title suggests, this book does not focus on governmental institutions, the political situation, economic trends, or security policies. Rather, it focuses on customs and the modern culture of reemerged independent states, as well as their attempts to respond to today's international challenges through national theater, music, literature, and art. The book reviews the historical roots of the region's national cultures and, to understand the history, destiny, and identity of the people, analyzes two major philosophers of the twentieth century: the Georgian Merab Mamardashvili and the Armenian Vladik Nersesiants.

My goal is to present the evolving, dynamic, and diverse cultures and customs of the people of the Caucasus republics and to show their small but important presence in the world. In my research I relied on existing American and foreign publications, which are listed in the bibliography and can be of help to those who want to learn more about the scholarly foundations of Transcaucasian cultures, and on conversations with my friends and colleagues in the United States and in the Transcaucasus region. My field trips to these countries at times of peace and war were the best sources of information. Better than any study, my personal impressions influenced the conclusions reflected in this book; all opinions expressed in this book are solely mine and do not represent the position of my employer.

Library of Congress rules of transliteration were used in this book for foreign words and personal names because there is no universally accepted system for romanizing the various languages. All personal names appear with the first name followed by the last name. Because of inconsistencies in citing Azerbaijani personal names in Russian and indigenous forms, the most commonly used name is given in the book. Dates of birth and death are provided for all major figures. The date system used is B.C. and A.D., though the A.D. notification is used only when the identification of a date can be confusing.

The Russo-Georgian war of August 2008 and recognition of South Ossetian and Abkhazian state independence by Russia changed the political landscape of the entire region significantly. These events and their consequences are not discussed in this book; all information is accurate through July 2008.

I would like to thank the many people who have helped me in the preparation of this book, but first of all my colleagues at the Library of Congress who took time to discuss the book with me and provided me with invaluable advice. I am especially thankful to friends and scholars Leila Alieva, Anushik Mazmanyan, and Natela Mosesova for their consultations, tips on sources, and personal photographs they kindly offered as illustrations for this book; and to the Budagashvili family for their suggestions on how to make this book better. Also, I appreciate the assistance provided by the staff of the Georgian embassy in the United States, especially that of Natia Zambakhidze.

I would like to extend my special gratitude to Robert Roudik for his editorial assistance, Greenwood Press editor Kaitlin Ciarmiello for her support and encouragement throughout the writing of this book, and Aptara, Inc. for their assistance and cooperation.

As always, this work is dedicated to my wife, Svetlana.

Chronology

MEDIEVAL TIMES

640–ca. 1000	Arabs occupy Azerbaijan.
645	Arabs capture Tbilisi.
653	Byzantine Empire cedes Armenia to the Arabs.
813	Armenian Prince Ashot I begins his 1,000-year rule of Georgia with the Bagratid dynasty.
1008	Bagrat III unites the western and eastern parts of Georgia known as Kartli and Colchis.
1099–1125	David IV the Builder establishes the Georgian empire.
1100s–1300s	Armenian and Georgian armies join European armies in the Crusades.
1223–ca. 1400	The Mongols invade the region.
1501	Azerbaijan introduces Shia Islam as the state religion.
1553	Georgia is divided between the Ottoman Turks and the Persian Empire.
1615–1616	The Persian Shah Abbas kills 60,000 Georgians and deports 100,000.

RUSSIAN COLONIZATION

ca. 1700	Russia starts its conquest of Caucasus.
1747	The Azerbaijani kingdom fragments into khanates.
1762	Eastern Georgian regions unite in the kingdom of Kartli-Kakheti.
1795	Persian forces take Tbilisi and the Georgian King Erekle II turns to Russia for protection.
1801	The Russian Empire dethrones the Bagratid dynasty and annexes Georgia.
1811	The Georgian church loses its autocephalous status due to Russification.
1813	Treaty of Gulistan divides Azerbaijan into Russian (northern) and Persian (southern) spheres.
1828	Treaty of Turkmanchay awards Nakhichevan and area around Yerevan to Russia.
1829–1878	Russia expands its possessions in Transcaucasus.

1846	Private land ownership is legalized in Caucasus.
1859	First oil refinery in the world is built in Baku.
1865	First technical high school and first high school for women open in Baku.
1872	Oil industry in Azerbaijan is privatized.
1875	Foreign capital is introduced in Caucasus.
1887	Industrial production of Armenian brandy starts.
1895	Ottoman Turks massacre 300,000 Armenian subjects.
ca. 1900	Radical revolutionary organizations begin to form in South Caucasus.
1902	Railroad connects South Caucasus and Europe.
1915	Turks massacre between 600,000 and 2 million Armenians.

PERIOD OF FIRST REPUBLICS

1917	Armenia, Azerbaijan, and Georgia form the independent Transcaucasus Federation.
1918	Independent Armenia, Azerbaijan, and Georgia emerge from defeat of the Ottoman Empire in World War I.
1920	
May–July	The Caucasus economies are nationalized.
1920–1921	Russian Red Army invades Transcaucasus.

SOVIET RULE

1922	Three republics form the Transcaucasus Soviet Federative Socialist Republic as autonomies and are admitted to the Soviet Union.
1936	The Transcaucasus Federation dissolves, and each republic becomes a full-fledged member of the Soviet Union.
1941–1945	The Soviet Union engages in World War II.
1943	Autonomy is restored to the Georgian Orthodox Church.
1945	Azerbaijani Academy of Sciences is established.
1946	Byurakan Astrophysical Observatory is established in Armenia.

1950s–1960s	Azerbaijan loses its status of a main Soviet oil producer following discovery of oil in Siberia.
1969	Heydar Aliyev is named head of Azerbaijan.
1970	Zviad Gamsakhurdia begins organizing dissident Georgian nationalists.
1988	Georgian Parliament announces a program to recuperate the Georgian language.
1988	Merab Mamardashvili's collected works are first published.
January	A mob in Azerbaijan kills about 100 Armenians in the city of Sumgait.
February	Nagorno–Karabakh government votes to unify the Azerbaijani region with Armenia.
December	Disastrous earthquake in northern Armenia kills 35,000, leaves 400,000 homeless, and totally destroys city of Gyumri.
1989	The Armenian Pan-National Movement is legalized.
March 19	Abkhazia declares its intentions to separate from the Republic of Georgia.
April 9	Soviet troops violently break up peaceful demonstration and kill civilian demonstrators in Tbilisi.
September	Azerbaijan starts a blockade against Armenia.
December 1	Armenia annexes Mountainous Karabakh.
1990	
March 9	Georgia declares sovereignty.
September 20	South Ossetian legislature declares the region's separation from Georgia.
1991	Caucasus republics declare their independence from the Soviet Union.
January	Soviet troops are sent to Azerbaijan to halt anti-Armenian pogroms and disperse public demonstrations.
May 26	Zviad Gamsakhurdia is elected president of Georgia.
September 23	Armenia declares independence.

POST–SOVIET INDEPENDENCE

1992	Azerbaijan and Armenia join the Commonwealth of Independent States, a loose union of the former Soviet states.

March	Eduard Shevardnadze returns to power in Georgia.
1992–1993	Fighting breaks out between Georgian and Abkhazian independence forces, with large-scale refugee displacement.
1993	The International Olympic Committee recognizes the national Olympic committees of the Caucasus republics.
May	The Organization for Security and Co-operation in Europe negotiates a cease-fire in the Nagorno–Karabakh conflict.
September	Georgians are expelled from Abkhazia.
October	Following the rebellion against President Abulfaz Elchibey of Azerbaijan, Heydar Aliyev is reinstated as president.
1994	Abkhazia proclaims its independence, and a Russian peace-keeping force of 2,500 moves in.
May 1	Georgia becomes a member state of the Commonwealth of Independent States.
May 16	Armenia and Azerbaijan sign an armistice treaty.
September 20	Azerbaijan and leading global oil companies sign the "Contract of the Century" oil exploration contract.
1995	European Union and Caucasus republics sign partnership agreements.
	Russia opens a military base in Armenia.
1996	
April 22	Georgia establishes partnership and cooperation treaty with the European Union.
1997–2002	The region experiences a series of presidential elections, passages of new constitutions, and fruitless peace negotiations.
1999	
April 27	Georgia admitted to the Council of Europe.
October 27	A shoot-out in Armenia's Parliament kills the prime minister, speaker of Parliament, and six other legislators.
2000	U.S. military advisers are sent to the Caucasus to train local armed forces.
2002	Russia extends its citizenship to people of Abkhazia and South Ossetia.

2003   The so-called rose revolution in Georgia results in the resigna-
               tion of the incumbent President Shevardnadze and his party
               because of flawed elections.

2004   Mikheil Saakashvili is elected president of Georgia and begins
               radical reforms.

2005   Azerbaijan's President Aliyev orders celebrations of major lit-
               erary events, republication of Azerbaijani classics in the Latin
               alphabet, and publication of the National Encyclopedia.

2006   Armenia, Azerbaijan, and Georgia join the European Higher
               Education Area and participate in the Bologna process.

2008   Presidential and parliamentary elections in all three republics
               are recognized as free and fair, confirming the continuity of
               democratic reforms.

1

Land, People, and History

THE THREE GEOGRAPHICALLY isolated republics of Caucasus—Armenia, Azerbaijan, and Georgia—reappeared on the world map in 1991, after they proclaimed independence following the collapse of the Soviet Union, of which they had been a part since the early 1920s.[1] However, for long periods of time these ancient states existed as separate nations, or as parts of neighboring empires. In the time of conflicts and international calamities, these relatively obscure nations used to attract international attention. The twenty-first century's challenges, civil wars in Azerbaijan and Georgia, and long-lasting ethnic conflicts, especially those in Abkhazia and Karabakh, again have made the region an area where the international community tries to promote peace, resolve conflicts, and experiment with all kinds of reforms in an attempt to prevent the rise of Islamic radicalism.

THE LAND

The Caucasus Mountains are a thousand-mile-long and two-hundred-mile-wide mountainous system that geographically divides Europe and Asia, and politically serves as the boundary between Russia and the Middle East. With Mount Elbrus (elevation 18,506 feet) the Caucasus is the tallest mountain range in Europe. On a map, the Caucasus looks like a small strip between the Black and Caspian seas, but the variety of natural conditions is abundant. A distance of fifty miles or even less distinguishes lowlands or plains from tall, rocky mountains; humid subtropical climate from dry continental zones;

and grape- and orange-producing areas from glaciers covered with permanent snow. Each area of the Caucasus has its own unique characteristics.

Geographic Terrain

Three physical features dominate the region: the Black Sea that forms a natural boundary to the west, the Greater and the Lesser Caucasus mountain ranges in the middle, and the Caspian Sea with some extensive flatlands to the east. The snow line is located at the elevation of about 7,000–10,000 feet, and about 2 percent of the entire territory, mostly in the north, is covered with 1,400 glaciers. In the southern part, permanent snow and glaciers are visible much less; only on the highest peaks such as Mount Aragats (elevation 13,309 feet). The mountains are crossed with crests and overpasses distanced about five to ten miles from one another, which creates a complex network of trails, used since ancient times for keeping economic and cultural ties among the people who populated the area. Although the mountains make travel in all directions difficult, these peaks have never been insurmountable thanks to the overpasses, and peoples of different ethnicities have moved through the area continuously.

The modern topography was formed about 25 million years ago when a geological upheaval pushed the earth's crust upward to form plateaus in the Caucasus range. Geological turmoil continues in the form of devastating earthquakes; seismic activity is probably the most common geographic feature of the area. More than 3,000 earthquakes were registered in the area during the twentieth century.[2] In December 1988, Gyumri, the second-largest city of Armenia, was heavily damaged by an earthquake. When the first humans settled in the area about 200,000 years ago, the land looked much different from today. No fewer than ten volcanoes were active in the mountains, and herds of white elephants roamed the area, coexisting with mountain lions, bears, and many now-extinct birds.

Although the mountains are largely characteristic of the region,[3] numerous lowlands and valleys form the landscape in the south and along both seashores. Major Caucasian rivers are the Terek, Kura (in Azerbaijan named Mtkvari), and its tributary, the Aras, which is fed by eight other rivers. The Kura is the longest river in the Caucasus; its delta flows into the Caspian Sea. The water from these rivers provides hydroelectric power and irrigation. Inguri and Rioni are the largest rivers that drain into the Black Sea. Most rivers in the Caucasus are not navigable, as they are shallow, change riverbed configurations often, and have fast water flows. Navigation is conducted primarily on the 60 miles of the Rioni River and 360 miles of the 909-mile-long Kura River. Dams built on the Kura and Aras rivers collect waters for reservoirs that feed hydropower plants and irrigational systems. There are more than 2,000 lakes in the Caucasus, but most are not big. Lake Sevan, the largest lake in the region, is about 55 miles at its widest point, about 250 miles long, and measures 330 feet deep. It lies about 6,250 feet above sea level, while the surrounding mountains rise 11,800 feet high. It is uncertain whether Lake Sevan will keep its status as the main supplier of drinking water in the region in the future, as its water level is constantly falling because the lake is used as a source for hydropower.

Climate

The climate, affected by European and Mediterranean factors, varies from subtropical and dry in the mountains to subtropical and humid along the seashores. It is cold in higher mountain elevations and temperate on both seacoasts. Elevation determines temperatures and precipitation in the mountains. High mountains do not allow cold winds from the north to reach the area and guarantee a nice warm climate all year round. The weather is colder and wetter higher up in the mountains. Along the seashores, annual precipitation is about one hundred inches. Temperatures vary from the low thirties, Fahrenheit, in the winter to the nineties in the summer.

The landscape also depends on the elevation. The upper zones of the mountains, up to the snow line, consist of alpine meadows, which are used as pastures. Forests are at elevations below them; however, the energy crisis of the 1990s led to deforestation when many people began to scavenge for firewood. Lower levels of the mountain slopes are covered with tea plantations, lemon and orange groves, vineyards, and, in the ravines, mineral springs with medicinal qualities that house famous resorts. Swamps in the lowlands were artificially drained in the middle of the twentieth century and transformed into grain and corn plantations.

Natural Resources

The flora and fauna of the Caucasus are extremely varied, and more than 6,000 types of plants, or more than twice the number found in all of Eastern Europe, grow there. Tens of different types of animals populate the mountains, among them impalas, hogs, bears, groundhogs, squirrels, otters, and martens. Rivers and lakes, and especially the seas, are full of marketable fish. Caspian sturgeon is the best-known local delicacy.

Caucasian subsoil is rich with mineral resources. Since ancient times, people have extracted copper, iron ore, silver, and lead from the mountains, and according to some historians, metallurgy was invented in the Caucasus. The invention of steel is attributed to the ancient Georgian tribe of Chalybes. Cuneiform found in the state of Urartu (territory of present-day Armenia) by archeologists report that kings of this state requested tax payments from some Caucasian tribes in the form of copper or other metals. The myth of Jason and the Golden Fleece, which the Argonauts wanted to obtain, supports information about the early development of metalworks. Golden fleece was the name of the lambskin filled with stuck golden sand. The first-century geographer Strabo reported that this was the way of gathering gold in Colchis, where underground streams pushed gold up to the surface.

Of great economic importance today is industrial exploration of manganese and molybdenum. Oil is of special importance among Caucasian resources too. Great oil reserves were found in Azerbaijani oil fields off the shores of the Caspian Sea. The amount of oil is so great that oil leaks out onto the ground and many roads in Azerbaijan are patched with oil rigs where oil is pumped out. Abundant Azerbaijani oil resources and international efforts to develop them may influence the international economy strongly because of the possibility of establishing new transcontinental transportation corridors and reducing the United States' dependence on Middle Eastern supplies. The Caucasus has abundant reserves of natural building materials too. The main material is stone, which is widely used all over the region. Clay and wood are also used in construction, as well as in different crafts, such as pottery and woodworking.

Because of almost unrestricted exploitation of Caucasus's natural resources during previous years, all three Caucasian republics experience similar environmental problems. The most significant problem is air and water pollution caused mainly by oil refineries and inefficient chemical and metallurgical industries. The worst air quality is in Azerbaijan's capital city of Baku, where the oil industry is concentrated. The Caspian Sea is polluted by oil leakages and the dumping of raw or inadequately treated sewage. The city of Sumgait, located about forty miles north of the Azerbaijani capital and with 275,000 inhabitants, was the center of the nation's chemical industry during the Soviet era. In 2007, the United Nations recognized Sumgait as the second worst place to live on the planet. Almost the entire city area is contaminated by heavy metals, oil waste, and other chemical substances. Almost all children in the area are born with deformed bones, genetic diseases, and mental retardation.

During the Soviet era, all three republics were pushed to use extremely heavy applications of pesticides to increase the output of scarce subtropical crops for the rest of the Soviet Union. Although many of the chemicals are not in use any more, groundwaters are still polluted, and scientists attribute the increase in birth defects and illnesses to the previous indiscriminate use of fertilizers.[4] Illegal fishing of sturgeon in the Caspian Sea is another acute environmental problem. Russia has officially prohibited the consumption of black caviar, but this step has not been followed by Azerbaijan or Iran, which have a large share of the global caviar trade.

Landscape and the Economy of the Republics

Landscape and geographic conditions affected the political formation of the three Caucasian states. The Republic of Georgia is located on the eastern slopes of the mountains, on the westernmost shore of the Black Sea. The Caspian seacoast and northern ridges of the Caucasus range form the territory of Azerbaijan. The landscape of Armenia, which lies between two other republics, is dominated by the Armenian plateau, which slopes gradually downward into the Aras River valley (see Table 1.1).

Armenia

Armenia is a country of treeless basalt cliffs. Grass, which is green only in early spring, burns under the strong sun in the summer and fall. Stone is the main feature of the Armenian natural and cultural landscape. For control over each small plot of land, Armenian farmers have fought for centuries. It is amazing that Armenian gardens are able to grow among the stones. The most populated area of Armenia is the Ararat Valley, located along the Aras River, which forms the border with Turkey to the west and Iran to the south. Being irrigated, the valley is intersected with roads and water canals under the poplars and is covered with plantations, gardens, and vineyards. In the south, small valleys are squeezed among the highest mountains. This part of the country has a subtropical climate; fruits, nuts, and grapes are the area's main agricultural products. Most of the Armenian population lives in the western and northwestern parts of the country, where the two major cities are located. Because of the cold and dry climate, the northwestern high mountainous plateaus serve mostly as pastures for cattle.

Today, Armenian enterprises produce copper, molybdenum, artificial diamonds, rubber, building materials, movable electric power stations, electronics, textiles, and silk. In the integrated Soviet economy, the Armenian skilled and educated population was used to manufacture goods that were used by people all over the Soviet Union. The thirty-five-mile-long Arpa–Sevan water tunnel built in the mountains is a subject of technological pride. However, heavy industrialization required that additional energy resources and nuclear power plants be built in seismic zones, endangering the lives of local people. Still, there is no firm opinion as to whether these stations are secure and will survive a strong earthquake. The substantial pollution of lands and waters is another result of the disproportional industrial buildup in Armenia. Mount Ararat, located in Turkish territory, and soaring 16,874 feet over the surrounding plain, is Armenia's national symbol. The name *Ararat* is from the Armenian word that means "life" and "creation." Historically located on the territory of the Armenian Kingdom, Mount Ararat has been revered by

Table 1.1
Statistical Profile of the Caucasian Republics

	Capital city	Size in square miles (U.S. equivalent)	Population (millions)	Median age/life expectancy	GDP per capita (US$)/annual growth rate	Natural resources	Major industries
Armenia	Yerevan	9,933 (Maryland)	2,972	31/72.1	$5,700/10.5%	Small deposits of gold, copper, and bauxite	Diamond processing, microelectronics, textiles, shoes, chemicals, trucks, tires, and brandy
Azerbaijan	Baku	28,866 (Maine)	8,120	28/65.9	$9,000/31%	Oil, natural gas, cotton, tobacco, and iron ore	Petroleum, oil field equipment, metallurgy, chemicals, and textiles
Georgia	Tbilisi	23,233 (South Carolina)	4,646	38/76.3	$4,200/10%	Manganese, copper, and grapes	Aircraft, electrical appliances, steel, wine, and wood products

Source: CIA World Fact Book (data for 2007), available at https://www.cia.gov/library/publications/the-world-factbook/.

the Armenians as a spiritual place and the home of the gods of the Armenian pantheon. In the nineteenth century, the mount was divided between the Russian and Ottoman Empires. The mount belonged to Armenia during the short period of independence after World War I (1918–1921), but the Treaty of Kars, which defined the border between Turkey and the Soviet Union in 1921, placed Ararat on the Turkish side of the border. Since 1936, Ararat is reflected on the Armenia's coat of arms, which is subject of regular diplomatic protests from Turkey.

Azerbaijan

The most rugged terrain is in the Southeast of Azerbaijan, which of the three Caucasian states has the greatest land area. Azerbaijan is dominated by the shoreline of the Caspian Sea, the Caucasus mountain range, and flatlands in the middle of the country. Landscape is characterized by dramatic elevation changes over short distances, from lowlands to highlands, with nearly half of the country considered mountainous. The word *Azerbaijan* is a distortion of the Greek word Atropates, given by the successors of Alexander the Great to the region of ancient Iran and inhabited by mysterious people known as the Albans. The word *Atropates* means "protected by fire," a reference to the

A typical Azerbaijani landscape. Courtesy of Leila Alieva.

fires in the Zoroastrian temples and to the to natural burning of surface oil deposits. Although the Albans disappeared from history, each and every ethnic group now present in the region claims ties to their ancient heritage.

Citrus fruits, tea, and rice are grown in the lowlands, while the slopes are covered with vineyards and orchards. Besides being a major producer of grapes, Azerbaijani agriculture is known for olives, saffron, pomegranates, nuts, vegetables, figs, and the sesame plant for seeds and oil. The fishing industry is important to the economy, with the catch consisting mostly of herring, carp, and sturgeon roe that is processed into caviar. Agriculture is the second largest industry after petroleum exploration, processing, and transportation, which is the backbone of the Azerbaijani economy. Because of the Soviet policy to change priorities for economic development, Azerbaijan was traditionally far away from investments and no major development projects were initiated there after World War II. At the end of Soviet rule, Azerbaijan had the lowest rate of growth in productivity and economic output among the Soviet republics. In the Soviet Union, each republic was responsible for its contribution to a particular field of economy. Under Soviet government regulations, Azerbaijan was responsible for the proper functioning of farmers' markets all over the former Soviet Union, supplying staff and managing logistics. This assignment slowed down the economic development of the republic and contributed to corruption. There are two autonomous territories within Azerbaijan: Nakhichevan Autonomous Republic is a special administrative district separated from the rest of Azerbaijan by a strip of Armenian territory bordering Turkey; the Karabakh area populated mainly by Armenians was another constituent republic of Azerbaijan. Despite the fact that the Karabakh legislature declared the region's independence from Azerbaijan in 1988, and that Armenian troops later occupied the territory, Karabakh, which constitutes about one-fifth of the Azerbaijani territory, remains formally a part of Azerbaijan.

Georgia

According to a Georgian legend, when God was distributing land among the peoples of the world, the Georgians were so busy eating and drinking that they lost their place in the queue and there was no land left for them. But when they invited God to join the party, he enjoyed himself immensely and gave them all the bits of land he had been saving for himself. Today, Georgia has the most varied topography as well as the most inclusive administrative system of the three countries. Two autonomous republics, Abkhazia and Ajaria, and South Ossetia Autonomous Province are part of the Georgian federation. Abkhazia and Ajaria are small territories in the northwest and southwest of Georgia, respectively, along the eastern shore of the Black Sea.

South Ossetia is the northernmost Georgian territory, which borders Russia's North Ossetia district populated by the same Ossetian people who were divided by state borders when the Soviet Union collapsed in 1991.

The usage of the word *Georgia* is relatively misleading. The Republic of Georgia has nothing in common with the state of Georgia in the United States, and although St. George is the country's patron saint, the name *Georgia* comes from the Arabic and Persian words *Kurj* and *Gurj*. According to ancient Greek historians, the country, which had been known as Iberia, was renamed by the Greeks to *Georgiana*, meaning "promised land." Georgians name their land *Sakartvelo* and themselves *Kartveli*. Present-day reference to Sakartvelo includes both the eastern part known in Georgian as Kartli (or Iberia in Greek) and the western region Egrisi in Georgian (or Colchis in Greek). These regions were separate state units until King Bagrat III united them in 1008, eliminating long-standing cultural differences.

Georgians are agrarians. More than half of all types of wheat known in the world are produced in Georgia. Wine making is one of the most important domestic industries. About 500 kinds of grape are grown in the country. Tea, tobacco, and corn are produced in the western part of the country. Oranges, other fruits, and grapes are common in the east. Animal husbandry, beekeeping, and hunting are among the traditional Georgian activities. The bottling of mineral water is a specific Georgian industry; the Borzhomi mineral water has medicinal features and can be used for treatments. Up to 100 million Borzhomi bottles were produced in the late 1980s, when production was at its peak. Resorts, spa areas, abundant historic places, and natural beauty make Georgia an attractive tourist destination. Today, the food processing and textile industries account for two-thirds of the nation's gross domestic product. Previously, large trucks were produced for decades in the city of Kutaisi, and locomotives built in Tbilisi were exported to all republics of the Soviet Union and the Eastern bloc. The national economy still did not fully recuperate after the collapse of the integrated Soviet economy. Agriculture is no longer as profitable as it used to be, local enterprises are idle, many of them have been plundered, and the power supply is erratic. Unemployment is high in all of the Caucasian republics, and many people are living on money transfers from relatives who emigrated abroad or moved to Russia because of better-paying jobs.

THE PEOPLE

The Caucasus is one of the oldest continuously inhabited regions in human history. More than forty ethnicities claim the Caucasus as their native land. Sizable ethnic groups related to cultures of neighboring nations have compact settlements within each of the Caucasian republics. They are, for instance, Greeks in Georgia, Kurds in Armenia, and Lezghians in Azerbaijan. This book, however, will focus only on major nations; other smaller national groups will be discussed in less detail or simply mentioned. As mountainous countries, all republics of the Caucasus have been naturally divided into separate regions that had little communication between them. This regional isolation has been reflected in the proliferation of ancient and medieval kingdoms and principalities, in the feuds between various parts of each country, and in the difficulty of rulers in establishing a single national polity. It is also reflected in the multiplicity of languages spoken by the minority groups, incomprehensible to their fellow compatriots in other parts of the country.[5]

All ethnic people attempt to confirm their historical supremacy in the fields of culture (invention of ironworking), religion (early adoption of Christianity), and politics (early establishment of statehood). They try to defend their territorial rights through the deepening of their roots in a given "homeland." At the same time, they associate themselves with the glorious deeds of distant real or imagined ancestors mentioned by classical authors.[6]

Ethnic Features

People of the Caucasus are among the longest-living people of the world. Another of their distinctive features is the desire to communicate with one another and visitors. Observers agree that with a high level of intellectual ability, they are quick witted and prone to volatility and mood changes. They are gifted in dancing, singing, creating poetry, and making crafts. They tend to take an optimistic view of life, are generous in terms of hospitality, and are fond of food and wine.[7] According to anthropologists, people who settled in the Caucasus Mountains about 6,000 years ago had very pale skin. Because of a popular nineteenth-century theory, which has now been disproved, that stated that all people with pale skin had originated in this area, the term *Caucasian* was used to describe people of the white race. Despite many cultural and linguistic differences, all of the people of the area have relatively similar appearances. All Caucasian people look like any other southern Europeans. They are usually tall, have bright faces, long and outstanding noses, and dark eyes and hair, although red-haired people with blue eyes are not a rarity. People of western Georgia belong to the so-called Mediterranean type and have softer features with lighter skin color. Blue-eyed people with lighter hair are more common among the Georgians than in the other two countries. Azerbaijanis are darker, shorter, and look similar to their Iranian neighbors.

Caucasian women have always been known for their beauty. According to a local legend, when God decided to marry, he ordered all beautiful women to visit him at Mount Ararat. God chose one of the first women, but while on their way to Mount Ararat, the rest of the beauties gathered in Georgia and

A Georgian peasant. Courtesy of Mr. and Mrs.
Omari Budagashvili.

remained there. Beautiful women gave birth to handsome men, and that is
how the nation of good-looking people was established.

Historical Roots of Armenians

All three cultures experienced completely different external influences.
Even before Christianity, Georgian culture was influenced by ancient Greece
because of its location along the Black Sea. At the same time, southeastern
European tribes settled in the territory of Armenia, and Asiatic Medes, Per-
sians, and Scythians resided on lands that today are part of Azerbaijan, where
Persian cultural influence turned to be the most formative.

The most ethnically homogeneous among the three Caucasian republics
is Armenia. Armenians make up almost 98 percent of the entire population.
Because of ethnic purges and bloody confrontations, most Azerbaijanis fled
Armenia between 1988 and 1992. Armenians are one of the most ancient
people on the planet. Their long, difficult, and often tragic history of creative
labor has enriched civilization with great examples of material and spiritual

culture. They attribute their descent to Noah's son Japheth. Ethnically they are linked to those tribes that migrated from southeastern Europe to Asia Minor late in the second millennium B.C. and to the residents of the Urartu kingdom that existed in the area from the thirteenth to the sixty century B.C. According to the migration theory, proto-Armenian speakers first arrived in the Tigris Valley in the twelfth century B.C. and merged with local inhabitants afterward.[8] Research conducted in the 1970s identified state formations that existed in the middle of the second millennium B.C. and claimed that the Armenian language was transmitted by the Urartian cuneiform.

Originally, Armenians resided all over the southern Caucasus mountains. Periods of independent existence interchanged with periods of occupation, when the country was plundered and destroyed. For thousands of years, masses of people were resettled and forced to live first in neighboring countries, and then far away from their motherland and all over the globe. Persecutions, massacres, and displacements made Armenians the most dispersed people in the area. Today, communities of Armenian emigrants are vibrant in many countries around the world, especially in France and the United States. Armenia is the most homogenous country in the region. After the Karabakh war began, almost all Azerbaijanis fled the country, and Russians attempted to emigrate back to Russia, where the economic situation appeared to be much better.

Until the active urbanization in the middle of the twentieth century, the majority of the Armenian population consisted of farmers who carefully preserved their traditional way of living, which was based on complex agricultural and cattle breeding, which depended on the continental climate and mountainous landscape. Field agriculture (production of wheat, barley, rye, millet) was combined with gardening (peaches, pomegranates, apples, walnuts) and grape and wine production. Depending on conditions, animal husbandry (cows, horses, pigs, donkeys, buffalos) took the form of pasturing or settled raising. Pasturing influenced food, transportation, family relations, and housing. Craftsmanship and the cottage industry, known for their quality and artistic value even outside of Armenia, were always of great importance to the nation's economy. Carpet and lace making, jewelry making, and stone carving were among the most popular crafts.

Today, in all spheres of Armenian life, we can see strong connections between historic heritage and dynamic development. The current-day artisans find their inspiration in historic artifacts and national treasures. Armenian theater, music, literature, film, and paintings bear national colors and reflect ethnic visions of the artists. The richness of Armenian cultural heritage and the heroic history of the Armenians, who regardless of being dispersed around the world,[9] keep fighting for the revival of their nation, attract the interests of people in other nations. With strong support from the diaspora, centers for the study of Armenian language, history, and culture have been created in many European countries and in the United States.

Azerbaijan's Population

Contrary to the millennium-long history of Armenian statehood, the consolidation of the Azerbaijanis as a coherent ethnic group took place only in the 1920s, although Azerbaijani scholars argue that Azerbaijani people descended from the local Albans, who fell under Iranian influence in the first millennium B.C. and began to assimilate with Turkic-language-speaking newcomers during the first millennium A.D. The first settlers of the lowlands in Azerbaijan came from the mountains. These people intermarried with Persian invaders and later mixed with Seljuk Turks who arrived in the eleventh century A.D. According to Joseph Stalin's nation-state policy, which required the existence of an Azerbaijani nation to populate the republic named Azerbaijan, the majority of Azerbaijan's population, formerly known as Turks, was reidentified as Azerbaijani in 1937.[10] However, even today, the Azerbaijanis associate themselves much less with the country as a whole than with a particular locality or a region from which they come.

Azerbaijan's population consists of a single ethnic group, and problems with ethnic minorities have been dominated by Armenian uprisings in the mountainous, western region of Karabakh. The population is concentrated in a few urban centers, as well as in the most fertile agricultural regions. The share of Azerbaijanis in the nation's population, which accounts for 91 percent of the total population, has dramatically increased during the past years because of a high birth rate, expulsion of Armenians, the entry of Azerbaijani refugees from Armenia, and the emigration of Russians and other minorities. About 13 million Azerbaijanis reside in the northern provinces of Iran. Noticeable Azerbaijani communities live in Moscow, Georgia, and neighboring regions of Russia.

The largest minority groups in Azerbaijan are the Lezghians (about 170,000) and the Avars. The majority of these groups reside in large numbers to the north of the Russo-Azerbaijani border in semi-independence. They are Sunni Muslims and speak their own language. From time to time these groups demand more autonomy and special rights to contact their relatives in Russia. That creates some instability in the border region and threatens the national unity of Azerbaijan. About ninety other small ethnic groups consist of 260,000 people, among them Kurds, Talyshin, Tats, Iranians, and others living in the South, and culturally related to the Iranians. The role of the non-Turkic groups that inhabited the area is considered to be minimal in Azerbaijan's ethnic genesis.[11]

As a result of numerous invasions and control by the Ottoman, Persian, and Russian empires, people who were recognized as titular ethnicities for these states, Armenians, Azerbaijanis, and Georgians, were often displaced. For example, the Republic of Azerbaijan contains only about 6 million of the world's estimated 19 million ethnic Azerbaijanis, with the rest living mostly in Iran and Russia.

Different Peoples of Georgia

The great majority of the world's Georgian population lives in the Republic of Georgia, whose boundaries were little changed since ancient times. However, Georgia is a multiethnic state. Ethnic Georgians account for 74 percent of the population, with significant shares of Abkhazians, Azerbaijanis, Armenians, Russians, and many other people. Although the majority of the population consists of Georgians, there are many areas where minorities dominate. The Laz, who live in the south of Ajaria, are a specific ethnic group. Other members of the group reside in Turkey. Armenians can be met in southern Georgia too, and Azerbaijanis in the eastern Georgia.

The genesis of ethnicities in South Caucasus has not yet been widely studied. Supposedly, the two Georgian ethnic cultures of Colchis and Kartli were formed between the fifth and second centuries B.C. Much later, they consolidated into a unified Georgian nation. Despite the fact that Georgians make up a very cohesive nation, there are several local ethnic groups, which have their own distinct traditions and dialects, although they all belong to the Georgian (Kvartveli) people. The Kartlians, in whose region the capital city of Tbilisi is located, have a reputation for aristocratic breeding, the Kakhetians are known for solid resoluteness, while in western Georgia, the Mingrelians are singled out for astuteness. The Gurians are boastful and ruthless, and tenacious. In upland Imereti, the Ratchans are known for thrift, industry, and physical strength. The Svans who live high in the mountains have a reputation for savagery. The Pshav, Khevsur, and Tush people of eastern Georgia hold to curious ancient rites and costumes, and until the mid-1950s, they wore medieval chain armor.[12] These differences were also reflected in their daily customs. For example, hospitality is a common trait of all Georgians. In western Georgia an invitation to a feast by Imeretians or Gurians is accompanied by lengthy invitations and refusals; however, in central Georgia Khevsurs would be offended if a guest who entered the house did not just start eating without a formal invitation.

Three major Georgian minorities are Abkhazians, Ajarians, and Ossetians. During Soviet times, all three minorities were assigned a special status, and the territories of their compact living were designated as autonomous republics within Georgia. Two of them, Abkhazia and Ajaria are predominantly Muslim. Because of the Turkish presence in Georgia, a small ethnic Georgian minority group known as Ajarians was established. Before Ajaria became part of

Georgia in 1787, following the Congress of Berlin resolution, it was part of the Ottoman Empire and included a Georgian population converted to Islam. Despite centuries of living in predominantly Christian Georgia, the Ajarians remained Muslim.

Whereas Ajarians who reside in the southwestern corner of Georgia along the Black Sea and bordering Turkey are ethnic Georgians who, during Turkish occupation in the sixteenth century, accepted Islam but preserved their Georgian language and traditions, Abkhazians have closer ties with the people of the northern Caucasus of the Russian Federation. Abkhazians were more strongly influenced by the Christian Georgians, and until recently Islamic identity did not play an important role in the national consciousness. Abkhazians are a relatively small ethnic group with their own language, which is not related to the Georgian language. The Abkhazian language is related to a group of Adyghe languages spoken by the northern Caucasian ethnicities residing within the Russian Federation. "It is an extremely difficult language in which the verb takes on a great deal of lexical and syntactical duties that we, as English speakers, would not expect."[13] Early residents of Abkhazia adopted Christianity around A.D. 550, under the Byzantine emperor Justinian I. In the eighth century, the independent Kingdom of Abkhazia was formed, and in the sixteenth century, Abkhazia came under the rule of the Ottoman Empire, and Islam largely replaced Christianity. In 1810, Abkhazia became Russia's protectorate, and in 1864, Abkhazia was finally included in the Russian Empire. In material culture, Abkhazians are very close to the Georgians. They have the same appearance, and even their last names sound similar. Major differences are preserved in folklore, ethics, rites, and customs. In 1921, after Georgia was occupied by the Red Army, Abkhazia was declared independent for a short time; however, later, during the Soviet gerrymandering, Georgian borders encompassed Abkhazia. Abkhazia is located along the Georgian border with Russia, and its economy is mostly agricultural, as it produces tobacco, tea, silk, and fruits. During the Soviet era, tourism was Abkhazia's major industry because of a high concentration of resorts along the Abkhazian Black Sea coast. Despite the fact that Abkhazia was the largest autonomous region in Georgia, the ethnic Abkhazians constituted only 2 percent of the entire nation's population, and within Abkhazia 44 percent of population was Georgian; 18 percent, Abkhazian; and 16 percent, Russian.

In order to simplify control over the nationalities, ethnic groups, and future republics within the Soviet Union, Joseph Stalin, whose first job in the first Bolshevik government was to monitor and facilitate interethnic relations, advocated the split of established ethnic groups and their division along the state borders. That happened with the Ossetian people, for whom two separate autonomous republics, North Ossetia in Russia and South Ossetia in Georgia, were created. Ossetians are an ethnic Iranian group that became Christian in the early Middle Ages under Georgian and Byzantine influence. A consolidated Ossetian kingdom was created in the eighth century, but in the thirteenth century, having been driven out by invading Mongols, they arrived from the north to the area where they reside now. Today many all-Georgian villages exist in Ossetia, and the Ossetian population is mainly concentrated in the towns of Tskhinvali and Java. Before the recent conflicts, two-thirds of the region's population was Ossetian and one-third Georgian.

In the 1990s, three large-scale conflicts emerged in the region following the reevaluation of neighborly relations by nations striving for independence. These were wars between Armenia and Azerbaijan, between Georgia and Abkhazia, and between Georgia and South Ossetia. These conflicts resulted in growing violence among the nations, which are extending their demands for land and natural resources. Smaller ethnic groups requested freedom and independence for them. Most of the time these conflicts were provoked by borders, which were set by the Bolshevik regime with the purpose of preserving the region's economic integrity without taking into account ethnic boundaries. The border problems between the states are still not resolved and borders remain undelimited. The chairman of the Border Guard Department of Georgia recently commented, "We have an administrative border, but we still do not know where the state border runs."[14]

Among other major ethnic groups who have long history of living in the Caucasus are Assyrians, Greeks, Meskhetian Turks, and Germans. The first Assyrian community was established in Georgia during the reign of King Irakli II, who secretly corresponded with the patriarch of the Assyrian church Avraam, aiming to collect forces against the Ottoman Empire. The resettlement of Assyrians continued when Georgia became a part of the Russian Empire. By the 1890s, there were about 5,000 Assyrians in Tbilisi. To avoid persecutions by the Ottoman Empire, Assyrians moved in large numbers to Georgia and Armenia during and after World War I. In 1947, the Soviet authorities deported thousands of Assyrians to Siberia and Kazakhstan. Only some of them were able to return to Georgia when the ethnic group was rehabilitated in 1954. According to the 2002 census, the number of Assyrians dropped to 3,299, which is 0.1 percent of Georgia's population. Today, Assyrians live in two compact groups in Tbilisi and some other towns and in several villages in Armenia. Because of social and economic problems, the Assyrians who traditionally engaged in trade and handicrafts are leaving the region in large numbers, emigrating to Russia and Western Europe.

Although the first Greeks came to western Georgia in the eighth and seventh centuries B.C., the ancestors of the contemporary Greek population arrived in Georgia from Asia Minor together with the Assyrians in the middle of the eighteenth century, when King Irakli II invited about 800 families of Greek artisans to work at the newly opened silver and copper plants. Following the Russo-Turkish War of 1828–1829, Tsar Nicholas I allowed Greeks from Turkey who were viewed as reliable Orthodox Christians to relocate to Georgia. After the Sovietization of the region in the 1920s, Greeks started to emigrate to their homeland.[15] A very small Greek community remains in Georgia now. These people suffer from the continuing economic crisis and are in a disadvantaged position because they do not speak the official Georgian language.

The Meskhetian Turks, who are Sunni Muslims, come from Meskheti, a mountainous, agricultural region of Georgia located along the border with Turkey. Their native language is Turkish, and by their specific traditional culture, they are close to the Turks of Anatolia; however, some features in their lifestyle and customs show their alliance with the people of the Caucasus, primarily the Georgians.[16] During World War II, about 95,000 Meskhetian Turks were exiled from Georgia to Central Asia. It is believed that Stalin's reason for their deportation was that there was a need to "clear" a strategically located region on the Soviet-Turkish frontier of elements suspected of pro-Turkish sympathies, so that Soviet military operations could be extended into northeastern Turkey.[17] Thousands died en route and thousands more in the harsh living conditions of exile. The Meskhetian Turks could not return to their homeland because it had been designated a "border zone," off-limits to all outsiders by Soviet authorities. Special residency permits, unavailable to Meskhetian Turks, were required to enter the region. Recently, they have attempted to return but were not welcomed by the Georgians, who claimed that the Meskhetians have lost their links to Georgia. In 2006, the U.S. government developed a program aimed to assist Meskhetian Turks in relocating to the Philadelphia area.

The Germans established their community of 7,000 individuals in Azerbaijan in the first decades of the nineteenth century, trying to escape the disastrous political and economic situation in Germany after the Napoleonic Wars. Six German colonies were founded in Georgia too. They settled in and around Tbilisi, and on public lands given to them for agricultural activities. There were eight German colonies in Azerbaijan in the towns of Ganja and Khanly. Before World War II, about 23,000 ethnic Germans resided in the South Caucasus. All of them were resettled and murdered in Siberia under Stalin's policies when Hitler's Germany attacked the Soviet Union.[18]

While part of the Soviet federal system, these republics were subject to the policy of nativizing: forming indigenous ethnic leadership through specially developed programs of training, recruiting, and promoting for service in the republic's political, economic, and cultural administration of people who belonged to the republic's titular nationality, such as Armenians in Armenia, Georgians in Georgia, and Azerbaijanis in Azerbaijan. Ethnic administrative elites, who were created in the middle of the twentieth century, remain in power even today, preserving the overrepresentation of the major ethnic group and limiting opportunities available to minorities.

HISTORICAL BACKGROUND

The complex history of the region reflects the area's geographic conditions and the diversity of the population. Its location at the crossroads of southeastern Europe and western Asia influenced the histories of the people forming the present-day republics of the South Caucasus. All three countries originated as trade routes between Europe and Asia, securing narrow land passage for those who traveled between the Black and Caspian seas. People from the Middle East, Mediterranean, Eastern Europe, and Central Asia met and communicated in the Caucasus Mountains. The nice climate, rich soil, and abundant natural resources attracted traders and invaders. Local people adopted a lot from the Greeks, Romans, Arabs, Turks, Persians, and Russians, but no one influence became dominant. Each nation was able to preserve its own ethnic traditions and specifics and use them as a background for further development.

Cimmerian and Scythian cavalry, troops of Alexander, marched over the area. Iran, Byzantium, and Turkey always wanted to establish control over the Caucasus. Arab and Mongol invaders, troops of Genghis Khan and Tamerlane were here and took their booty. However, the history of Caucasus does not consist exclusively of wars. Despite the fact that the rulers were constantly fighting against one another, ordinary people wanted to coexist peacefully. Intensive commercial and cultural relations existed among neighboring countries.

Obsidian and flint stone tools can be traced to the lower Paleolithic period. Early farming society became involved in hunting in the sixth millennium B.C. The first permanent dwellings with stone foundations are attributed to this time period. Later, bricks were used to construct the walls of the houses, and men were involved in pottery and metalworks. The Iron Age started there at the end of the second millennium B.C. According to a Georgian version of local history, iron was first invented by the ancestors of modern Georgian people, who migrated to the area at the southeast corner of the Black Sea. They supplied the Mittani kingdom and ancient Egypt with iron; the Abkhazians claim their authorship to the invention of iron, although 1,000 years later.

Early Societies

First tribal unions were established in the southern Caucasus at the end of the Bronze Age, when the need to defend the lands from Assyrian incursions, known since the thirteenth century B.C., became a necessity. The number of tribes involved varied between forty and sixty, but eight of them were the largest and strongest with the Uruatri tribe at the head. Later, in the ninth century B.C., this union was transformed into a centralized state named Urartu, which existed for several centuries. The first known tsars of Urartu were Aramu (860–846? B.C.), Sarduri (mentioned in 834 B.C.), and his son and grandson, Menua and Ishpuin. The dynasty of Sarduri's successors ruled until 590 B.C.. Dozens of tribes and other statelike formations were included in this strong monarchy, which competed with Assyria, the mightiest state of the ancient Orient. The largest part of the future ethnic territory of Armenians was within the Urartu borders.

Urartu was an economically prosperous state. Irrigation systems based on channels and water reservoirs built by the slaves supported the agriculture in river valleys. Mountainous pastures were used for seminomadic cattle breeding. Breeding of horses and camels needed for the tsar's troops also developed here. The craftsmen had fine skills working with bronze, iron, precious stones, clay, and wood. A temple complex Tesheiba, which served as the residential and administrative center of the ruler, and was discovered near the present-day city of Yerevan, is an example of the city culture at that time. The brick-stone palace consisted of 120 rooms with huge reservoirs for grain and wine, armories, clothes, and china. Inhabitants of the city did not conduct their own economic activities and received everything they needed from the treasury. The city was destroyed by an enemy incursion accompanied by fire and plundering. The excavation of a large number of Scythian arrowheads allows one to conclude that the history of the city ended in the sixth century B.C. under attacks of the northern nomads. Many treasures belonged to the temples and clergy. In 714 B.C., while ravaging the Urartian city of Musasir, the Assyrians took from a local temple six golden shields decorated with dog heads, twelve silver shields adorned with heads of lions and dragons, and many bronze statues of local gods. The trophies also included a military arsenal, 1,000 pounds of silver, and about 200,000 pounds of copper. Local people worshipped wood as a symbol of life, and they expressed their knowledge in cuneiform. They had their own system of measurements and digits, which under the Persian influence was based on the "two-thirds of a hundred" unit favored by the Persians. The Armenian kingdom, which replaced Urartu in the sixth century B.C., became the first real Armenian state, and was very soon thereafter included in the Achaemenid empire, where it remained a separate province until the incursion of Alexander the Great's troops in the fourth century B.C. During this period, the current Armenian nation was formed.

At the beginning of the first millennium B.C., independent proto-states were created in the Caucasus. The genesis of ethnicities has not been studied very well. The Armenian nation was formed approximately between the fifth and second centuries B.C. within the framework of the *Armina Supria* state formation. The ancestors of Georgians formed somewhere around this time two related cultures of the Colchis and the Kartli, which were later consolidated into one nation. In the territory of present-day Azerbaijan, there existed the state named *Caucasus Albania*. Historical evidence confirms the existence of close economic and political ties between the Caucasus and the Hellenistic world. Ancient Greek myths brought to us the story of Jason, who together with his Argonauts had sailed to the eastern end of the Black Sea to retrieve a golden fleece from the Colchis, today's Georgia. According to another myth, angry Zeus ordered Prometheus to be chained to the cliff of the highest Caucasian mount for stealing fire. This myth is likely based in reality, because the Caucasus was an area of early metal production, where torches of natural gas were burning that came to the surface from underneath the ground.

The Colchis was governed by an independent ruler and comprised many large towns with well-developed crafts. This level of development restricted Greek colonization and prevented the Greeks from influencing the local economy and the social environment. Georgian historians insist that Georgian statehood grew directly out of the kingdom of Colchis, which survived and developed independently on the same territory from the twelfth century B.C. until the sixth century A.D., and was not subjugated by anybody, including Urartu, Assyria, Media, or Persia.

The ancient Georgian state formations, Colchis between the sixth and fourth centuries B.C. on the eastern shore of the Black Sea and the Kartli kingdom between the fourth and third centuries B.C., in the mountains of eastern Georgia were constantly defending their integrity and national independence. Persia, Rome, and then Byzantium attacked this territory and divided it into small parts. Archeological excavations show that these states were rich, and the coins found in large quantities prove that city life and trade were highly developed there. Colchis, a far corner of the ancient world, reached the peak of its development around the second century B.C. Colchis was famous for its gold and precious metals. While other nations were surviving in the Bronze Age, local people in Colchis were fusing iron. Gold was used for household and ornamental purposes. Robes were decorated by ornaments sewn with golden threads, and drinking vessels were melted from gold or silver. Drinking vessels were of special importance here because wine was invented in this land and widely consumed.

Knowledge about Colchis comes from several dozens of graves excavated in the vicinity of the ancient city of Vani in the western part of modern-day Georgia. The first archeological discoveries in the territory of this ancient city, which is covered by vineyards now, were made in 1975. It appears that Vani was the central city of the state until it was destroyed around 50 B.C., when the

A Colchis golden goblet (second century B.C.). Photograph by Badri Vadachkoria provided by the Embassy of Georgia to the United States.

province turned under full Greek influence. Excavations show that the people of Colchis used goods imported from neighboring Greece and Persia. Among the things produced domestically were necklaces made of small golden beads cast as tortoises, birds, crouching gazelles, or rams' heads. Golden plaques with pictures of eagles, ducks, and Sphinxes were attached to the clothes. As a result of the excavations, objects such as massive silver belts depicting banquet scenes and golden diadems with engraved scenes of lions killing boars and bulls were discovered. Statuettes and other decorative objects reflect Greek elegance. According to Strabo, the Georgian population was divided into four groups—elite with the tsar at the top and consisting of clergy, knights, and landlords, and slaves.[19]

Medieval States

Armenia became a developed and prosperous sate under King Tigranes II the Great (95–56 B.C.) when its territory included lands between the Caspian and Mediterranean seas. The state was based on agricultural communities, a strong army of many slaves and war prisoners, and a city population active in metallurgy, the main industry of the time. High cultural achievements are attributed to this time also. Under a strong Hellenistic influence, theater and architecture were established, and folklore epics described the fight of Armenian people against foreign invaders. The court poets glorified Tigranes's rule as twenty-five years of nonstop successes. However, because of the lack of economic integration, the Armenian state was weak and the Roman Empire occupied it. Contemporary information about other people of the Caucasus was provided by Strabo in the first century A.D. He provided a thorough account of life in Iberia (then Georgia), which according to him was full of large cities and settlements. Also, he gave a description of people who lived in northern Azerbaijan, a territory known then as Albania. Strabo stated that farming, cattle breeding, and wine production were the main economies of the Caucasus Albans, who were divided into twenty-six tribes united under the power of one tsar.

A series of slave uprisings in Armenia and parts of Georgia in the first and second centuries A.D. proved the inefficiency of slavery. At the same time, land ownership was established. Fertile lands of the Transcaucasus were always the subject of attacks from neighboring Iran and Turkey. The Arshakid dynasty, which ruled Armenia until 428, was supported by the Byzantine Empire. This union was confirmed by the acceptance of Christianity in Armenia in 301, contrary to the Zoroastrianism professed in Iran. With this act, Armenia became the first nation in the world that elevated Christianity to the level of a state religion. Although the official date of the acceptance of Christianity as its state religion is A.D. 301, the actual date may be as late as A.D. 314. Armenians claim that Tiridates III (A.D. 238–314) was the ruler who officially Christianized his people.

Tsar Arshak II (350–367) tried to strengthen his power and built a large city of Arshakovan, where all fugitive slaves and peasants received rights of free men. Immediately, the valley around the city was full of people who served in the tsar's 90,000-strong army. This endangered the aristocracy, which asked Iran for assistance, and all men and women of Arshakovan were murdered by the Iranians. Arshak's successor, Pap (369–374), continued the policy of state expansion, fighting for more independence for the Armenian church from Byzantium, but the ongoing secularization of church possessions aggravated relations between him and the clerics who killed the tsar. In 391, the Byzantine Empire occupied Armenia, and the institute of tsars was eliminated; lands under Iranian control were incorporated into Iran in 428, when the Arascid monarchy of Iranian origin was abolished. Since then, no single ruler has ever controlled the entire country, which at that time had a territory five times greater than the territory of the present-day republic.

The western part of the Caucasus was populated by the Georgians. Iberia and Kartli were the most advanced areas with established feudal relations and land ownership by aristocracy. The clan of the Bagratids, who were to rule Georgia for the next thousand years, was established in the third century. For purposes of prestige, they proclaimed the dynasty's descent from David and Solomon of Israel, although they originated in the territory of northern Turkey. In 331, King Mirian accepted Christianity and proselytized among his subjects. The first written documents originated around this time. The introduction of Christianity in Georgia influenced the development of philosophy and theological studies. Developed schools of rhetoric existed in Georgia in the fourth century, and the first census was conducted in the seventh century. Temples built at that time still serve as examples for modern Georgian architecture. Under the influence of Christian Armenia and Georgia, a script appears in the lands along the Caspian Sea inhabited by the so-called Albans, who were under the control of the Iranian ruling dynasty of Sasanids. When the Byzantine Empire established its control over this territory, Antropatena, an Azerbaijani proto-state was created.

Foreign Invasions

In the sixth and seventh centuries, the territory of the present-day Caucasian republics was divided between Byzantium and Iran with a larger part recognized as one of the provinces of Sasanid Iran. Persian rule was characterized by increased taxation and the introduction of monetary taxes. Zoroastrianism was the dominant religion of that time and King Khosrov I introduced it forcefully. In 571, the Caucasian people revolted against religious discrimination, and Byzantium took them under its protection. The war ended in 591 with the defeat of the Iranians; the lands were returned to Emperor Mauritius (582–602), who ruled through the appointment of military governors. The governors transferred land from one state to another as a trophy in ongoing wars between them.

Like everywhere during feudal times, religious institutions performed political, legal, and cultural functions. Because the countries of the Caucasus were not politically independent, the church was the only institution that attempted to unify the people and represent all ethnicities residing in the region. Christianity was the common religion for all people of the region. Slavery did not play a significant role in Caucasian society. Feudal relations were based on relations between a landlord and the vassal agricultural community.

After creating the caliphate with its center in Baghdad in spring 654, and after the mountain paths became open, Arabs moved into the area of the southern Caucasus, expanding Islam by force. The Arabs did not stay in the Caucasus permanently but made rapid attacks, looting villages and taking prisoners. Since the middle of the seventh century, all of the people of the Caucasus defended their lands from the Arab attacks and had no protection from Byzantium. They united under Theodoros Rshtuni, who signed a treaty with the Arabs, creating a dependent state with the right to have its own army with up to 15,000 knights and not paying duties to the Arabs. Because of a relative balance between the Arabs and Byzantium, the Caucasian countries preserved their independence. The entire period of the Arab occupation was an endless cycle of revolts, defeats, and expulsions of occupants. The strongest was the uprising in Azerbaijan, which started in 816 and lasted for more than twenty years. While under Arab rule, the lands of the Caucasus were ruled by a caliph's representative, who appointed local rulers for Albania, Armenia, and eastern Georgia. The previously popular belief that the invasion of Arabs had some positive consequences, because Islam brought some elements of culture to the region, has been discarded by scholars. It appears that before the Arab occupation, the cultural development of the region was much higher than in the areas where the Arabs resided. Future achievements of the so-called Muslim culture were based on accepting the culture of Caucasian and Central Asian peoples.[20]

During the following centuries, Armenia was from time to time divided between Iran and Byzantium. Much damage was inflicted by the occupation of Seljuk Turks in the eleventh century. This fight against oppressors is described in the great Armenian epic of David of Sassoon. During these years, the forceful resettlement of the Armenians was so intensive that in eleventh century, the Armenian kingdom was established on the periphery of the Byzantine Empire. Armenian villages existed in the territory between Egypt and Crimea, and between India and the Balkans. Armenians were first known as city dwellers and craftsmen, but later, especially after the Mongols ravaged the country in the thirteenth century, Armenians became involved in agriculture.

The Golden Age of Georgia

The Seljuk Turks who invaded Byzantium in the eleventh century devastated western Georgia. However, King David IV, also known as David the Builder (1089–1125), who united separate Georgian states into one kingdom, overcame the crisis. Smart, educated, and having a strong will, he became one of the best military and political leaders in Georgian history. King David IV gathered the population in valleys of eastern Georgia, concentrated all government power in his hands, and created a new 45,000-man army, which consisted of resettled nomads from the north who received land plots in exchange for their service. David stopped paying contributions to the Turks and secured Georgia's independence. Additionally, he made some territorial acquisitions, adding a part of Armenia to Georgia. By the middle of the eleventh century, all small medieval Armenian kingdoms were incorporated into the

Byzantine Empire, and then lost to Seljuk Turks after the battle at Manazkert in 1071. After that, Ani, the old Armenian capital, was ruled by Muslim dynasties. In 1123, Georgia's King David IV recovered Ani for the Christians, but lost it three years later.

David's successes were multiplied by his grandson George III (1156–1184), who elevated his daughter Tamar (1184–1207) to the throne because he did not have a son. The international political situation was in Tamar's favor. Because Constantinople had been captured by crusaders, Tamar was able to get rid of the Turks' control and acquire large parts of Armenia and Azerbaijan, which had been devastated by Turkish occupants. Expanding Georgian power into Armenia, Queen Tamar (1184–1212) extended Georgia's control as far west as the Caspian shores and as far south as the Aras River. At that time, the country's population was more than 5 million. After northern Armenia and Azerbaijan were included in Georgia, small principalities, mostly under Kurdish rulers, were established in different parts of the region. The monarch ruled by divine right, though the existence of feudal institutions prevented the royal power from becoming a despot. During Queen Tamar's reign, there was a movement, although unsuccessful, to limit the royal prerogative and establish a legislative body with authority equal to that of the ruler. Under Tamar, hospitals opened and two academies were established. Newly built bridges, roads, and inns for traders contributed to the development of trade and international relations. This period of the twelfth and thirteenth centuries is recognized as the golden age of Georgian culture; the age of creation of literary, architectural, and artistic monuments, which are still the source of inspiration for contemporary Georgian artistic thought.

Late Feudal States

Since the middle of the thirteenth century, the people of the Caucasus found themselves under the hardships of the Mongol yoke. Only Georgia and northern Armenia, controlled by Georgia, remained unoccupied, although they were forced to provide up to one-fifth of the entire male population to the Mongol army. The Mongol occupation brought real devastation to the Caucasian lands. In the fifteenth century, Khan Timur (or Tamerlane) invaded Georgia seven times. During the 1403 attacks, his troops destroyed more than 700 villages, fortresses, monasteries, and towns, and threw about 7,000 people down a cliff in the Armenian city of Van. The attackers took skilled craftsmen into imprisonment, and traders tried to stay away from these risky areas. Terror and impoverishment forced people to run away from their homes. Armenian settlements were established in Ukraine, Crimea, and India. For many centuries, these countries could not restore the level of their economic development that had existed before the Mongols. The culture of the region was damaged significantly too, because the most valuable written texts and monuments of art and architecture were destroyed. Only a few monasteries continued to rewrite the rescued books, while the national culture, especially Armenian culture, was developed abroad.

In the sixteenth century, Iranian shahs established a small statelike formation based on the union of different Azerbaijani clans and family groups and imposed the Shia version of Islam on the population. A growing Muslim religion and the division of lands between Iran and Turkey had the most negative impact on Armenia. The non-Muslim population was cruelly exploited, murdered, or sold on slave markets all over Asia. In 1578, for example, 60,000 Armenians were pushed into exile. Because of similar pressures by Muslims, Georgia developed better connections with Russia. The first requests for Russian assistance were sent from Georgia by the Kakhetian King Levan to the Russian tsar Ivan the Terrible. Georgian loyalty to Russia was formally expressed in 1587 by King Alexander.

Tragic events continued in the Caucasus during the seventeenth century also. The development of international trade, which was concentrated in the hands of the Armenians, led to the growth and enrichment of cities, but in 1604, the Iranian shah Abbas I exiled 350,000 Armenians and increased taxes. A series of brutally suppressed uprisings continued until 1633. The same policy was conducted in Georgia, where Shah Abbas I wanted to exterminate the entire native population and use the freed lands for the resettlement of Turkish tribes. Contemporary chronicles reported that a Georgian peasant worked the plow with one hand and clenched a rifle with another, afraid of being killed or taken into captivity. Up to 12,000 Georgians were captured and kidnapped into Turkish or other Middle Eastern slavery annually. About 300,000 Georgians were resettled to Iran when Shah Abbas wanted to transform Georgia into a Persian province. In 1634, the Kakhetian King Teymuraz initiated a campaign aimed to unite two separate parts of Georgia, Kartli and Kakheti. Some economic developments occurred in the cities during the 1640s, when the role of Tbilisi increased. Georgian traders used the time of peace to reestablish their connections with Europe and the Near East. Turkish and Persian occupation of Armenia continued in the seventeenth century.

In the first quarter of the eighteenth century, when the Safavid monarchy in Iran collapsed, Georgian kings attempted to strengthen their union with Russia in order to use Russian force against Iran and to make their country free. King Vakhtang VI supported the Russian tsar Peter the Great in his war against Persia, but Russia did not have enough power to protect Georgia, and King Vakhtang had to find refuge in Russia. Georgians who emigrated together with him founded a separate Georgian colony in Moscow, which is remembered through the naming of Moscow's streets with Georgian names. Several famous Georgian and Russian scholars, politicians, and military commanders were born into this colony. After that, eastern Georgia was under Turkish rule, and was then transferred to Iranian control until 1747, when it became independent after the death of Nadir Shah.

In 1762, Erekle II (1720–1798) acceded to the throne and united Georgia. The first European power that recognized newly independent Georgia was France, which hoped to turn Erekle against Russia and use his help in controlling Persia.[21] As an independent king, Erekle exchanged letters with the emperor of Austria, promising to attack Turkey in Asia if subsidized. Independence contributed to the economic development of the country, where free trade and guild activities were permitted. Glass and cannon factories were immediately established in Tbilisi, the coinage of domestic money was restored, and the city population increased rapidly. Georgia's strength helped lead to the Kuchuk–Karnaiji peace treaty in 1783, under which Turkey removed all of its military garrisons from Georgian territory and agreed not to request any payments. However, this did not mean that Turkey had no aggressive plans in regard to Georgia any more. In order to prevent further Turkish aggression, Erekle II initiated the conclusion of the Georgievsky treaty, which defined the status of Georgia as a Russian protectorate. The Georgian king recognized himself as a Russian subject, and Russia in exchange accepted the obligation to defend Georgia from foreign aggressions.

Within the Russian Empire

Wars in Georgia affected the people in Azerbaijan and Armenia during the entire eighteenth century. Using the relative weakness of Iran, Turkey invaded Armenia in 1722, and about 30,000 people were murdered during the siege of Yerevan. Between 1747 and 1795, Armenia experienced almost constant devastating incursions from Iran and Turkey. Azerbaijanis thought that disintegration and internal barriers could help them to preserve independence, and more than thirty small khanates, emirates, and other statelike units were established. In the late 1760s, Fatali Khan of Kuba, one of the small statehoods, expanded his possessions and acquired other lands. In 1775, he applied to Russia for protection and military assistance. Instead, in 1787, Russia initiated the unification of eastern Georgia and northeastern Azerbaijan and placed its troops along the entire Caucasian coast of the Caspian Sea, preparing for the admission of Azerbaijan into Russia.

In 1785, the Iranian ruler Aga Mokhamed-Khan Kadzhar invaded Georgia. Russia was able to send only two battalions in addition to a small unit from western Georgia. Despite the heroic resistance, Georgian troops could not stop the aggressor who approached Tbilisi. The inhabitants of the city took up arms and went forth to meet their foe. The city's musicians accompanied them, inspiring the fighters with their music. When the invaders entered the city, Tbilisi was completely destroyed. Those inhabitants who had not been murdered were driven off to Iran, where they were taken into bazaars and sold into slavery. The Georgian king Giorgi appealed to Russia for help. Russia wanted to gain possessions of the South Caucasus and declared war upon Persia and Turkey. As a result of Russia's victory in this war, the lands of Azerbaijan and Armenia were added to Russia's list of possessions. However, the actual Russian colonization began only after the conclusion of an 1804 treaty. After Russia's victories in two Russo-Persian wars of 1804–1813 and 1826–1828, all territories north of the Aras River went to Russia under the Turkmanchay treaty, which substituted Persian occupation for that of the Russians. The Caucasus became a colony of Russia, and its territory was admitted to the Russian Empire as a separate province, with Tbilisi as the center of the provincial administration.

Despite the fact that the Caucasus is a fertile region, the people who inhabited it were poor. According to law, serfs were cruelly punished for the smallest disobedience. The law in Georgia read: "If a peasant strikes his master, his arm will be chopped off; if in his rage he curses his master, his tongue will be torn out."[22] Although the people of the Caucasus found themselves under tsarist oppression, devastating attacks by the Turkish and Iranian armies ended. The tsarist state did not interfere in daily activities of local people, and the newly acquired lands were mostly used to extend Russia's strategic influence in the Middle East.

The Russian government understood that education was an important element of Caucasians' assimilation. In 1848, a Caucasian educational district was created, and the Russian school system was extended to the newly acquired territories. In addition to the district schools, four two-grade parish schools were set up in the highland areas to offer basic literacy courses. Other measures established schools for girls, for Muslims, and for those wanting to learn trade skills. Sixty government scholarships were distributed annually to enable Caucasian graduates to attend Russian universities. However, the policy treated the Caucasian population unevenly. More schools were built for Georgians than for Armenians, and many fewer for Azerbaijanis and highland Caucasians. Allocated budgets revealed similar inequalities and the government's assumptions that Georgians were better suited to take advantage of the civilization that the empire offered.[23]

Russia's presence helped to develop the region's economy. The economy became more stable and trade increased. A large timber industry was created in Georgia, new intensive farming techniques were introduced, and education was provided to most of the Georgian population. In general, the standard of living increased too. At the end of the century, Russians owned nearly 60 percent of land in the region, while the majority of the merchants were Armenians.[24] This disparity led to growing nationalism and resulted in a strong socialist movement. While ruling the southern Caucasus, the Russians applied the divide and conquer policy. Islamic Azerbaijanis conflicted with orthodox Christian Russians, who they viewed as a threat to their way of life, while the Christian nations of Armenia and Georgia accepted Russian rule more easily. The Russians attempted to set one ethnic group against another by giving favors in economic development and by building roads or public institutions. As Russian favor shifted back and forth, resentment between ethnic groups grew. Communists used the same policy during the Soviet era too.

In the nineteenth century, Baku was the fastest-growing city in Russia. After oil was discovered in the Caspian Sea, rapid industrialization began and was followed by an influx of Russian and international entrepreneurs and workers from all over the area. Oil extraction became the main form of business activity in the area, conducted mostly by the Russians, British, and Armenians, because local Azerbaijanis lacked the needed qualifications. By 1898, the output of oil in Azerbaijan exceeded that of the entire American oil industry. The first oil tanker, oil refinery, and wooden oil pipe were manufactured in late-nineteenth-century Azerbaijan. Despite the fact that the newly arrived nonnatives received the highest-paying jobs in the oil industry, the Azerbaijanis remained poor and uneducated, and a segregated society was created in Azerbaijan with interethnic tensions affected by high taxes and food shortages imposed by World War I. Industrial capitalism modernized the entire Azerbaijani society, distinguishing the country from the rest of the Muslim world and bringing European values to all spheres of social and political life.[25]

Armenian Question

The part of Armenia that fell under Russian control was almost half the size of the historic Armenian state, and a large western part remained under Turkish control. Armenia prospered during the nineteenth century, mostly because Russia viewed Armenians as true allies in the Caucasus and gave them a favorable status. Close ties with Russia resulted in a further Europeanization of Armenia. At the 1878 Congress of Berlin, where the disposition of the Ottoman Empire had been discussed among the European powers, an independent Armenian delegation unsuccessfully attempted to raise the issue of European protection of the Armenian state. That and a series of revolts aimed to achieve independence from Turkey in 1894 antagonized the Turkish sultan, who viewed the Armenians as an alien element within his empire. In 1895, the sultan ordered a massacre of Turkish Armenians. It is estimated that about 300,000 Armenians were killed over the following two years.[26] To improve his image, the Turkish sultan Abdul Hamid II ordered some supposedly effective reforms for the Armenian provinces, but they were not implemented. The European powers did not want to risk the partition of Turkey and did not press the sultan, while Russia, engaged in controlling the Armenians in its territory, was not interested in western Armenian affairs either. Armenian nationalism was an obvious threat for the stability of the Russian Empire. In order to increase assimilation, in 1903 the Russian government ordered schools and churches closed in Armenia, and all Armenian church property was seized in 1905. Until this year, the Russian policy had been one of ruthless repression, which resulted in increased revolutionary activity by the Armenians against the government. After 1905 a new governor of the Caucasus, Illarion Vorontsov-Dashkov (1837–1916), inaugurated a conciliatory policy and put an end to the Armenian separatist drive. Peace, order, and justice were returned to the Armenians, as well as some nationalist rights. "The Armenians were still, however, a thorn in the Russian side."[27] The Armenian members of the Russian legislature lined up with the left-wing parties, and activists were prosecuted and sent to exile in Siberia. In 1912, there was a show trial of 500 of the most important Armenians who had been accused of high treason; however, all but 50 were acquitted. Most seriously, the Armenians were stricken by the Young Turks' government, which in spring 1915 accused the Armenian community of helping the Russians during World War I and ordered mass killings and deportations of them. The exact number of victims is unknown, but the range is estimated between 600,000 and 2 million.[28] Those remaining fled Turkey together with the retreating Russian troops and settled within the borders of the Russian Empire, mostly in Tbilisi and Baku.

Old town Tbilisi on the shore of the Kura River. Photograph by Badri Vadachkoria provided by the Embassy of Georgia to the United States.

Because American Protestant missionaries have been active among the Armenians since the beginning of the nineteenth century, they were among the first who reported on the massacres during the war and raised large sums of money for Armenian relief. Armenian suffering attracted support from all over Europe. British children were told to remember the starving Armenians when they failed to clean their plates, and the French prime minister Georges Clemenceau wondered how it could be possible that "at the dawn of the twentieth century, five days from Paris, atrocities have been committed with impunity, covering a land with horror—such that one cannot imagine worse in time of the deepest barbarity."[29] Lloyd George echoed this opinion and requested that the essential condition of peace in the Caucasus be the "redemption of the Armenian valleys for ever from the bloody misrule with which they had been strained by the infamies of the Turks."[30]

World War I and Independence

During World War I, the people of the southern Caucasus had different allegiances and aspirations. For Armenia and Georgia, Russia appeared as the only defense from Turkish occupation. Azerbaijan hoped for Turkish help in overcoming Russian rule and implementing pan-Turkic ideas. Using the defeats of Russia and the Ottoman Empire in World War I and the collapse of the Russian Empire in 1917 to their advantage, the leaders of the three states of Armenia, Azerbaijan, and Georgia were convinced that the survival of their nations depended on their own efforts and strengthening mutual defenses. The Transcaucasus Federation was established in 1917, after the Russian tsar abdicated the throne. The federation did not survive for long. After the Bolshevik revolution in Russia, pro-Communist groups in Azerbaijan, which consisted mainly of Russians and Armenians, declared Azerbaijan a Marxist republic. Simultaneously, Muslim nationalists separately declared the establishment of the Azerbaijani People's Democratic Republic in May 1918, and formed the Army of Islam supported by Ottoman Turkey. Its independence was undermined by internal political infighting, and the pro-Russian Bolshevik faction won. To prevent a new Turkish occupation and neutralize Bolshevik followers, on May 26, 1918, Georgia declared its independence under the support of Germany. Azerbaijan did the same on the next day, having assurances of Turkish benevolence. Armenia declared its independence on May 29, 1918, repudiating all claims to Armenian populated territories under Turkish occupation. Unlike Georgia and Azerbaijan, Armenia was devoid of the bare essentials of life and was surrounded by hostile forces. Unlike the neighbors, Armenia did not inherit arsenals, storehouses, administrative machinery, or the financial, commercial, and industrial resources of the previous regimes. With a population of starving refugees, nearly 200,000 people died in Armenia during the next year as a result of ensuing famine and epidemics.[31]

The major European powers, including Bolshevik Russia, recognized the independence of the Caucasian republics.

During the Paris peace talks, all powers expressed their intention to secure peace for southern Caucasus. It was expected that U.S. President Wilson would offer the mandatory power of the United States, at least for Armenia, at the Versailles peace conference.[32] The French Foreign Office wanted a large Armenia under French protection, which would provide a field for French investment and the spread of French culture. The British saw certain advantages for themselves in taking a mandate of the region—the protection of oil supplies coming from Baku on the Caspian to the port of Batumi on the Black Sea, and the creation of a barrier between Soviet communism and British possessions in the Middle East. However, these sentiments were not followed by practical measures. The U.S. Senate did not consent to take the mandate in 1919, and the powers did not have the will to enforce the decisions of the San Remo conference, which in April 1920 made provisions for an independent Armenia. This can be explained by the fact that the Caucasus was far away, surrounded by enemies, and the allies had few forces in the area. The roads there were primitive, and the railroads had been badly damaged. Moving troops and aid into the area when resources were stretched thin was a major undertaking. While help was far away, the enemies were close at hand. The Russians were advancing southward and could no longer tolerate any independent state in the Caucasus. On the other flank, Turkey resented the loss of its territory.[33]

During the following two years of unstable independence, and attempts by the three states to keep their independence on the periphery of Russia's fluctuating borders, all three republics conducted free and democratic elections, guaranteed equal suffrage rights to all citizens, including women, established obligatory free elementary education, and passed laws regarding the social protection of disadvantaged individuals.

During the short period of independence, these states remained poor and unstable, and had to survive "the brigands, the deserters from the Turkish Army, White Russian forces, disease, and hunger."[34] They were not able to resist Russian attacks from the north and Turkish ones from the south. Despite the fact that at the end of 1918 British forces from Mesopotamia were moved into the Caucasus to occupy the oil fields of Azerbaijan, the Black Sea port of Batumi, and protect the Transcaucasus railway, the Bolsheviks moved into the region in 1919. Lord Curzon warned about the danger of leaving the region "at the mercy of a horde of savages who know no restraint and are resolved to destroy all law,"[35] but by the end of 1919, all British troops were withdrawn from the region. When it became obvious that Soviet Russia would take over the entire Caucasus, Britain recognized the three little states and sent them some weapons. The Allies asked the League of Nations to protect the newly independent states but it refused, claiming that the league was not really in existence.

Soviet Rule

The Soviet troops entered the southern Caucasus in spring 1920, and the Bolshevik offensive started with the taking of Azerbaijan. Then the Bolsheviks were supported by a pro-Communist rebellion in Armenia. In September 1920, Azerbaijan signed a treaty with Russia to unify its military force, economy, and foreign trade with those of Russia. Armenia's independence was recognized by the Allies and Turkey in 1920 by the Treaty of Sèvres. According to the treaty, all disputed territories in what had been the Ottoman Empire were supposed to be included in Armenia. However, these provisions of the treaty were not implemented and lands of western Armenia were not returned to Armenia. Squeezed between advancing Turks and the Red Army that already had occupied Azerbaijan, Armenia agreed on secession to Bolshevik Russia in December 1920. As soon as the Red Army echelons arrived in Yerevan, hundreds of former government officials and non-Bolshevik political leaders were imprisoned, the army officer corps was exiled, and a regime of retributions and requisitions was imposed.

In March 1921, Russia and Turkey signed a treaty that normalized relations between the two countries. According to the treaty, Turkey dropped its claims to all non-Armenian territories in return for Russia's abandonment of attempts to redeem for Soviet Armenia territories other than those that were already occupied by the Red Army. Thus, the new Turkish boundary was extended to the Aras River, incorporating the fertile Igdir Valley and Mount Ararat into Turkey. Also, the treaty stated that the Nakhichevan district would not be a part of Armenia and would remain an autonomous region in Soviet Azerbaijan.

Despite the fact that a treaty between Russia and Georgia provided for a continuation of Georgia's independence, in February 1921, Russian troops moved into this republic too. As a punishment for partial and nonimmediate acceptance of Bolshevik rule, 5,000 Georgian noblemen were executed under Stalin's order. After the Soviet troops occupied Georgia in 1921, they formed the Ajarian Autonomous Soviet Socialist Republic in the far southwestern corner of the country. Abkhazia was given a separate status of an independent Soviet republic in 1918, but in 1921, it was placed within the borders of Georgia, and in 1930, its status was downgraded to an autonomous republic. The South Ossetian Autonomous District was established in 1922 in the territory of a central province of Georgia. Some argue that this was granted by the Bolsheviks to the Ossetians in return for their assistance in fighting against democratic Georgia and favoring local separatists because this territory had never been a separate principality before, although large Ossetian communities in Georgia were established in the sixteenth and seventeenth centuries.[36]

According to the Bolshevik policy on nationalities, it was believed that national differences would not exist in the Communist society, where people would share common ideological and class values regardless of their ethnic roots. Following this concept, the Transcaucasus Soviet Federative Socialist Republic had been created as an independent state. On December 30, 1922, the Soviet Union was formed, and the Transcaucasus Republic joined the Soviet Union as one of four constituent member states. It remained a federation of constituent Armenia, Azerbaijan, and Georgia until the union's new constitution was adopted on December 5, 1936, which gave the status of a full union republic to each of the Caucasian republics. Nakhichevan, an Azerbaijani enclave completely separated from Azerbaijan by Armenia and Iran, and declared a Soviet republic in 1920, was downgraded in 1924 to an autonomous republic within Azerbaijan with some local powers. This status remains unchanged even today.

During the 1920s, under conditions of ideological control and political pressure, all three governments made tremendous efforts to develop a national culture and education, to establish contacts with artists and intellectuals abroad, and to create an environment of better security and material well-being than before. Later, during the rule of Joseph Stalin (1879–1953; in absolute power from 1926 to 1953), these republics were industrialized and educated under prescribed conditions, and nationalism was harshly suppressed. To strengthen the political hold of the Communist Party, police terror was used. In 1930, 530 popular revolts occurred in the villages all over the Caucasus.[37] The largest rebellion lead by a young but popular Mola Mustafa (1906–1937?) took place in the northern Azerbaijani town of Sheki, where 2,400 people, including members of the Communist Party, overthrew local government in an attempt to establish an Islamic republic. The Soviet troops could not suppress the uprising and restore the order for more than two weeks, and they could not apprehend the leader of the rebellion for the next two years.

Being an integral part of the Soviet Union for more than seventy years, the three Caucasian countries suffered from all possible Communist repressions, including Communist purges, muss murders, and deportations. Expecting the war with Nazi Germany, the Soviet authorities persecuted everyone who had potential contacts with the foreigners. In 1938, all Azerbaijanis in possession of an Iranian passport were expelled from the republic, mostly to Iran, where a sizable Azerbaijani majority exists now. After World War II, the Soviet

Union tried to acquire this territory and occupied Iranian areas populated by Azerbaijanis. But under strong pressure from Western powers, the Soviet Union retreated in 1946. Following that, the Iranian government suppressed Azerbaijani culture and did not allow any contacts across the border.

The countries of the southern Caucasus were not invaded by Hitler's troops during World War II. Hospitals were placed in these republics, and together they contributed almost 1 million fighters to the Soviet army. The republics were an important source of textile, fuel, and munitions. During less repressive years, Stalin's successors Nikita Khrushchev (in power 1953–1964) and Leonid Brezhnev (in power 1964–1982) furthered the industrialization of the region and promoted the social mobility of the people. During the late Soviet years of the 1970s and 1980s, names of all three Caucasian republics were synonymous with bribery, corruption, favoritism, and illegal shadow economies. New leaders, who were sent by Moscow to improve the situation and clean up the old state and party apparatus, soon adjusted themselves to the corrupt political system they had inherited. After Stalin's death in 1953, Communist elites in each republic were given more power and relative independence. Although open political opposition remained tightly restricted, expressions of moderate nationalism were viewed with greater tolerance and statues of national heroes, including saints, were erected in the three republics.[38]

At the end of the 1980s, the people of the Caucasian republics were much different people from those who had initially been included in the Soviet Union. Seventy years of experience of living in cities, of education, and of work cooperation made them much more sophisticated, modern, and Westernized people. Yet, very strong limits were placed on their freedom of expression. The Soviet political system could not accommodate the newly educated people. In all the Caucasian republics, a tension was building among the demands of the coming globalization, nationalist aspirations, and the narrow framework of the Soviet life. People in all republics were becoming more conscious of their language, history, and culture than ever before in their history, and they tried to find outlets for real expression of their national pride and interests.

Post-Soviet Developments

In 1991, the Soviet Union disintegrated, and its constituent republics, including those of the Caucasus, became independent states. On August 23, 1990, Armenia was the first republic in the Caucasus that formally declared its intention to become sovereign and independent, with the Mountainous Karabakh region an integral part of what had become known as the Republic of Armenia. The Armenian nation was defined broadly to include not only those living in the territory of the republic but also the Armenian community worldwide. On September 23, 1991, following the results of a referendum in which 99 percent of the voters favored independence, the legislature passed the country's declaration of independence.

In contrast to Russia and other Soviet republics, in the Caucasus, the dissolution of the Soviet Union was viewed as an achievement and a wonderful opportunity for further progress. While part of the Russian Empire and then the Soviet Union, Armenia and Georgia never forgot their great former statehood and the golden age; Azerbaijan always had dreamed of an independent exploration of its petroleum reserves too. After decades of Soviet mismanagement and exploitation, it was believed that oil resources in Azerbaijan were exhausted, but explorations of offshore fields in the Caspian Sea in 1991 suggested reserves in the range of 4 billion barrels of crude oil. Since 1991, these countries have been trying to overcome Soviet legacies, including corruption and widespread crime. They faced similar tasks of rebuilding devastated economies and strengthening fledging democratic institutions. But the escalating military conflicts and economic problems have almost led to a total collapse of these states.

In the 1990s, after obtaining independence, all three states looked like they were about to fall apart. Chaos, confusion, and self-destruction, typical of any failed state, appeared to be the main feature of the Caucasian republics. The Caucasian states developed amid the debris of great power, with anti-Communist and anti-Soviet sentiments dominating people's minds. These states were not prepared for independence because "the process of immanent national progress was severed for a long time. These countries did not have the opportunity to live through all of the evolutionary stages that would have transformed them from a state-bureaucracy into a nation-state."[39] The old structures were falling apart, while new, complicated ties based on clans and hierarchies appeared. The state-building process was extremely difficult for Azerbaijan, as it had no real state formation to celebrate before the establishment of the Azerbaijani Soviet Republic in 1921; this experience was hardly useful under new circumstances. Relations between the republics and Russia, which was the strongest among the post-Soviet states and concentrated ties with the economies of newly independent states, were severed because the states wanted to enjoy their newly acquired freedom and take obvious steps to secure their statehood, such as the expulsion of Russian (foreign) troops and the creation of their own border guards. For Russia, these actions meant opposition to the attempt to reintegrate post-Soviet states under Russian leadership.

The economies of all three states greatly declined in the early 1990s, affected by the dislocations caused by the breakup of the Soviet Union, conflicts,

A protest staged by the opposition party in Baku. Courtesy of Leila Alieva.

trade disruptions, transport and communication disruptions and stoppages, and the lingering effects of the 1988 earthquake in Armenia. In Armenia, for example, in July 1993, approximately 1 million people of the 1.7 million-strong labor force were either formally unemployed or forced to leave.[40] That was a result of the total collapse of the integrated Soviet economy, ongoing privatization, and institutional restructuring. Although this situation was typical for all countries of the region, in Armenia all hardships were even greater because of the continuing blockade imposed by the neighboring countries as a result of the escalating military conflict.

Although economic figures began to improve at the end of the 1990s, the economies remain fragile. Investors in oil and gas resources have fueled economic growth in Azerbaijan in recent years at the expense of other sectors of the economy. Widespread poverty and regional conflicts have contributed to high emigration from all three states, and remittances from emigrants have provided major support for the remaining population. According to some estimates, around one-quarter of each village population moved outside of their native place to seek work elsewhere amid the economic instabilities of life in the new republics. While few young women traveled further than a neighboring town with some working factories, almost every family has somebody who had moved abroad, usually to Russia, in search of economic opportunities.[41]

In general, the present-day life of rural communities across the contemporary Caucasus is not very different. When the various collective farms in the Caucasus closed in the early 1990s, assets were handed to liquidation committees, who parceled out land, equipment, and animals in arrangements that were most often advantageous only to committee members. Since then, almost all rural residents have worked as small-scale farmers, raising fruits, vegetables, and animals to feed themselves, and living off of the cash profits from the sale of oranges, grapes, honey, hazelnuts, walnuts, cherries, and, when they defy authorities, a local vodka made from mulberries. Men who have horses also work year-round to cut trees from the forests, draw them back to their yards, and burn them in covered pits to make charcoal, a job that could earn them as much as the equivalent of US$4 a tree.

In regard to the democratization process, the 2006 World Bank's annual report on democratic governance ranked Armenia among the better-performing half of countries in terms of government effectiveness and regulatory quality, and slightly below world norms on four other indicators: accountability, stability, rule of law, and anticorruption. No regress has been reported in Armenia in recent years. Georgia ranked slightly below Armenia on all indicators, except for accountability and anticorruption, and it seems to have made recent progress on all indicators but stability. Azerbaijan was ranked below the other two regional states on all statistic indicators, but it seems to have made some progress in regulatory quality.

The newly independent states that arose in the post-Soviet expanse made progress toward democratization, and transplanted to local soil the democratic constitutions and political systems officially approved in the West, particularly those with a semipresidential and presidential rule. According to the current constitutions, these countries are presidential republics in which state power is divided among the legislative, judicial, and executive branches. Each of them is independent and is guided in its activity by the provisions of the basic law and corresponding legal regulations.

Since becoming independent, all three republics have had relatively free democratic elections of their legislatures and heads of states, who are limited to two consecutive terms. Although presidential institutions are the strongest, the role of the legislatures is increasing. The legislature received a voice in appointing the prime minister, in addition to having its term increased up to five years in Armenia and four years in Georgia and Azerbaijan. Also, the legislatures have some responsibility for appointing judicial and media regulatory personnel. In May 2007, Armenia held legislative elections, and five parties divided 131 seats. The leading party is the Republican Party of Armenia. A less democratic transition of power occurred in Azerbaijan, where ailing leader Heydar Aliyev (1923–2003) ran for reelection against his son Ilhom Aliyev (b. 1961). A few days before the elections, the father withdrew from the race, and Ilhom Aliyev won the elections with 77 percent of the vote, beating seven other candidates. Protests alleging a rigged vote resulted in violence and spurred detentions of more than 700 oppositionists. Trials resulted in several dozen imprisonments. Most political prisoners were pardoned by the president in March 2005, after a strong intervention by the Organization for Security and Co-operation in Europe. The tradition of jailing opposition leaders during election campaigns and accusing them of plotting coups continues.

Georgia, on the other hand, appears to have a good record of democratic power transitions during the postindependence period. After the first popularly elected democratic government of Zviad Gamsakhurdia (1939–1993) failed and left into exile, the former Communist leader of Georgia and Soviet foreign minister Eduard Shevardnadze (b. 1928) was elected president. As he demonstrated the inability to conduct economic and democratic reforms, the opposition forces launched the peaceful so-called rose revolution. The rising generation of politicians used popular discontent with Shevardnadze's regime and the unfolding systemic crisis to escalate themselves into a revolution, which went peacefully because the government was weak and already discredited. The young reformers pushed the old Communist Party elite from the political scene, and elevated the incumbent president, Mikheil Saakashvili (b. 1967), to the top office after he received 96 percent of the popular vote. In 2004, the Georgian constitution was amended, giving more power to the executive branch at the expense of the legislators. In order to fight corruption, the revolutionaries reformed the police, armed forces, and the judiciary. Local administrations were placed under strict control of the central government.

The success of Georgian political reforms was questioned in late 2007, as a result of the increased instability. Several opposition parties united into the National Council, which launched demonstrations in Tbilisi demanding that legislative elections be held in spring 2008 instead of late 2008 as had been set by a recently adopted constitutional amendment. Their demands escalated to include Saakashvili's resignation. Security forces dispersed demonstrators and several dozen individuals reported injuries. An independent television station that transmitted the opposition's views was stormed by police and closed. The president declared a state of emergency for fifteen days, receiving enhanced powers. He claimed that the demonstrations were part of a coup attempt initiated by Russia and ordered three Russian diplomats to leave the country. In order to resolve the crisis, new presidential elections were scheduled for January 2008, and Saakashvili was reelected with 53 percent of the vote. During the legislative elections in May 2008, the party of the president received more than 60 percent of the parliamentary seats, while the opposition got about 15 percent of the votes.

Regional Conflicts

Since the Soviet collapse in 1991, the South Caucasus states did not enjoy peace, stability, and democratization fully; mostly because of ethnic conflicts, which impose on all countries a burden of arms races and refugee crisis. In terms of numbers, the region has become the most unstable in the post-Soviet era in regard to the intensity and length of its ethnic and civil conflicts. The ruling nationalists harbor various grievances against one another. This is particularly the case between Armenia and Azerbaijan, where discord has led to the nearly complete displacement of ethnic Armenians from Azerbaijan and vice versa.[42] There is an opinion that ongoing fighting between ethnic groups and civil warfare began because of the revival of long-repressed cultural yearnings.[43] Few of the region's borders coincide with the ethnic population. Attempts by territorially based ethnic minorities to secede are primary security concerns for all three states. The secessionists have failed to gain international recognition.

The longest and bloodiest conflict is the war between Armenia and Azerbaijan for the possession of a small, mostly Armenian populated territory within Azerbaijan, named Mountainous Karabakh. The region became especially important for Armenians after their lands were divided between Russia and Persia in the sixteenth century. Until 1828, this land was ruled by Armenian princes and had preserved an element of autonomy. Later, this became an area of Armenian refuge for those who fled Persia and the Ottoman Empire. For Azerbaijanis, the Mountainous Karabakh province has some significance too, as it is the area where the country's modern identity emerged under the Muslim khans.

The conflict began in 1988 and has resulted in 30,000 casualties and more than 1 million refugees and displaced people in Armenia and Azerbaijan.[44] In 1988, Karabakh petitioned to become part of Armenia, sparking ethnic conflict. The Karabakh's intention to secede from Azerbaijan and become a part of Armenia provoked an outrage in Azerbaijan and ethnic cleansings and mass killings of Armenians occurred in different towns. In December 1991, a Karabakh referendum, boycotted by local Azerbaijanis, approved the region's independence and a local legislature was elected, which later unsuccessfully appealed for international recognition. Following military activities,

Mountainous Karabakh military forces, which are part of the Armenian Ministry of Defense, controlled 20 percent of the Azerbaijani territory. A Russian-mediated cease-fire was agreed to in 1994; negotiations continue on the core principles of the agreement.

Several Georgian minorities expressed their desire for separatism in the late 1980s, when South Ossetia requested to join its territory with North Ossetia in Russia, and Abkhazia renewed its secession attempt, which was first undertaken in 1978 when local officials demanded the incorporation of their republic into Russia. After the breakup of the Soviet Union, this issue was raised again, and the Abkhazian representative body declared Abkhazia an independent state. Separatism has always been popular among the Abkhazians, who claim their original rights to land and try to prove that they arrived to the area first. In May 1989, the Abkhazians asked a well-known oracle who lives in a famous cave to tell them when their ancestors came to settle in Abkhazia. Unsurprisingly, the oracle confirmed that the Abkhazians were the original inhabitants of the area, providing a timely boost to nationalistic views. Abkhazia's legislature declared its independence in 1992, prompting an attack by the Georgian national guard. The conflict resulted in 10,000 dead and 300,000 displaced people, mostly Georgians who were driven out of their homes in Abkhazia. Many of them were forced to walk to Tbilisi through high mountain passes in the cold October weather; several died on the way. According to various estimates, the separatists in Abkhazia have between 3,000 and 5,000 men-at-arms, about 50 tanks, and 90 artillery systems. Although Georgia and Abkhazia agreed on a framework for political settlement and the return of refugees, the repopulation of Abkhazia did not happen, and Russian troops deployed along the Georgia–Abkhazia border remain in the conflict area. Without political and financial support from Russia, the Abkhazian separatist movement would not survive; therefore, Georgia views the Abkhazian conflict as a continuation of a fight for the state's independence and integrity, and national resistance to Moscow's efforts to take Abkhazia away. Approximately 80 percent of the present-day Abkhazian population has been recognized as Russian citizens and has had Russian passports issued to them. Georgia considers this a breach of its territorial integrity, and does everything possible to prevent this independence from international recognition. Ajarian demands for independence were stopped in 2004, when the Georgian central government extended its authority over the region.

A similar secession movement was initiated by the South Ossetians in 1990. Georgian actions aimed to return the region under Tbilisi's control triggered a conflict in which 2,000 to 4,000 people were killed. According to a Russian-brokered cease-fire, Russian, Georgian, and Ossetian peacekeeping units totaling 1,100 men established their camps near Tskhinvali, the capital of South

Ossetia. President Saakashvili increased border control and limited smuggling operations in the region. He also sent police, military, and intelligence personnel into the region. In response, Russia sent several hundred paramilitary elements. Regardless of the different peace plans proposed by Georgian authorities, in November 2006, a popular referendum was held in South Ossetia to reaffirm its independence from Georgia. Ninety-nine percent of voters supported the referendum. In response, the Russian authorities actively started to hand out Russian citizenships to South Ossetians and issue them Russian passports too. Both conflicts are receiving a growing geostrategic importance because of Russia's presence in the north and Georgia's friendship with the United States and aspirations to join NATO.

There are significant distinctions between the conflicts in Georgia and Azerbaijan. First of all, the conflicts in Georgia are formally internal, initiated by the "homegrown" separatist forces of Abkhazia and South Ossetia, whereas the Karabakh conflict is an interstate conflict, which broke out as a result of Armenia's occupation of the Azerbaijani territory in an attempt to protect ethnic Armenians living in the area. The conflicts in Georgia did not entail an invasion of the country by foreign armed forces, although the Russians attempt to be present there; the Karabakh conflict has resulted in the occupation of 20 percent of Azerbaijan's territory by the armed forces of Armenia.[45]

Besides the ongoing conflicts, which are nearing peaceful resolutions as a result of international involvement, all three countries are interested in peaceful and friendly relations with their neighbors and with those who can provide assistance to them. All countries expressed their interest in joining NATO and strive to meet the requirements. In 2003, the Caucasus Stability Pact was signed among Armenia, Azerbaijan, Georgia, and the European Union, providing for a regional security system and drafting political and economic measures that could contribute to the prosperity of the region.

NOTES

1. The word *Caucasus* is applied to describe the mountains, region, and the territorial affiliation of people residing in the territory of the three countries researched in this book.

2. Mikhail Kosven, *Narody Kavkaza* [People of the Caucasus] (Moscow: Nauka, 2002), 11.

3. Many mountain passes are closed by snow from October until early July, isolating the communities during this period.

4. Glenn E. Curtis, ed., *Armenia, Azerbaijan, and Georgia: Country Studies* (Washington, DC: Federal Research Division, 1995), 26.

5. Ronald Suny, *Looking toward Ararat: Armenia in Modern History* (Bloomington: Indiana University Press, 1993), 18.

6. Graham Smith, Vivien Law, Andrew Wilson, Annette Bohr, and Edward All-worth, eds., *Nation-Building in the Post-Soviet Borderlands: The Politics of National Identities* (Cambridge: Cambridge University Press, 1998), 64.

7. David Lang, *The Last Years of the Georgian Monarchy, 1658–1832* (New York: Columbia University Press, 1957), 5.

8. Smith et al., *Nation-Building*, 50.

9. More than half of the world's 6.5 million Armenians are scattered outside the borders of the Republic of Armenia as a result of persecutions that forced people into exile and forceful reduction of the state's territory.

10. Mark Saroyan, "Beyond the Nation-State: Culture and Ethnic Politics in So-viet Transcaucasia," in *Nationalism and Social Change*, ed. Ronald Suny (Ann Arbor: University of Michigan Press, 1996), 404.

11. Smith et al., *Nation-Building*, 52.

12. Lang, *Last Years*, 6.

13. Donna Urschel, *Eighth Kluge Staff Fellow, Interview with Paul Crego, Library of Congress Gazette* 19, no. 5 (February 1, 2008): 9.

14. Ekaterina Arkhipova, "The Borders between Azerbaijan, Georgia, and Russia: Soviet Heritage," *Central Asia and the Caucasus*, no. 6 (2005): 33.

15. Mamuka Komakhia, "The Greeks of Georgia: Migration and Socioeconomic Problems," *Central Asia and the Caucasus*, no. 6 (2005): 150.

16. Parikrama Gupta, "De Facto Stateless: The Meskhetian Turks," *Central Asia and the Caucasus*, no. 5 (2006): 127.

17. Ibid.

18. Sudaba Zeynalova, "Germans in Azerbaijan: A Retrospective Analysis," *Central Asia and the Caucasus*, no. 6 (2005): 144.

19. Strabo, *The Geography of Strabo* (London: G. Bell & Sons, 1903), 2:327.

20. Kosven, *Narody*, 47.

21. Lang, *Last Years*, 159.

22. Cited by Yuri Anchabadze, *Staryi Tbilisi* [Old Tbilisi] (Moscow: Nauka, 1990), 171.

23. L. H. Rihnelander, *Viceroy Vorontsov's Administration of the Caucasus*, in Suny, *Looking*, 99.

24. Margaret Kaeter, *Nations in Transition: The Caucasian Republics* (New York: Facts on File, 2004), 19.

25. Leila Aliyeva, "Promoting Cooperation and Integration in the Wider Black Sea Area," in *Establishing Security and Stability in the Wider Black Sea*, ed. Peter Volten (Amsterdam: IOS Press, 2007), 157.

26. Rouben Adalian, *Remembering and Understanding the Armenian Genocide* (Yerevan: National Commission, 1995), 24.

27. Roderic H. Davison, "The Armenian Crisis, 1912–1914," *American Historical Review* 3 (April 1948): 482.

28. Adalian, *Remembering*, 26.

29. Margaret McMillan, *Peacemakers. The Paris Conference of 1919 and Its Attempt to End War* (London: John Murray, 2001), 380.

30. Ibid.

31. Richard Hovanessian, *Caucasian Armenia between Imperial and Soviet Rule*, in Suny, *Looking*, 276.

32. McMillan, *Peacemakers*, 389.

33. Ibid., 412.

34. Ibid., 448.

35. Ibid., 454.

36. Smith et al., *Nation-Building*, 62.

37. Bruce Grant, "An Average Azeri Village (1930): Remembering Rebellion in the Caucasus Mountains," *Slavic Review* 63, no. 4 (2004): 714.

38. Curtis, *Armenia*, 53.

39. Iury Sulaberidze, "The Nature of Political Split: The Rose Revolution," *Central Asia and the Caucasus*, no. 1 (2007): 79.

40. Wolf Scott, *Emergency and Beyond: A Situation Analysis of Children and Women in Armenia* (Geneva: UNICEF, 1994), 22.

41. Grant, "Average," 709.

42. Jim Nichol, *Armenia, Azerbaijan, and Georgia: Political Developments and Implications for the U.S. Interests* (Washington, DC: CRS Report for Congress, 2008), 8.

43. Kaeter, *Nations*, 10.

44. Some observers believe that this war has continued for so long because individuals at the highest levels of government make good money by keeping the war going. See, for example, Thomas Goltz, *Azerbaijan Diary: A Rogue Reporter's Adventures in an Oil-Rich, War-Torn Post-Soviet Republic* (Armonk, NY: M. E. Sharpe, 1998), 19. One example was an Azerbaijani commander who kept bodies in refrigerators so that he might draw his dead men's combat pay.

45. Kamal Makili-Aliyev, "Problems in Implementing and Observing the Law of War in the Central Caucasus," *Central Asia and the Caucasus*, no. 2 (2006): 74.

2

Urban and Rural Developments

ARCHITECTURE IS AN important component of the Caucasian culture. The entire region is a large open-air museum of architecture, where objects from different centuries and even millennia are collected. Many temples, military fortifications, and churches have survived from the fourth or fifth century. Baku is considered a masterpiece of medieval Middle Eastern architecture, Tbilisi is known for its European-style labyrinthine streets, and the rose-colored tuff stone covering the building facades is the architectural signature of Yerevan. Because of the mixing of cultures, the architecture of nearly every city in the Caucasus combines European and Oriental traditions and styles. The Caucasus countries are a unique lesson in architecture. More than 1,500 years ago, native workmen were the first to apply circular domes and other difficult techniques in constructing churches. Many buildings show consideration taken in regard to the seismic conditions of the region. During the early medieval period, the commemorative monuments were mausoleums, memorial columns, and obelisks. With the Arab occupation of the region, experiences and traditions in architecture were lost in Armenia and Georgia; in Azerbaijan, Islamic architectural monuments, such as minarets, mosques, mausoleums, and Muslim schools, appeared. During the late medieval period in the region, civic buildings and monastic complexes with integrated libraries, scriptoria, hostels, refectories, residential apartments, and trade shops were built in such a way that each element created harmony with the other elements and with the surrounding landscape.

After the region's annexation by Russia, local religious architecture ended. Architects worked on objects of modern civic architecture and city planning. New types of administrative and residential buildings were built in the Russian classical design. Changes took place in city planning. Yerevan, Gyumri, Baku, and Tbilisi were built according to predesigned city plans. The influx of foreign investors at the end of the nineteenth century provoked an architectural boom. The most elegant buildings representing European architecture were created during this period.

Soviet rule during the twentieth century dramatically changed construction policies and city development. This was a period of rapid urbanization, urban sprawl that resulted from the mass migration of people from rural areas to the cities, the development of transportation, and the mass construction of drab cement apartment buildings on the cities' outskirts. Many historic buildings were destroyed in order to clear space for monumental Soviet architecture, which, according to Communist ideologists, was supposed to serve as propaganda. In the late 1990s, the changes in architecture mirrored the political development of the countries in the Caucasus. Municipal services were hit by economic problems. In the 1990s and 2000s, there was almost no urban development, and in many areas the quality of urban living even decreased. Disruptions in transportation, utility services, and waste removal became common. Only recently have some improvements appeared. During the same period, old Soviet monuments were removed and often replaced by modern art sculptures. Foreign architects were invited to construct new buildings; they introduced Western steel and glass skyscrapers, which are often criticized for their dissonance with local traditions. Restoration work has mostly stopped, and architectural monuments are suffering from excessive commercialization. A few nongovernmental organizations that aim to preserve national architectural treasures and promote national architectural traditions have been formed in all the republics, but they are small and weak, and cannot significantly affect the situation.

HISTORICAL ORIGINS OF CAUCASIAN ARCHITECTURE

An old Caucasian proverb says, "There is no city without a fortress." In previous times, a city's fortress determined the city's defense, influence, economic status, and organization of public services; all over the region the definition of a city and a fortress often coincided. Strong walls, deep moats, steep ramparts, and high turrets were not just a means of security; they also symbolized dignity and splendor. Usually, cities consisted of several smaller rectangular fortresses located along the banks of a river or on the edge of a cliff over a valley. The first information about cities located in the southern Caucasus dates from the first millennium B.C., and the residents of Yerevan are proud of the fact that their city is 300 years older than Rome.

Architectural construction began in the region during the Stone Age. Circular and rectangular dwellings of the third and fourth millennia B.C. were excavated near Yerevan. The most ancient buildings preserved in their entirety are Armenian churches built between the fourth and seventh centuries A.D. These single-nave basilicas had an outer narthex containing a small altar for those who had not been baptized or were in repentance. Domes were later incorporated into the structures, and the placement of a dome in the middle of a church building became a model for church construction for the next several centuries.

The main characteristic of the churches of the Caucasus is their stone-faced rubble masonry. Unlike the bricks and mortar of Byzantine structures, Armenian and Georgian churches were sheathed with thin slabs facing a core of fieldstone and mortar. The churches were built according to the cruciform design of the free-cross form of domed structures.[1] The designers of the initial structures paid particular attention to the interior. Decorative elements were added to portals and doors, windows, and eaves. Inside, the walls were made of finely cut stone and for the most part did not feature frescoes. The best example of early Christian Armenian architecture is the cathedral of Zvartnots, built in 641–661. The three-story structure featured a central dome, a cruciform floor plan, and it was encased in circular shell. The entire structure was 150 feet high. Mighty columns with eagles sculpted on their capitals were placed behind the four main pillars that connected each apse. The columns formed the rotunda for the second floor. They were decorated with sculpted grapevines and pomegranates, as well as images of the builders with tools in their hands.

One of the few medieval architects mentioned by name in contemporary sources is the Armenian Trdat (950–1020). Trdat is believed to be the architect of all the main churches built in the second half of the tenth century. Churches built by Trdat differ from early medieval domed basilicas with their pointed rib arches that spring from profiled piers, slender blind arcades of the exterior walls, and an enlarged space under the dome. These features determined the development of Caucasian architecture for the following seven centuries.[2]

Four-pillared prayer halls were built in the thirteenth and fourteenth centuries. At that time, churches were decorated with frescoes depicting scenes of the Nativity and the Annunciation. Independently standing bell towers became construction novelties of the late medieval period. Sometimes, the bell towers were used as mausoleums because, according to church rules, burials were not allowed inside of churches. In the nineteenth century, three-nave basilicas became the most popular type of church structure.

48   CULTURE AND CUSTOMS OF THE CAUCASUS

Table 2.1
UNESCO World Heritage Sites in the Caucasus

Armenia	Cathedrals and churches of Echmiadzyn and the archeological site of Zvartnots
	Monasteries of Haghpat and Sanahin
	Monastery of Geghard and the Upper Azat Valley
Azerbaijan	Walled city of Baku with the Shirvanshah's palace and Maiden Tower
	Gobustan rock-art cultural landscape
Georgia	Bagrati cathedral and Gelati monastery
	Historical monuments of Mtskheta
	Upper Svaneti

Source: UNESCO official Web site (http://whc.unesco.org/en/list).

UNESCO WORLD HERITAGE SITES IN THE CAUCASUS

In the 1990s, the United Nations Education, Science, and Culture Organization (UNESCO) recognized a number of historic places and monuments in each of the Caucasus republics as world heritage sites (see Table 2.1). Each recognized building is unique from a architectural point of view, demonstrating styles and techniques that native builders used in constructing places of worship, palaces, and defensive fortresses. The most intact architectural complex is the entire inner city of Baku that maintains the city's medieval appearance.

UNESCO protected 500-year old towers of a Svani village. Photograph by Badri Vadachkoria provided by the Embassy of Georgia to the United States.

The eight-floor Maiden's Tower, constructed in the twelfth century on a forty-foot foundation that dates to the seventh century B.C., is the visual symbol of Baku. The tower is the remaining part of the fortress that defended the city, and its defensive walls extended into what used to be the shallows of the city's port. Each of the eight floors of the tower is crowned with a stone cupola. Behind the tower, a labyrinth of small streets lined with pastel-colored houses leads to the complex of a fifteenth-century palace of Shirvanshah, one of the last independent rulers of Azerbaijan in those times. Spread over three terraces that tower above each other, the structure contains residential and official quarters, the tomb of the shah, a mosque with a minaret, a bathhouse, a mausoleum of court scientists, and an opening of the Eastern Gate built later.

In Armenia, the cathedral and churches of Echmiadzyn illustrate the evolution and development of the Armenian central-domed cross-hall type of church. The cathedral at Echmiadzyn, the oldest Christian temple in all of Eurasia, built in 480, is located in a walled compound with gardens and various structures. It has a traditional Armenian design, with the dome resting on four massive pillars linked to exterior walls by arcades. A three-tier belfry and a number of rotundas that surmount the apses were added in the seventeenth and eighteenth centuries. The patriarchal palace, which is the official residence of the catholicos, is located in the western part of the monastery. Adjacent is the Spiritual Academy.

Two other monastic complexes of the tenth century that are protected by UNESCO in Armenia, the Haghpat and Sanahin monasteries, are known for their collection of *khachkars*, carved memorial stones erected between the twelfth and fourteenth centuries and found only in Armenia. Like many other Armenian churches, these monasteries consist of asymmetrically placed buildings around the main cross-winged dome-type cathedral.

The main Georgian historic complex is the city of Mtskheta, located thirty miles southwest of Tbilisi; its churches date back to the eleventh century. Until the sixth century, Mtskheta was the capital of Georgia, and it has remained the religious center of the country throughout its history. The Svetitskhoveli (Pillar of Life) cathedral was built in the eleventh century, then destroyed by invading Mongol armies in the thirteenth century and rebuilt in the fifteenth century. It contains the burial vaults of Georgian rulers. The cathedral stands at the confluence of the Kura and Aragvi rivers, a place considered the holiest place in ancient Georgia. According to legend, the church was built on the spot where Christ's crucifixion robe was dropped to the ground in 328, having been brought from Jerusalem by a Jew from the Caucasus region; fragments of the robe are kept inside the cathedral. One of the Mtskheta monasteries is famous for being the burial place of the first Christian king of Georgia, Mirian, and his wife, Nana. Ruins of the sixth-century Jvari Temple are also nearby.

Other examples of the medieval architecture of Georgia are the wonderful mosaics and wall paintings protected by UNESCO in the eleventh-century Bagrati Cathedral, named after Bagrat III, the first king of united Georgia. The Gelati Monastery in the city of Kutaisi is also protected, as is the entire mountainous area of Svaneti, located in the northwestern part of the republic. Its villages have houses and towers that are at least 500 years old, and tiny churches decorated with medieval silver casting instead of painted icons.

CITIES AND VILLAGES OF THE CAUCASUS

In all of the South Caucasus republics, highly developed urban areas lay adjacent to tranquil villages, where the rural way of life has been preserved for centuries. Capital cities are the major urban centers, and the smaller towns all across the region follow the trends developed in the capitals. The largest of the three capitals is Baku, with a population of 2 million. Yerevan and Tbilisi each have 1.1 million inhabitants. All three are charming cities with a cosmopolitan atmosphere and tree-lined walkways where people sit on benches, kids play soccer, and the elders play dominoes. Many sidewalk cafés are along the streets. The real heart of each big city in the Caucasus is a farmers' market, a colorful and vibrant maze of produce stands and small shops. Cajoling vendors make the markets resemble Middle Eastern bazaars.[3]

Each capital city has neighborhoods that were formerly reserved for the ruling elite and now are home to the wealthier classes. State officials, recognized scholars, scientists, and artists populate these neighborhoods. In Tbilisi this neighborhood is Vake, in Yerevan, the area around Theater Square; in Baku, the neighborhood is the streets surrounding the old town. Such neighborhoods boast cleaner streets and better provision of utilities. The most upscale retailers try to open stores there too. Some of the older stores have signs that famous artists made for them long ago. The outskirts of the cities are filled with similar and bleak rows of high-rise apartment buildings. These areas are divided into so-called miniature districts, and are often named by numbers or the personal names of local historical figures.

Outside of the big cities, people continue to live in single-family detached houses. Thomas Goltz describes in his *Azerbaijan Diary* such a household, whose home is

unprepossessing when viewed from the street, but looks like a veritable palace within. Set on about two acres of fruit trees (cherry, pomegranate, apple, pear), the estate of a comfortable, two-story main house flanked by a second kitchen/den unit with an attached marble sauna and bath, separate digs for grandma, and a shack out back for the master's Russian gardener-cum-slave. In addition to tending to the fruit trees, and weeding the large tomato, eggplant, and pepper garden, the Russian was entrusted with looking after a long, low-sung hothouse discreetly tucked behind some bushes at the far end of the compound [where flower bulbs to be sold in northern Russian cities were grown].[4]

Most of the buildings are made from stone, the main building material in the region. Numerous cement mixes are popular along the Georgian coast, and tuff stone is the major building material in Armenia. Wood and clay are also used, even in very prosperous settlements of northern and eastern Georgia, and in mountainous Azerbaijan. Stoneworkers and sculptors were and still are highly respected in the area. They always have tried to establish a connection between interior design and exterior decorations. Pictures of animals, botanical forms, and abstract geometric designs cover walls, pillars, and portals. Builders were always held responsible for their work and were supposed to restore the building and compensate the owner if the building fell apart because of builder's faults. However, this responsibility extended only to cases when the walls fell apart toward outside of the house and the ruins covered the surrounding surface. If a building collapsed on itself, those who built it were not liable.

While today most of the city dwellings are multistory houses converted into condominiums with standard apartments, individual households used to be the main type of housing. In the nineteenth century, a typical village house consisted of two parts, a living area and the area for domesticated animals. Depending on the status of the family, the house might have separate areas for different types of food. Typical traditional houses, called *saklia*, were two- or three-room structures made out of bricks or clay. The guests stayed in the front room, and the host family lived in the kitchen or the remaining bedrooms. Each area had a high shelf for plates and pitchers. Mirrors, shawls, and such weapons as swords, long knives, *kinzhal*, pistols, and rifles hung on the walls. The furniture consisted of trunks, cabinets, rugs, and pillows. Massive ceilings were based not on stone walls but on strong wooden piles built within the building. The hearth was the center point of the house, and sometimes even had a sacred meaning. An oath given at the hearth was considered to be especially obligatory.

Soviet-style modernizations turned the Caucasus republics into industrialized countries. The provincial towns, which previously resembled Persian or Turkish villages, now have modern Western-like looks and amenities. The specifics of each republic's urban development are discussed in the following sections.

Armenia

Yerevan, the capital and largest city, was established in 782 B.C. Before the early nineteenth century, the city had only a few multistory buildings. The rest of the dwellings were small buildings with flat roofs, similar to those built in the neighboring villages. The city was dirty and dusty. Today, no area of the city is a reminder of its past.

Present-day Yerevan was built according to a centralized plan. Colorful buildings and a combination of traditional Armenian and Russian styles characterize the architecture of modern Yerevan. Republic Square, the main square with fountains, is framed by buildings that house the national art gallery and the museum of national history. Synchronized colored lights and music are features of the fountains built in Republic Square in 1970. The pedestrian boulevard, covered with light-colored basalt tiles, is the main avenue that bisects the main square and the city. Rings of boulevards with fountains and flower beds encompass the city center. Pink-colored facades of tuff stone buildings help to keep the festive mood.

New districts are located on hills that surround the city, and the green slopes have been transformed into parks. The city is decorated with many fountains, ponds, pools, and monuments dedicated to poets, writers, and statesmen. Equestrian statues remind visitors of mythological and real Armenian heroes. Another city park is located in a gorge along the Hrazdan River, where an artificial water reservoir and public beach have been created. The southern, valley-like part of Yerevan is occupied by industrial enterprises. Behind them are agricultural lands and wineries.

Most of the rural settlements look like small towns with paved and electricity-lit streets and modern two-story houses, which are often decorated with ornamental paintings. There are multistory apartment complexes too. However, many settlements did not recuperate from the December 7, 1988, earthquake, which devastated one-third of the republic. The refugees and earthquake survivors continue to live in schools, hotels, metal containers, and other buildings that were never intended for habitation. Newly constructed individual houses are built from natural stones or bricks with all the modern features of comfort. A traditional and important part of each house is a vegetable and fruit garden, located next to the house. Armenian villages are relatively big. Several hundred people usually live in the medium-size villages, and the population of large villages exceeds 1,000 people. Most such settlements have their own school building, movie theater, library, and store. Earlier, the villages were separated into quarters, which were often named after large families that resided close by. Although today in villages this separation into quarters is not so obvious, old family names are still used to define different areas of villages.

Industrial buildings, stables, and warehouses are usually located outside the residential part of a village. A cemetery is often located beyond the formal village boundary. While visiting cemeteries, local people bring food with them and have picnics to remember their deceased relatives and friends. Also, in almost every village there is a memorial to the local people who fell on the fronts of World War II. These memorials are usually in the village's main square, on a high school's premises, or in a park.

In the mountainous areas, villages seem much more authentic and ancient. Steep slopes of the mountains have naturally created a difficult settlement plan, with crooked, narrow, and short streets that can hardly be expanded to make them passable for cars. Village houses reflect regional climate changes. In the north, builders take into account long and cold winters, and in the south, a small, light summer cottage is almost always constructed in the middle of a garden. During hot summer months, families relocate to their cottages. Traditional old buildings, named *glkhatun*, which literally means "house with a head," are still in use as separate sheds or storages. These are square buildings with walls made from natural stones and roofs made from wooden logs supported by a pyramidal pillar inside the house. Roofs are covered with thatch. As a rule, *glkhatuns* did not have windows, and light entered the house through the exhaust hole in the middle of the ceiling. From the outside, such houses look like small smoking hills covered with grass. In the northern areas, residential and work parts of the houses shared the same roof and houses had only one entrance. In the south, the residential and work parts were usually separated. Several clay stoves and fireplaces were used inside the homes for heating, cooking, and baking. In the mountains, houses were built very close to one another, and the roof of one house often served as a patio for another; for defense purposes, village houses were often connected with hidden passages. Since the early twentieth century, shingle roofs have become more popular, with traditional houses becoming a rarity and visible only in remote pastures.

Azerbaijan

Ancient fortresses, palaces of feudal rulers, mosques, mausoleums, and bathhouses built in a typical Middle Eastern or Central Asian style are the traditional structures of Azerbaijan. Baku, the capital of Azerbaijan, is situated in the southwestern part of the Apsheron Peninsula. The city's main houses and administrative buildings are built in the style of an amphitheater along the bay of the Caspian Sea. Scientists date the first settlements back to the second millennium B.C. The city of Baku was mentioned for the first time in an Arab manuscript from the eighth century. Until the nineteenth century, Baku existed within the walls of the city's fortress, Icheri Sheher. The fortress's twelfth-century appearance and nearly 200 medieval buildings have been preserved.

Baku expanded outside the city walls during the oil boom of the late nineteenth century, which led to an architectural explosion and the construction

Old and new quarters are next to each other in downtown Baku. Courtesy of Leila Alieva.

of buildings in the neoclassical, neo-Gothic, North African Maghrebi, and rococo styles. The main railway station was built in 1884, in what is known as the Cairo style. The art nouveau Mailov Brothers' Theater was built as an opera house in 1910. Multistoried buildings full of balconies, arches, niches, and other architectural details, as well as fashionable mansions in different architectural styles, were built around the fortress. The city used to have an equally varied cultural life, but, unfortunately, its diversity mostly came to an end with the exodus of the non-Azerbaijani population in the 1990s. Armenian churches in downtown Baku were boarded up and have been partially desecrated.[5]

The architecture of the Soviet time reflects the aesthetic whims of the Communist leadership. The Amernikend, a model village built in 1925, provided apartments for 10,000 workers associated with the oil industry.[6] The buildings were especially designed to shield their inhabitants from the winds that blew during much of the year, and the front steps were raised to keep sand out of the hallways. Stalin's Gothic style, evident in the government house on the seafront, soon replaced constructivism, a Soviet architectural style popular in the 1920s and 1930s, which declared the supremacy of social purposes over art. More recent buildings and subway stations reflect traditional Azerbaijani and Islamic themes.

Today, Baku looks like many other Middle Eastern cities. Its esplanade runs along the seashore, and restaurants sell kebabs, local pancakes, and Azerbaijani sweets. Colored lanterns light outdoor eating places along the boulevards. A beautiful seaside park is located next to the harbor. Because Baku is the oldest explored oil field in the world, tens of miles of viaducts, elevated highways, derricks, and oil platforms extend into the sea. The Apsheron Peninsula has sandy beaches, summer cottage settlements, and resorts. There are many monuments of medieval architecture: watchtowers, mosques, baths, and civil constructions in the surrounding villages, which are becoming popular residential areas. Because of economic difficulties, housing construction in Baku almost came to a halt during the 1990s and only recently reappeared.

An important development of modern-day Baku occurred in the transformation of a former festive park, named after the Bolshevik Sergei Kirov, who established Communist rule in southern Caucasus, into rows of steel and glass tombstones between dwarf pines. These monuments commemorate those killed for the cause of Azerbaijan's independence. The park has been renamed to Martyr's Alley. Many graves belong to the victims of the Armenia–Azerbaijan war, and the majority of monuments have inscriptions from the Muslim holy book, the Koran. There are also graves of people of other religions. The most unique monument is a jar that contains a pickled human heart ripped from a body of an Armenian foe and placed on the grave of a nineteen-year old soldier by his mother.[7]

Unlike Armenia or Georgia, Azerbaijan has not undergone sufficient urbanization, and the living conditions in small towns are almost the same as in rural areas.[8] The younger industrial towns, built in the middle of the twentieth century, of Sumgait, Mingechaur, and Dashkesan combine modern Soviet architecture with elements of national decoration.

Usually, old Azerbaijani settlements were large, the buildings were separated from the street by a windowless stone or clay wall, and rarely was greenery seen behind the walls. A typical Azerbaijani house was a two-story brick building with a flat roof covered with mud. The first floor was used to keep animals, to store and prepare food (food was cooked on an open fire), and for other household purposes. People lived on the second floor. Unlike in the lowlands, mountainous villages consisted of houses called *garadams*, cottages with stepped, vaulted ceilings. *Garadams* were built on logs stacked one over another, with the bottom log supported by thick pillars in the corners of the dwelling. Smaller logs were placed higher, and while the construction continued, they made a kind of a ceiling, which was covered from the outside by planks, straw, and soil. A small hole for ventilation was left at the top of the ceiling. In northwestern Azerbaijan, in the area where silkworms were produced, the houses had clay and alabaster walls and four-sided tiled roofs. A large attic used for growing the silk worms was located under the roof.

Today, many Azerbaijani villages have been totally rebuilt and redesigned. Tiles and shingles have replaced old roofs, and houses now have large windows, screened patios, and terraces. Despite the fact that modern furniture is in many houses, the tradition of sitting or lying on the floor on small pillows is still alive, and floors and walls are covered with rugs and carpets.

Georgia

Tbilisi, the capital of Georgia, is located in the southeastern part of the republic. For many centuries, Tbilisi was the center of not only Georgia but also the entire region. Officially, Tbilisi is 1,550 years old, but settlements on the place of the modern city were erected much earlier. It is believed that the city was established in 458, when King Vakhtang Gorgasali ordered defensive walls to be built around his settlement. In Georgian, the word *Tbilisi* means "warm." According to legend, the city was established by a king who was chasing a wounded pheasant and saw how the exhausted bird entered the waters of a warm spring and regained its strength. Warm sulfuric springs with medicinal qualities still exist in the old part of Tbilisi and feed several thermal baths. The establishment of the city is connected, however, not to the springs but to economic factors. At Tbilisi, the Kura River becomes especially narrow, and a crossing existed here for centuries. Today, eleven bridges connect the two shores of the river in the center of the city, which is squeezed between the mountains; southern and northern industrial zones are located on the outskirts. Because of the stretched-out shape of the city, its main streets run along the embankments of the Kura River.

The main street, Rustavely Avenue, is located on the right bank and is the main public transport artery. Stylish public buildings along the street testify to the city's prosperity at the turn of the twentieth century. Today, cafés and tourist shops that sell locally produced arts and crafts are located in the nineteenth-century buildings with arcaded open galleries on the upper floors. The cross-streets are smaller and narrower. The farther from the river the streets are, the more steeply they climb toward the mountains. The restored residential houses with small courtyards and colorful carved wooden balconies and galleries climb up like ladders along the old town's streets, which end up at the foot of Mtazminda, the highest mount that dominates the city. Its name means "holy mount." A television tower, a restaurant, and an exhibition pavilion are located at the top of the mountain, which offers scenic views of the city. A funicular railway built in 1902 and a chairlift are the two most popular ways to reach the top of the mountain. An entertainment park on the mountain is the leisure destination for many city residents. Ruins of the old defensive wall, fortress gates, and towers below Mtazminda remind visitors of the citadel that stood at this place in the Middle Ages. The Mother Georgia monument was erected in the citadel in 1957; it is a gigantic statue of a woman with a sword and a wine cup, symbolizing the fact that Georgia has always met its enemies with a sword and its friends with wine made from local grapes.

Because the Turks almost completely destroyed Tbilisi in 1795, it has hardly any buildings older than the late eighteenth century. Churches are the exception. Most of the churches date to the twelfth and thirteenth centuries; however, some sixth- and seventh-century churches are preserved too. Georgian churches are characterized by floor plans that resemble a cross. Seventeenth- and eighteenth-century artists decorated many Georgian churches, including those constructed in the earlier periods, with mural paintings and frescoes. Among the subjects depicted are biblical scenes, as well as the lives of the saints, martyrs, and local princes. Some of the paintings reflect traditional Georgian dress and manners of the time. Many portraits of Georgian historical characters exist solely as part of church frescoes.[9]

Most Georgian monasteries and fortresses were built in the thirteenth century during the rule of Queen Tamar. A legend that explains the fast, large-scale construction says that Tamar was an avid traveler, accompanied by a large

Cafes and galleries line streets in Tbilisi's old town. Photograph by Badri Vadachkoria provided by the Embassy of Georgia to the United States.

retinue. Before leaving the palace, each woman who accompanied the queen was to take a handful of mortar in a special pocket attached to the sleeve of her dress. When the queen and her entourage were on a high mountain where the queen liked the view, Tamar ordered the women to pile up the mortar at that spot. Usually, it was enough to build a fortress. Then the men lined and transported stones from the bottom of the canyon or from the banks of a river to the construction site at the top of the mountain. After that, construction workers arrived to put soil around the construction spot and used it instead of scaffolding. When the construction neared the end, the soil was taken down for everyone to see the new building on an unassailable mountain.

Old gabled houses are preserved in some parts of the country, but modern two-story buildings with glass-covered galleries along the front and pyramid-like roofs covered with red tiles or gray shingles dominate in rural areas. In Georgian villages, buildings are placed very close to one another, but each house has its own garden and vineyard. Despite the fact that modern houses are relatively similar to one another, the building materials vary. In eastern Georgia, the preferred construction material is stone, often river boulders, while in western Georgia, houses are built from bricks or cinderblocks. The kitchen is usually separate from the living quarters in a special dwelling. When a new large house is built, the old one is often transformed into a kitchen.

In Abkhazia and Mingrelia, houses are round or semicircular with wicker walls and thatched roofs. In the mountains of central Georgia, in Svaneti and Khevsureti, old stone buildings look like small fortresses, mostly because of the medieval defense towers surrounding them. Along the seacoast, large villages and small towns are situated one after another, beside the nation's main railroad and motorway. There, oversized houses are located deep inside orange or other fruit groves, which are separated from the street by tall fences and metallic gates. Grapes or ivy almost always cover fences, balconies, and teahouses inside the gardens.

CONTEMPORARY URBAN PROBLEMS

The majority of the region's population lives in urban areas where modern amenities were introduced during the second half of the twentieth century. Because the region is a product of the Soviet system, municipal services have not been provided in their full entirety, and today all cities in the Caucasus experience housing, transportation, communication, sanitation, and many other problems inherited from the Soviet era. Economic disasters associated with military conflicts and economic collapses after the breakup of the Soviet Union in the early 1990s, enormously increased the difficulties of daily urban life. Many utility companies were closed because of the lack of fuel supply, the dramatic price increase of transportation, and the lack of regular municipal services. The irregular supply of cooking gas and electricity forced women to cook on kerosene or wood-burning stoves, a slow and dirty process, and to change their daily routine and prepare meals or heat water for washing clothes and bathing in the middle of the night when electricity was on. Without electricity, water pumps were off, and modern high-rise apartment complexes did not have running water for a large part of the 1990s.

Because residential areas have extended further from city centers, many people spend about an hour or more to get to work every day because of inadequacies in the transportation infrastructure and the distance between areas of housing and employment. While ownership of private cars is still below the level normally associated with a modern industrial state, their number is constantly increasing, which makes traffic congestion almost unbearable. All cities in the region were developed during the Soviet time when the idea of individual car transportation was not even considered and attention was paid to the development of public transportation, which did not keep pace with demand. Such problems as infrequent and unreliable service, expensive prices relative to the average income of local workers, and low numbers of buses, trams, and trolleys are common throughout the region. Only recently have city trams, trolleybuses, and buses come under management by the same city department, but taxis, suburban railways, and the underground subways remain independent enterprises. There is no connection between systems operated by different but neighboring jurisdictions. Because of a lack of investment during the Soviet period, Yerevan's tramway system is insufficient. In the 1980s, many lines were unjustifiably eliminated in Baku. Because of the economic problems of the 1990s, new means of transportation were rarely acquired, and work stopped to develop new high-speed rapid transit systems in Yerevan, including underground tramways. The impoverished population regularly stole electric wires used to supply power to trolleybus lines and sold them as recycled scrap metal. Because buses are cheaper and simpler to operate, and easier for providing access to new housing areas, they became the main mode of transportation all over South Caucasus. However, because drivers sometimes abandon routes, use buses for personal reasons, or disregard the established time schedule, service remains unreliable. Fixed-route minibustype taxis that parallel bus routes or provide connections to otherwise inaccessible areas appear to be a better, though more expensive, alternative. All three capital cities have metro systems, which remain rather limited carriers of traffic because of their insufficient length and area coverage. Built in 1965 in Tbilisi, in 1968 in Baku, and in 1981 in Yerevan, each metro system carries slightly more than 100,000 people annually. Existing transportation problems are worsened by unsatisfactory road conditions. Of the three capitals, Yerevan probably has the largest potholes, often as deep as the radius of an automobile's wheel.

Of all of the inherited urban problems, housing is the most acute. Although the Soviets invested heavily in housing, they failed to provide resources to house the millions of people who left their farms to work in the factories. Since the 1960s, thousands of housing units had been built in the Caucasus every year, but their size and quality were below Western standards. The results of this effort are visible in almost every city and town, where all areas except for the historic center are filled with identical drab, gray, concrete multistory apartment buildings. Often, these overcrowded areas are populated even though there are no lines of communication or transportation. Today, most people use cell phones, and telephone landlines rarely extend to the newly built areas.

Despite the fact that living conditions are often inadequate, the price for real estate in the region has increased significantly, reaching US$150 per square foot for a new condominium in any Caucasian capital city. Most real estate development occurs on the city's outskirts, where large apartment complexes are built on empty lots, and downtown, where old buildings, abandoned many years ago, are razed and substituted with new residential and commercial real estate—in the hope that demand will rise in the future.

Buildings that are more than a hundred years old in hilly areas of Tbilisi or in the old town of Baku are often damaged, some of them heavily; nevertheless, they are all still occupied. Some such buildings have missing walls or huge cracks in ceilings and walls. The entire region experiences heavy seismic activity, and the next big earthquake will likely destroy these buildings and result in a large number of casualties. In September 2005, two damaged buildings collapsed with few casualties in Tbilisi. None of the countries has an official program to relocate residents or help banks and developers rebuild the damaged areas. Meanwhile, real estate developers and banks expect the national or city governments to step in and relocate people from the damaged buildings. If relocation should happen, the vacated properties will become available for new developments.

Sanitary conditions and waste collection are other problems that affect the lives of city inhabitants in the Caucasus. Recycling is in its early stages of development because waste disposal has never been a priority before.[10] When city services were paralyzed during the 1990s, housewives usually dumped plastic buckets of refuse into large metal containers, which were emptied twice per week. With the upturn of the economic situation in the republics in the late 1990s, the organization of garbage collection improved. Iron bins were placed in strategic locations in neighborhoods and are emptied periodically. In most cases, these places are breeding grounds for rats. Large residential high-rise complexes usually have their own garbage compactors. The drop bins on each floor of the high-rise buildings end in large rooms with metal doors leading to the exterior of the building. Periodically they are opened and emptied by garbage trucks. The organic refuse is brought to large animal farms where it is used as forage.

Today, newly elected governments attempt to undertake complex reforms on the municipal level and make it profitable for local businesses and authorities to change the city infrastructure. For this purpose, each republic restructures and privatizes utility companies, adopts new management models applicable to transportation networks, and tries to make water supply and sewage systems efficient. Social housing programs have been developed, and conditions for public–private partnerships to construct housing have been created. However, there are not enough resources to implement these programs. Armenia and Georgia are recipients of the Millennium Challenge funds, aimed to finance small projects to improve quality of life in particular communities. All of the countries receive World Bank loans to develop their infrastructures; the assistance of private donors is important too. Road reconstruction in Armenia, for example, is paid for by money collected from the diaspora.

Notes

1. Murad Hasratian and Zaven Sargsian, *Armenia: 1,700 Years of Christian Architecture* (Yerevan: Moughni Publishers, 2001), 14.

2. Christina Maranci, "The Architect Trdat: Building Practices and Cross-Cultural Exchange in Byzantium and Armenia," *Journal of the Society of Architectural Historians* 62, no. 3 (2003): 301.

3. Mary Chatwin, *Socio-Cultural Transformation and Foodways in the Republic of Georgia* (Commack, NY: Nova Science Publishers, 1997), 27.

4. Thomas Goltz, *Azerbaijan Diary: A Rogue Reporter's Adventures in an Oil-Rich, War-Torn, Post-Soviet Republic* (Armonk, NY: M. E. Sharpe, 1998), 9.

5. Ibid., 16.

6. Fred Halliday and Maxine Molyneux, "Letter from Baku: Soviet Azerbaijan the 1980s," *Women and Politics in the Middle East*, no. 138 (1986): 32.

7. Goltz, *Azerbaijan Diary*, 16.

8. Sergei Rumiantsev, "The Influence of Urbanization on Forming the Social Structure of Azerbaijan Society," *Central Asia and Caucasus*, no. 30 (2004): 107.

9. David Lang, *The Last Years of the Georgian Monarchy, 1658–1832* (New York: Columbia University Press, 1957), 137.

10. Chatwin, *Socio-Cultural Transformation*, 86.

3

Family, Marriage, and Education

FOR MANY CENTURIES, the family was the institution that preserved national traditions of the Caucasus. Within families, people acquired their self-identification, cultural background, manners, and professional skills. In Armenia and Georgia, women were always respected; education was an esteemed achievement. Similar patterns were found in Azerbaijan, where Islamic fundamentalism has no historic roots. Since becoming independent in 1991, the Caucasian republics have experienced painful developments, including wars and extreme economic hardships, which have had a tremendous impact on every aspect of social life, especially on relations within the family. Because of widespread poverty, such basic aspects of life as adequate housing, access to health care, availability of food, security, and educational opportunities are the primary concerns of almost all families. Trying to adapt to the changing conditions and ongoing stress, the institution of the family has survived thanks to extended family networks, despite the necessity of many to emigrate in search of better income. Impoverishment, mass unemployment, and termination of caregiving services that the state traditionally provided changed women's status in Caucasian society and forced them to accept new social roles. Under the new circumstances, highly educated people became underpaid, and young people changed their attitudes toward education. Today, while the countries are still in a difficult transition, Armenia, Azerbaijan, and Georgia are returning to their traditional, though modernized, values. Despite the fact that marriage is more often viewed as a tradition than a necessity, starting a family remains an important goal for youths of the region. As soon as a woman gets married, she is challenged by the difficulties of balancing work and family. Higher education, which is being adapted to fit the Western model, is now more essential for success in the world, and educational opportunities are opening up in these countries.

MARRIAGE AND THE FAMILY

Tradition of Family Relations

For the majority of the people in the Caucasus, life revolves around the family, which is a very important social element. The family has always been the institution that protected people from cultural assimilation and physical destruction. People of all Caucasian nations have proverbs that generally describe the family as a fortress, where a man wards off external danger and a woman preserves domestic order and harmony. While public institutions are not well developed, extended families remain as social units that are capable of providing effective cooperation and security. Most of the population would likely feel vulnerable without a respected, well-connected family. Respect, in most cases, is based on a man's ability to earn enough to support his wife and children, and to maintain the family's socioeconomic position in the community.

Throughout the region, nuclear families are of similar type and form. Families usually include five to eight people of two or three generations, including husband and wife, their children, and sometimes the parents of one of the spouses. In rural areas, families are bigger, and depending on commercial or medical needs, may include relatives from three or four generations. Usually, families include people of the same religion and ethnicity. Today, marriages between people of different social statuses occur more often than they did before.

Paying formal respect to a man and an elderly person within the family and in greater society is an organic part of Caucasian culture. Mountainous people have particularly long lives. The percentage of people older than ninety years is about 3 to 7 percent higher among people living in the mountains than among those living in the lowlands. Researchers attribute this fact to the respect of the population for the elderly, especially within the family. Respect for elders is emphasized through established ceremonies, which are similar among all Caucasian people. For example, it is not acceptable for younger people to sit or lie in the presence of an elderly man. This rule applies even to younger family members, who should not keep their hands in their pockets, start conversations, interrupt elders, answer questions briefly, speak loudly, dance, smoke, drink, scratch themselves, or dress sloppily. The head of the family usually has a special chair, which, as a sign of respect, is placed next to the hearth. Similar respect is shown to older brothers. It is common for a younger person to walk on the left side of an older person, and in villages it is still taboo to pass an older man. Girls are expected to be even more modest and polite than boys are. There are some Georgian proverbs that emphasize the respect demonstrated toward the elderly: "The elderly is the savory shadow," "One, who does not have an older person has no luck," "When an old tree fell down, ants started to attack," which means that a family will be vulnerable without an elder person in the house.

In Georgia's mountainous communities, patriarchal family relations with all relevant social institutions have been preserved for centuries. Because households were labor intensive, most families were large with strong labor forces. It was common for all sons to continue to live in their parents' house even after marriage; the wife of the oldest son was usually superior to the other wives living at the family's estate. Even if some members of the family moved out and lived independently, the land always remained common property. Until the middle of the twentieth century, family relations were based on the separation of labor. Because of this separation, women were often confined in the house and busy with housework, which was never considered prestigious. Sometimes women were involved in agricultural work, but mostly as men's assistants. The head of the household was usually the elderly man, and the rest of the family was subordinate to him. The power of the head of the household allowed him to determine the duties of all other family members, approve or disapprove marriages and divorces in the family, resolve disputes, and use corporal punishment in the case of disobedience. A sick and old father could transfer his leadership duties to his oldest son, who was expected to continue to ask for his father's advice and was not considered a true head of the household. Some ethnic communities in Georgia (Pshav, Svani, Kartli) elected the heads of large families. In such families, even the youngest son had the opportunity to inherit power after his father's death if he had better skills than the older brothers or if his older brothers did not reside in the same household.

If after the father's death a property division threatened the household, the mother could become the head of the household. The authority of the senior woman was traditionally high. Men usually did not interfere in female activities, and the oldest woman monitored all affairs relating to the other women and maids in the house. She divided work and maintained order on the women's side of the house. Neither daughters nor daughters-in-law could do anything without reporting to the matriarch or asking for her permission. She decided on punishments for the women and protected them from male abuse. In this capacity, she was highly respected and was often the only woman whose opinion men would take into account.

The patriarchal family remains strong, especially in the highlands and in Azerbaijan, because of the tradition of subordinating the younger to the older and the women to the men. Customary and religious norms are still applicable if the elders endorse them. For example, in the case of a father's death, the son's share can be twice as big as the amount of property received by the daughter, while the widow may receive only one-eighth. In Azerbaijan, for example, men usually represent their families in circumstances dealing with the authorities or the community, but in Armenia women have had voting rights at village assemblies for many years.

Neighboring families are often connected by blood and establish tightly knit communities, which are also based on the general principle of age hierarchy. Prior to the 1930s, older people in the Caucasus lived in a comfortable atmosphere of respect and authority. Elder leaders were often mediators and arbitrators in conflicts, and they represented their communities as guarantors of rights. It was unheard of to disrespect or disobey elders. Those who demonstrated such behavior were severely punished or even expelled from the community. It was obligatory to invite elders to family celebrations and offer them the first and best part of a meal. This tradition was significantly undermined by the Bolshevik revolution, after which young people were promoted to fill local vacancies in courts and official institutions. To undermine the traditions, older people were purposefully repressed, sent into exile, or murdered. Although the elderly are still customarily respected, many traditions have been lost, the authority of the older people is not as strong, and their opinions do not matter as much as they used to.

Urbanization and technical progress have damaged family traditions as well. The norms of civil law, which have applied since the 1930s, modernized family relations and formally equalized the status of men and women. Today laws in all three countries prohibit gender discrimination and impose equal responsibilities on men and women regarding the upbringing of children, care for the elderly, and rights in the division of family property. Soviet policies aimed to unify family life and eradicate religious rites and local marriage traditions eliminated the differences in family relations and weakened patriarchal traditions, which today are stronger in Islamic communities than among Christian ones.

Respect for the elders is often sanctioned by the state to secure public approval of government policies. Formal status does not guarantee informal leadership in the family. Women and children may demonstrate respect for the oldest man but actually listen to the person they recognize as a leader. According to research conducted in the 1990s, in more than one-third of families, husbands and wives resolved all important questions together; approximately 23 percent of households in each republic reported that women were heads of the household.[1]

Marriage Rites

Most people regard marriage highly, and it is a sign of prestige. Traditions related to marriage are universal in the region. Weddings are conducted at a relatively early age. Family laws of all three republics establish marriageable age at eighteen years old for men and seventeen years old for women, and the governments strictly enforce these provisions. In rural areas, where there are almost no career prospects, women do not face the difficult decision of having a baby or pursuing professional success. Most women who do not plan to attend a university get married between eighteen and twenty years of age. If a woman wants to earn a university degree, she is more likely to get married in her third or fourth year of study, around the age of twenty or twenty-one. Young men sometimes marry between the ages of twenty-three and twenty-five, and sometimes twenty-seven years old, but the public opinion considers this quite late. Unmarried women have lower social status and often remain with their parents or married siblings. The migration of unemployed men outside of the Caucasus for extended periods of time in search of work creates a disproportion percentage of men compared to women and reduces women's marriage prospects. This situation has contributed to the increased number of teenage marriages and the growing age gap between husbands and wives. Forced marriages have not been reported, but parents pressure their girls to take the prosperity of future husbands into account more than they did before.[2]

Marriages are regulated by numerous ceremonial rites and rituals, including marriage ransoms, payments of bridal fees, preparations of dowries, the stealing of a bride, and prearranged marriages by parents, though the opinions of the couple are taken into account. All these traditions have economic justifications; they were introduced in times when women were considered part of a labor force and potential mothers of future community members. In Georgia, grooms used to pay brides' parents between five and twelve cows. In Armenia, gifts were given to the bride, and together with the dowry, the gifts were her property if a disaster struck. Earlier, the community strongly monitored the ban on marriages between relatives, and the family codes of all three republics have incorporated this ban. The authorities exercise control and request proof that the marrying couple has no blood relations in order to register to marry. Specific rites vary depending on the locality. It is believed that marriage rules known to people of Armenia and Georgia are based on principles of the ninth-century Byzantine law adopted during the rule of Emperor Leo the Wise.

Usually there are three stages of marriage: preliminary, which is the selection of a bride and related negotiations about the marriage conditions; second, the wedding, which includes the celebration and relocation of the bride to the groom's house; and third, the after-wedding customs.

As a general rule, young people meet independently and let their relatives know about their decision to get married. Before the formal engagement, the parents try to learn as much as possible about their future relatives. The tradition of an agreement between parents of the children for an arranged marriage is of the past. Even if the groom's parents are involved in selecting the bride, they always give the young people an opportunity to meet and express their own opinion. When the young people have agreed to get married, the groom's father, uncle, and two or three close relatives go to the bride's house to propose the marriage to the bride's family. This is often a formality, and the bride and her parents pretend to not expect such a visit. Even if the parents of the bride agree, they cannot express their agreement immediately. They say that they need time to discuss the issue with relatives. Especially in Armenia, a second or even third visit by the groom's father is not rare. After the bride's parents agree, they offer food and wine to the guests. A gift to the bride, usually an engagement ring, is given. In previous times, a formal engagement was later conducted; today, however, the engagement is combined with the conclusion of the marriage agreement. Engagements and weddings can be months and sometimes even years apart. Previously, weddings were conducted in the autumn after the harvest. Today, weddings are celebrated all year round.

All weddings require thorough preparation. Food, beverages, and gifts are stored well in advance. Pastries and cakes are baked a few days before the wedding at the home of the bride. Usually, weddings begin on a Friday night and end on Sunday evening. Before the wedding, the bride's girlfriends meet at her house to view the dowry and the dress. The girls' celebration often turns into a dance attended by young men and the groom's friends. According to an old tradition, the bride dances with a handkerchief in her left hand and money in her right hand. During her dance, she stops to greet all guests personally, shaking hands with them and receiving more gifts.

The formal wedding begins when three or four of the groom's friends, relatives, or neighbors attempt to steal a chicken from the bride's household. The owners pretend that they do not notice this stealing attempt and only when the "theft" has been accomplished do they catch the intruders. However, they pardon them when the thieves say that they came to confirm the groom's intent to marry. Then the wedding begins. The thieves return to the house of the groom together with the entire wedding procession but without the bride; the stolen chicken is to be given to the mother of the groom. At the same time, the guests gather at both houses. They eat and dance. The groom and bride are ritually bathed, and the groom wears his wedding suit, which is usually a specially tailored dark-colored suit adorned with a red flower or a ribbon in the buttonhole. When the party is ready, they leave to pick up the bride.

Customarily, the groom buys the wedding dress for the bride and brings it with him. He does not give it to her immediately but holds the dress as ransom. Before the bride puts on her veil, her friends try it on with the hope that they will get married soon too. Then the father of the bride gives his daughter to the groom and her future father-in-law. After that, the procession moves on to the groom's house for further celebration. It may stop on the way at the church for a religious ceremony and at the state registry office or at the local city hall for an official civil registration of the marriage, as none of the Caucasian republics recognize common-law marriages. In order to be legal, a marriage must be registered by state authorities. The couple's entry into the groom's house is the culmination of the marriage, and a festive celebration begins with the breaking of porcelain plates, which is the sign of a good omen. The feast may continue for a day or two. Most gifts given to the newlyweds are money, although close relatives may present them with jewelry.

In recent years, old marriage rites and traditions, which were viewed as roots of national identity, have been revitalized; however, they are less strict than before. For example, newlyweds are now allowed to sit with the guests and eat during the celebrations. In addition to state legalization and the registration of the marriage, almost all couples who marry perform religious ceremonies, which were prohibited during Soviet rule. Marriages between people of different religions are rare and generally met with disapproval. The high rate of ethnic endogamy is explained by the relatively high homogeneity of the society, ethnic consciousness, and sociodemographic factors.[3] Among other factors affecting the decrease in the number of intermarriages during the past ten years are language, increased religious activity, education, and the preservation of family ties. Presently, in each republic, more people than before speak their native language, and that is the only language they are able to speak. The lack of a common language for interethnic communication creates barriers in contacts among the people and decreases the possibilities of meeting members of other ethnic groups. Usually, the relationships that lead to marriage are established during the period of college education. Because today most people receive their education within the republic they are from, their chances of meeting people of other ethnicities are lower. In Azerbaijan, the decline in intermarriages has been strongly affected by the growing influence of the Islamic religion.

Divorce

Although the emancipation of women during the twentieth century destabilized family relations and simplified divorce procedures, families are traditionally stable in the Caucasus. The patriarchal family was not focused on personal aspects of a marriage. In such families, economic reasons and the necessity of securing the continuity of the family facilitated and preserved marriages. Subsequently, it was not easy to divorce. Only certain reasons could justify divorce, such as the wife's infidelity, her inability to have children, conflicts with relatives, or the absence of skills necessary to run the household. Although men and their families had almost unlimited power over women, women were traditionally allowed to dissolve marriages at their initiative when a husband embezzled his wife's dowry, violently abused her, could not support his family financially, or was unable to have children or perform his sexual functions. However, this occurred relatively seldom. Men of the Caucasus are expected to take a good care of women, and to defend and protect them from any possible offenses; most men continue to fulfill this historical role. Economics contributes to family stability too. Because of the subordinate positions of women in society, men are almost always the owners of industry, land, and other real estate. Regardless of written legislation, customary laws permit women to have only movable property in their possession, which makes women vulnerable in case of divorce.

Following traditional views of marriage as an inseparable institution, society does not approve of divorce. Despite the fact that divorce procedures are relatively easy and favor women, divorce rates in all of the Caucasus are minimal, and in rural areas the divorce rate is about three times less than in the cities.[4] According to the United Nations Office of Statistics, the crude divorce rate, or the number of divorces per 1,000 people, is 0.6 for Armenia, 0.8 for Azerbaijan, and 0.4 for Georgia. In comparison, the rate in the United States is 3.6.[5]

Uncontested divorces, with no unresolved disputes over division of property or payment of alimony, and divorces with no minor children involved can be granted by a local civil registry office. A waiting period of three months for possible reconciliation must pass between the date that the application is filed and the final registration of divorce. Contested divorces must pass through the local court. The trial judge may postpone the ruling and suggest reconciliation. A man may not request a divorce if the family has a child younger than the age of one. The judge decides on issues of custody, alimony (usually 25 percent of the man's income for one child and 50 percent of income for two or more children), and division of property if such issues arise. Divorce does not terminate parental rights, and divorcees may either keep their married last names if they had adopted the spouse's last name before or return to their maiden name.

Children's Upbringing

In the Caucasus, raising children was always the main focus of any family. Infertility and lack of children were considered the most serious family tragedy. It appears that this view has changed today. Only Islamic Azerbaijan, with four children in a family on average, has a positive population growth rate, and its birthrate is about 50 percent higher than in Christian Armenia and Georgia, where the population is declining and the birthrate is 10 and 12 per 1,000 people, respectively. Despite government measures to support families and encourage women to have more children, birth control measures are becoming more popular. Scholars mention that among the factors that have caused parents to act more responsibly in regard to starting families are the economic situation, the increasing employment of women, government efforts to expand literacy among young people, and the availability of birth control. This situation contradicts traditions of the Caucasus, where prior to World War II, the birthrate was about nine births per woman. Even in the 1960s, in Armenia and Azerbaijan the birthrate was more than 40 per 1,000 people.

Many rites, beliefs, and superstitions surrounded the birth and early life of children. Newborns were usually dusted with salt because of beliefs that salt has protective features, especially among Armenians. Salt was kept in special jars, and everybody who entered the house with a newborn was supposed to touch the jars first and then see the mother and child. The restrictions on visiting the mother with the child had partially mystical, partially logical hygienic reasons and prevented the child from becoming infected. Because today almost all births occur in hospitals, the traditions associated with the birth of a child are almost extinct.

The most popular method of child upbringing is the personal example of adults. When children are present, adults control their behavior. Punishment and encouragement are widely used. Corporal punishment is not approved by public opinion, but it is not rejected entirely either. According to common opinion, corporal punishment proves that parents are bad educators. Usually, convincing children and explaining things are the most accepted ways to raise children. Parents almost constantly remind their children that they are responsible for their actions for the good name of the family and should not disgrace their parents. Sometimes as a form of punishment children are not allowed to leave the household premises and play with peers or watch television for a specified period of time.

Parents and grandparents often feel that it is their duty to teach youths traditional craftsmanship and folk dances. In villages, children are involved in productive labor activities starting in early childhood. Children who are five or six years of age already have simple daily duties that they have to perform, but the involvement of children in household activities depends on the social and professional status of the parents. In the cities and in families where mothers have more time to spend with their children, children become

Georgian children help their parents with agricultural work. Courtesy of Mr. and Mrs. Mikhael Budagashvili.

involved in work later. Labor duties are minimal during the school year be-cause most parents believe that children's main duty is to study. Physical ed-ucation is traditionally important, especially for boys. In rural areas, children learn how to ride horses, and in cities they participate in various athletic ac-tivities. The most popular sport is soccer, and children play it throughout the region. Because religious life was revitalized after the breakup of the Soviet Union, attendance at religious services during the holidays has become a fam-ily activity. Often children attend religious Sunday schools.

THE ROLE OF WOMEN

Social Status of Women

Tradition secures and cultivates the modest behavior of women and their supportive and subordinate role in family relations. These stereotypes largely exclude women from public and economic life, reserving for them a greater role in reproduction, child care, cooking, and housework. The Virgin Mary is often referred to as the ideal model of a woman. In contrast to Muslim society, which views women according to religious laws, Georgians have always given women a high place in community life. Special cults are associated with the Virgin Mary, St. Nino the Apostle of Georgia, and Queen Tamar, the symbol of Georgia's golden age. It is expected that Queen Tamar, who symbolizes women's traits of perseverance, beauty, kindness, and fearlessness against great odds, is a female model for young women.

The forced modernization during the Soviet period brought fundamental changes to Caucasian society. Women constituted half of the workforce in each republic. In the early 1990s, well more than two-thirds of doctors and more than half of teachers in the region were women.[6] Becoming more urban and more industrial, women became more mobile and literate. Among women all over the Caucasus, literacy rose from 19 percent in 1926 to 62 percent in 1939, and to 100 percent in the middle of the 1980s.[7] Education, the lessening role of the church, and a metropolitan life brought social patterns similar to those in Western European countries. Women assumed double roles—one of the family-oriented mainstay and the other as a professional in the public sphere.[8] However, during most of the twentieth century, despite the fact that the overwhelming majority of women were employed outside their households, and that their earnings were not significantly lower then those of men, men were traditionally considered the breadwinners. Today, these views have become even more popular. Ongoing military conflicts, underemployment, reduced subsidies and benefits (which existed during the Soviet era), the collapse of infrastructure, and male labor migration weakened the status of the family and worsened the position of women, leading to the reaffirmation of the traditional gender traditions. This is revealed by the fact that women, especially young women, often are not invited to a table attended by men. They serve the men but eat separately. However, during important meals, women take turns serving and sometimes sitting at the table. Women with higher positions outside the home are more likely to mingle with male guests. Although religious practices in Azerbaijan are less restrictive than in other Muslim countries, the women have to follow their traditional roles. Especially in rural communities, women who appear unaccompanied or smoke in public, or who visit restaurants, are subject to disapproval. Nevertheless, the majority of Azerbaijani women have jobs, and a few have attained leadership positions. In 1993, President Heydar Aliyev appointed surgeon Lala-Shovket Gadjieva (b. 1951), a champion of women's rights, to be his vice president. Later, she was transferred to a diplomatic position and represented Azerbaijan in the United Nations.

Daily Life of Women

The traditional role of women gradually changed during Soviet rule. Women were graduating from universities in equal numbers as men, and they

were working in every profession, though they rarely occupied positions in upper management. Traditionally, men dominated positions in industry, metallurgy, mining, government, military, and the police. Work in the health-care,
education, and culture sectors, as well as in textile and food-processing industries, was considered more suitable for women. Because of the relatively high
standards of living, families did not have a serious need to keep women employed. Most women preferred to leave the labor force for years to raise young
children, or they combined household responsibilities while seeking less demanding jobs with fewer hours and lower pay. This process contributed to
the feminization of some professions, mostly teaching, medicine, and office
work.

In Abkhazia, the northwestern region of Georgia, prophecy and art of ora-
cles is a traditional and still respected female occupation. The Abkhazians are
likely the only people of the Caucasus who continue to believe that a shaman
may find out who caused a certain illness and the necessary remedy. There
is a woman who is trusted with the knowledge of healing in almost every
Abkhazian settlement. According to observers, sometimes during treatment
sessions these women have ecstatic inspirations and cry out the name of a
person who caused the illness and the demands of the angered divinity.[9] At
other times, the shaman converses with the divinity, whom she questions and
from whom she receives answers. After a while, she may announce what kind
of sacrifice is to be conducted. Various ritual actions, such as walking an animal around the sick person and then taking the animal to the forest to carry
the sickness away, are performed too. The rites are executed by selected other
women for whom the shaman serves as an instructor. Large sums of money
are usually paid for such services.

In every Caucasus republic, women much more than men have been subject
to negative aspects of the economic transition, to detrimental consequences of
war, and to the dramatic reduction in the social security previously provided
by the state. Many women have been burdened by increased responsibilities to
provide care for other family members and the need to assume essential economic roles.[10] Because of the irregular supply of electricity and cooking gas
in the mid-1990s, water pumps did not work, and women carried water from
wells to their apartments in high-rise buildings for washing and bathing. They
cooked using wood-burning stoves. Small-plot farming was used for subsis-
tence, and women added to their housework the additional burden of physical
labor in the fields and caring for livestock. Because of widespread poverty, hard
labor, and the need to survive, "for most people daily life is still a matter of
just getting by."[11] Making ends meet is hard in any of the republics, regardless
of what sector of the economy one works in and despite the fact that all three

republics have among the highest growth rates of gross domestic product in the world since 2005.[12]

Migration due to unemployment, especially from rural areas, by men between eighteen and sixty years old, has affected family relations significantly. About 1 million people have left each of the three countries since their independence. As a rule, men migrate to other regions of a republic, or to Russia, Iran, or Turkey, where they work as seasonal laborers and bring their earnings home at the end of the season. Wives and children are left at home and experience serious problems trying to make ends meet. In some cases, young wives who remained in their husbands' homes were forced into sexual relations with their fathers-in-law or brothers-in-law. Some men establish new families in the places where they work. There have been reports of abandoned wives committing suicide.

Military conflicts have affected the position of women too. A small number of women accompanied men to the front lines as cooks or nurses and, on rare occasions, as fighters or prostitutes. For the most part, women remained home, maintaining the family economically and morally inspiring men through their patriotism and by giving birth to future soldiers. Society expected women to take on to this role, and women readily conformed to these expectations. Because of wars, women lost their husbands or sons, and many became either refugees or internally displaced as a result. In Azerbaijan, in 2003, 71 percent of nearly 1 million refugees were women, and 60 percent of them were living in tents in refugee camps or in railroad boxcars, with the remainder living in abandoned buildings and other temporary housings. Women attempted to organize peace movements, but the greater society did not view this effort seriously. In September 1993, the famous Georgian actress Keti Dolidze called on all peace-loving women to ride a train, specially hired for the occasion, to travel to Abkhazia and demand peace. The hope was that up to 60,000 women would gather, but just a few thousand got on the train and even fewer arrived in Abkhazia. This was probably the largest female peace rally in the region,[13] but it did not bring positive results.

Because they have found themselves in need, many women have showed entrepreneurial skills and occupied positions in the informal economy. They have become self-employed home-based workers, street and market vendors, small-scale farmers, and dayworkers. The most active sphere of female business was the sale at open-air markets of consumer goods purchased in neighboring countries. Women also made use of their skills knitting, sewing, embroidering, and baking and sold their products. Because society does not approve of the active involvement of women in business and does not allow them into established networks, women are usually less successful entrepreneurs than men. Privatization has been a male event, and 90 percent of business own-ers are men. Traditional beliefs that women achieve success through immoral means still prevail. Despite the fact that in each republic the constitution pro-vides for equal rights and freedoms to men and women, employment is highly gendered and women earn approximately 50 percent of what men do.

The elimination of state services and the introduction of fees for previously free services has added extra demands on working mothers. Family mem-bers with health problems are commonly cared for at home by mothers and grandmothers using traditional home remedies. Similarly, reductions in state-funded social security benefits for the elderly require family members, usually women, to care for parents and grandparents. Education is gendered as well. As funding has declined, parents have become more selective in educating their children, and more boys than girls in low-income families now receive formal schooling.

In recent years, the arrival of foreigners has created some opportunities for women who can offer their services as interpreters, translators, tour guides, and office managers. However, women are almost totally excluded from pub-lic life. Their representation in parliaments is minimal, with 4.6 percent in Armenia, 10.5 percent in Azerbaijan, and 9.4 percent in Georgia,[14] while

An urban Azerbaijani woman at her country house. Courtesy of Leila Alieva.

during the Soviet era women constituted approximately 40 percent of parliamentarians in each republic. Nino Burdzhanadze (b. 1964)—a leading political figure in Georgia who was a speaker of the nation's legislature and acted as the nation's president in 2007—is rather a unique exclusion. During the parliamentary elections that were held in 2005–2007 in all three republics, none of political parties showed interest in women's issues or women's rights. Those women who are in a position of influence view as their priorities the fight against the existing gap in salaries between women and men, protection for pregnant women, and measures to reduce the number of unwanted pregnancies through affordable contraception. As a response to challenges of economic restructuring and war, women's advocacy movements have emerged in every republic.

EDUCATION AND SCIENCE

Educational Reform

Education has always been respected in the Caucasus, and it has been a particular priority in Armenia and Georgia, countries with more than a 1,000-year history of literacy. Traditionally, a university education was of lesser value in Azerbaijan, but the entire population can read and write. The main structures and principles of current education were established during the short period of independence after World War I, and then further developed during the Soviet period. Because of the Soviet system of free and mandatory education, in the 1980s, all the republics achieved almost total literacy. Educational rates were the highest in Georgia. More than 15 percent of adults had graduated from a university, and about 60 percent of the population had a specialized secondary education. Approximately 70,000 people were employed in the research field in Georgia in 1990. In Armenia, the share of university-educated people was about 14 percent. A high percentage of Azerbaijanis obtained higher education too, mostly in scientific and technical subjects. Because of the role of the oil industry in the Azerbaijani economy, several universities and vocational institutes train people to work in the oil industry.

The early years of independence were difficult for educational institutions. The lack of funds resulted in the poor maintenance of school buildings, low salaries for teachers, and closures during the winter months because of heating oil shortages. In all three countries, supplies of books and study materials were inadequate, and only recently has the situation begun to improve. The main feature of current education in the Caucasian republics is the attempt to comply with international standards so that the diplomas issued by local educational establishments are recognizable abroad, especially in the West.

In 2005, Armenia, Azerbaijan, and Georgia joined the European Higher Education Area and became participants in the Bologna process, which aims to make standards of academic degrees and quality assurance comparable throughout Europe.

Constitutions of all three republics provide for their citizens' right to education. This right is guaranteed with free secondary education in public schools, which is compulsory, state control over educational standards, and the creation of opportunities to access professional and university education.

Since 1991, higher education and science have been the objects of important financial and management reforms in all of the Caucasian republics. The reforms were influenced by two major factors. One was the economic crisis and impoverishment of the state, aggravated by the disruption of the old administrative system. The second was an attempt to acquire Western values and standards and integrate the national educational system into that of the West.[15] The changes addressed individual educational institutions and the whole system. The main principles of the reform were management decentralization, diversification, the establishment of new educational institutions, changes in curricula, the introduction of new mechanisms for management and finance, and the introduction of new levels of academic degrees. However, a lack of resources, poor management, corruption, inertia, and conservatism are strong obstacles to such change. The implementation of changes was complicated by such factors as obsolete curricula, inflated and immobile faculty, inefficient state funding, and the lack of commercial motivation by private institutions.

System of Education

The education system in each republic consists of several components: preschool education for children between the ages of three and six; general secondary education (grades 1–11), and higher education in colleges and universities. After graduating from the ninth grade, all schoolchildren have to decide whether they want to study for secondary education at a regular high school (grades 10–11), a specialized secondary educational establishment, which combines a high school education with some professional knowledge (four years of study), or a vocational school (three years of study). Anyone who has received a secondary education diploma is eligible to attend a university or another institution of higher learning, and then postgraduate education. Nonstate educational institutions of all levels exist too. Although legislation in all three countries provides for the existence of specialized teacher-training institutes, and allows teachers to be employed at all levels of primary and secondary education, about three-quarters of teachers are university graduates.

In the course of implementing reforms, all of the republics divided school management between the ministry of education and the provincial and community administrations. The involvement of the local population in school affairs is encouraged, but it remains minimal.

Before independence, there were two types of schools in each republic. Although the curricula were identical, the language of instruction varied. Some taught in Russian, while others provided classes in the language spoken by the majority population. The study of Russian was compulsory in all schools, as was the study of the native language of the republic. This ensured that all high school graduates had knowledge of both the state language of the Soviet Union and the state language of the republic. Soviet curricula also required the study of a foreign language, usually English or German. In deciding upon the basic language of instruction in schools, local educational authorities were to consider the wishes of parents. Presumably Armenian school children were to be sent to Armenian-language schools and Russian children to Russian-language schools; however, this was not the case, because the language of college and university instruction was always Russian, and those parents who wanted a good education for their children used to enroll their children in Russian schools to prepare them for university.[16] Today, Russian is recognized as one of the selective foreign languages, and there are state schools in each republic that teach students in Russian and have extra classes in the local state language. These schools are mainly oriented toward ethnic Russians who reside in these states. In 1988, the State Program for the Georgian Language, aimed to preserve and revitalize the language, was introduced and was soon followed by similar programs in Armenia and Azerbaijan. These programs introduced a set of measures that upon their implementation transformed local universities into national institutions with classes in native languages. Classes taught in English are conducted by Western professors at universities supported by foreign donors.

Traditionally, children with physical and mental disabilities were educated in special schools operated outside the general educational system, and they were usually placed in special boarding schools. Today, more efforts are made to educate them in general schools and integrate them into society. Boarding schools exist for children with special needs, such as especially gifted children or juvenile delinquents.

There are now opportunities for learning for those who are in low-paying jobs or unemployed. Evening schools for dropouts and those who had no chance to attend school have been established across the region. Businesses interested in obtaining an educated workforce have opened adult education centers. Courses in professional retraining or skills that the market demands are offered by universities and the state. These modern lifelong learning initiatives emphasize job-related vocational training to improve employability and competitiveness.[17]

To develop students' interests and ensure their psychological, aesthetic, and physical education, there is an out-of-school education system that includes creative and aesthetic youth centers, music and art schools, clubs and camps for young naturalists, technologists, and environmentalists, and sporting schools and resort camps. There is no comprehensive state policy in this area of education after the collapse of the Soviet Union, and students' organizations depend on the sponsorship and leadership of different nongovernmental institutions, churches, and political parties.

When the three republics were part of the Soviet Union, the universities were state owned and subordinate to federal authorities in Moscow, which decided on curricula and matriculation. Moscow also established annual enrollment numbers, with quotas for locals depending on economic needs but not students' demands. There was no broad liberal education; students had to immediately select a professional specialization. The area of a student's major was chosen at the time of application and could not be easily changed. Education was free, and depending on their grades, most full-time students received stipends from the state. Up to 40 percent of the entire student body were part-time students in evening or correspondence courses.[18]

After the republics became independent, they decentralized their higher education systems. Private educational establishments were permitted, and state universities were allowed to charge tuition to cover their expenses. Today, higher and postgraduate professional educations are completed in three degrees. There are bachelor's degrees, degrees for certified specialists, and master's degrees in both state and nonstate educational institutions. Postgraduate studies include master and doctoral courses. At state universities, a certain number of slots in free programs is usually set aside for candidates with the best admission test results, and the constantly increasing number of students is admitted to the programs, which charge tuition and therefore have less competitive admission. State institutions are largely conservative and underfunded, while private universities aim for profit at any price, without pursuing any other goals. Both trends undermine the quality of education. Increased demands for faculty and opportunities for additional salaries have enabled many state university professors to continue their work at private institutions. Financial resources at private institutions are scarce, and they usually rent rooms from schools for part of the day. Several universities have opened on the premises of existing academic research facilities. They attract staff and resources of the institutions and teaching there means supplemental income for staff. The motivation among students to acquire a good education is still very high, because education is often a key to a good career. Studying abroad increases employment opportunities substantially for students. Most of graduates who return to their home countries find employment in international organizations, government, or foreign businesses, as these are the better-paid positions.

Scientific Developments

In each republic, the research institutes of the national academies of science are the centers of scientific work, though usually they are in dire financial situations. New research groups that depend on short-term contracts and grants work independently or associate themselves with these institutes. Originally, scholarly research was separated from the universities in the Caucasus. The universities were supposed to teach and institutes of the academy were supposed to do research. Such division of professional work turned out to be counterproductive. At universities, lecturers, aggravated by the necessity to look for supplemental income in order to survive, teach for so many hours that they do not have the energy, time, or inclination to conduct research. Scientists at the research institutes have little access to teaching positions or to research grants, which are frequently distributed not on the quality of a proposal, but unevenly to research groups with better connections or formal status.

Despite the disruption of scholarly research in the 1990s, the area has great intellectual potential. The South Caucasus is the birthplace of many great scientists. Works of the fifth-century historian Movses Khorenatsi serve as the original sources for studies of many countries; the works of the seventh-century geographer, astronomer, and mathematician Anania Shirakatsi are well known; the physicians Mkhitar Geratsi (thirteenth century) and Amirdovlat Amasiatsi (fifteenth century) contributed a lot to the development of diagnostics and pharmacology. Universities, academies, and scientific centers have existed all across the region since early medieval times. Science and education were highly valued, especially among the Armenians. Until recently, scholars, writers, and artists were the most popular people. Their opinions were respected more than politicians and their speeches.

The world scientific community especially recognized the works of Armenian scientists in physics, astronomy, chemistry, biology, and Oriental studies. The best-known Armenian scientist of the twentieth century is Viktor Ambartsumian (1908–1996), who founded the school of astronomy in Armenia and established the Byurakan Astrophysical Observatory in 1946. The observatory became the main regional center for astrophysics research, where the theory of the transfer of radiation through matter had been developed. Ambartsumian discovered stellar associations and showed that most stars were born in unbound and expanding associations rather than bound clusters. He came to believe that the stars were born explosively. Extending this to galaxies, he was the first to emphasize the importance of activities and explosions in the nuclei of galaxies, long before quasars and black holes were discovered.

The researchers of the Institute of Experimental Medicine, located in the Abkhazian city of Sukhumi, also were successful. In the 1980s, a collection of almost 7,000 apes was gathered at the institute, which was established in 1927. Some apes belonged to the tenth generation of primates raised at the institute. The Sukhumi apes were used for all kinds of medical and biological research, and even participated in space flights to research the impact of space conditions on human organisms. Most of the studies were conducted in the field of neurology and pathology, and were aimed to discover new types of viruses. Because of the war between Abkhazia and Georgia, and an almost total lack of financing since the 1990s, the number of apes has decreased to 2,400. In an attempt to save at least the most unique research species from bullets and starvation during the Abkhazian war, the institute's specialists kept them at their own homes. Today, the research work has almost stopped and the institute is a tourist attraction.

Because of the economic difficulties of the 1990s, the advantages of intellectual potential have mostly been neglected, and all three countries depend on Western expert advice in the fields of scientific development. Education and research in social science, economics, and law, which are important for the building of a democratic society, are in a particularly bad condition. Many prominent scientists who have contacts with Western scientific centers went to work abroad; others have established private organizations and moved to more commercial fields, becoming engaged in less intellectual activities.

NOTES

1. Ia. S. Smirnova, *Semia I Semeinyi Byt na Kavkaze* [Family and Family Customs in Caucasus, in Russian] (Moscow: Nauka, 1995), 206.

2. Nora Dudwick, "Out of Kitchen into the Crossfire: Women in Independent Armenia," in *Commonwealth or Empire? Russia, Central Asia, and the Transcaucasus*, ed. William E. Odom (Washington, DC: Hudson Institute, 1995), 243.

3. Brian Silver, "Ethnic Intermarriage and Ethnic Consciousness Among Soviet Nationalities," *Soviet Studies* 30, no. 1 (1978): 108.

4. Smirnova, *Semia*, 247.

5. UN Office of Statistics, *2004 World Demographic Report*, http://unstats.un.org/unsd/demographic/products/dyb/DYB2004/Table25.pdf.

6. Ronald Suny, *Looking toward Ararat: Armenia in Modern History* (Bloomington: Indiana University Press, 1993), 184.

7. Suny, *Looking*, 153.

8. Mary Ellen Chatwin, *Socio-Cultural Transformation and Foodways in the Republic of Georgia* (Commack, NY: Nova Science Publishers, 1997), 121.

9. Andrejs Johanson and Park McGinty, "The Shamaness of the Abkhazians," *History of Religions* 11, no. 3 (1972): 253.

10. Mehrangiz Najafizadeh, "Women's Empowering Carework in Post-Soviet Azerbaijan," *Gender and Society* 17, no. 2 (2003): 294.

11. Thomas Streissguth, *The Transcaucasus* (San Diego: Lucent Books, 2001), 65.

12. World Bank, *2007 World Development Indicators Publication*, at http://web.worldbank.org/WBSITE/EXTERNAL/DATASTATISTICS/0,,contentMDK:20394802~isCURL:Y~menuPK:1192714~pagePK:64133150~piPK:64133175~theSitePK:239419,00.html.

13. Tamara Dragadze, "The Women's Peace Train in Georgia," in *Commonwealth or Empire? Russia, Central Asia, and the Transcaucasus*, ed. William E. Odom (Washington, DC: Hudson Institute, 1995), 251.

14. *The Situation of Women in the South Caucasus*, Report of the Council of Europe Parliamentary Assembly, February 6, 2007, at http://assembly.coe.int/Main.asp?link=/Documents/WorkingDocs/Doc07/EDOC11178.htm.

15. Tamar Mikadze, "Crisis in Higher Education and Educational Migration from Georgia," *Central Asia and the Caucasus*, no. 5 (September 2002): 104.

16. Yaroslav Bilinsky, "Education of the Non-Russian Peoples in the Soviet Union," *Comparative Education Review* 8, no. 1 (1964): 82–83.

17. Joseph Zajda, "Lifelong Learning and Adult Education: Russia Meets the West," *International Review of Education* 49, no. 1 (2003): 123.

18. Theodore Gerber and David Schaefer, "Horizontal Stratification of Higher Education in Russia: Trends, Gender Differences, and Labor Market Outcomes," *Sociology of Education* 77, no. 1 (2004): 51.

4

Thought and Religion

TRADITIONALLY, THE CAUCASUS was the borderline between Christianity and Islam. Armenia and Georgia are predominantly Christian, although there is a strong Muslim minority in Georgia; Azerbaijan is a Muslim country. In Georgia and Armenia, the development of Christianity was inextricably linked with the emergence of the state, and in Azerbaijan, Islamic faith was a strong unifying factor. A specific feature of religion in the Caucasus is its close relationship with national identity. Religion determined unique historical fates of people in the Caucasus. Nationhood, language, and the national church actually merged in the Caucasus republics and were always associated with secular dissident groups, which promoted political independence of the nations. That explains special relations between national churches and nationalist movements. Some researchers believe that religio-ethnic symbiosis had been reinforced by centuries of incursions from Persia and Turkey, and annexation by Russia,[1] although in Azerbaijan, growing Islamism is not fueled by anti-Western or anti-Russian sentiments. Long histories of ecclesiastical independence were the basis for further association between national cultures and churches. Cultural developments of these three countries, especially in literature, learning, art, and architecture, occurred under a strong religious influence. During the Soviet era, the authorities attempted to suppress religion. Many churches became ethnographic museums, and people were forced to use public venues to conduct their traditional rituals. However, for all three major nationalities in the South Caucasus, national culture was indivisible from religious tradition.

In Armenia and Georgia, literary sources indicate the acceptance of Christianity from the top down, omitting references to any gradual missionary efforts. However, because these statements were written much later than the events described, they cannot be considered the eyewitness accounts they claim to be. It has been argued that Armenia was the first state to adopt Christianity as the official religion, in 301, predating Constantine's edict of toleration by fifteen years, after extensive contacts with proselytizing Christians. The preaching of the Christian Gospels in Georgia dates back to 328, and the Georgian conversion is placed at 331 on the timeline.

ARMENIAN APOSTOLIC CHURCH

The official name of the Armenian Church is the Armenian Apostolic Church, but it is also referred to as the Gregorian Church. It considers Sts. Bartholomew and Thaddeus as its founders, with St. Thaddeus as its first formal head. Because the Arascid royal dynasty came to its end in 427, the church in Armenia took the place of a national leader, transcending the feuding of the noble families. In Armenia, Byzantine occupation brought Greek culture, which continued to influence Armenians through the Middle Ages, although Armenian Christianity broke its relations with Byzantine orthodoxy very soon. Originally, religious services were conducted in Greek or Syriac, and only after the introduction of an independent script at the end of the fourth century did the services begin to be conducted in vernacular.

The Armenian Church is in communion with the Eastern Church of Egypt, Syria, and Ethiopia, which believe that the human and divine natures of Christ constitute a unity. The Armenian Apostolic Church split from the rest of Christendom in 451, by rejecting the acts of the Council of Chalcedon, which convened to resolve the Monophysite heresy concerning the divine and human nature of Christ. This decision made the Armenian Church legally and theologically independent from the early Middle Ages. In the periods when Armenians did not have their own state, the church played the role of a religious and political leader, preserving Armenian culture and expanding written traditions. In contrast to the Georgian and other Orthodox churches, the Armenian church rejected the council's Christological position. To this day, it maintains a modified Monophysite interpretation that nevertheless rejects the mingling of the two natures of Christ.

The Armenian Apostolic Church is headed by the Supreme Catholicos of All Armenians, the most respected Armenian and the most important representative of the Armenian people. Translated from Greek, the word *Catholicos* means "concerning the whole," "universal," or "general," and is used as a title for the patriarch of any certain eastern church. The first Catholicos of Armenia

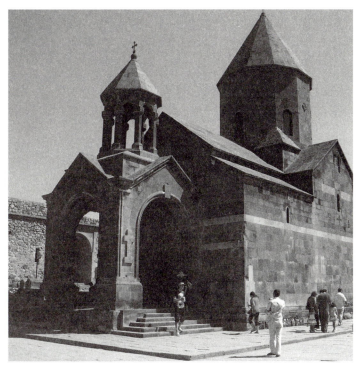

Khor Virap Church in Armenia's Ararat Valley. Courtesy of Anushik Mazmanyan.

and of all Armenians was St. Thaddeus, one of Jesus' apostles, who brought Christianity to Armenia. The present Armenian Catholicos is Garegin II (b. 1951). He was elected Catholicos in 1999, after taking an active role in Armenia's social life. He was instrumental in helping people after the 1988 earthquake, and he participated in building several schools and churches. He actively introduced modern technologies and telecommunications into daily church life too. After being elected Catholicos, he established good relations with Pope John Paul II, and when the pope visited Armenia in 2001, he stayed with the Catholicos. He was the first Armenian Catholicos to visit Turkey, in 2006, blessing the Armenian community of Istanbul and affirming the Armenian genocide. During his visit to the United States in October 2007, he offered the opening prayer for the day's session of the U.S. House of Representatives. The Catholicos of Armenia is sometimes called the "Catholicos of Echmiadzyn" after the city, which is the administrative and spiritual center of the Armenian church. The Armenian alphabet was created and the Bible translated in Echmiadzyn. The monastery there promoted Armenian art, literature, music, philosophy, medicine, and astronomy (the monastery is described in more detail in Chapter 2).

During the Soviet era, Armenian Christianity had not been subjected to intense repressions as national churches were elsewhere in the Soviet Union. It was considered a lesser threat to Communist ideology than any other religious denomination, and antireligious campaigns during Communist rule were always mitigated in Armenia. Sometimes, when needed, the Soviets even used the church for their own purposes. During World War II, Soviet Communist authorities turned to the church for support in mobilizing masses to fight Hitler's Germany. The Armenian Church, along with the others in the Soviet Union, played its role in the nation's defense and its clergy campaigned tirelessly for the "fatherland." Their efforts impressed Stalin to the degree that, at war's end, he summoned Archbishop Chorekjian, who at that time was the formal leader of the Armenian Church, to Moscow and decorated him with the Defense of the Caucasus Medal, a respected Soviet military award. Although the Catholicos was often criticized for having too friendly relations with the Soviet regime, this subservience did not erode the popularity of the Armenian hierarchy nor the church in general. The Armenian Church has historically played a central role in civic and political affairs, and there is some evidence of continuity to this day. It also has had a more participatory and democratic organization than the Georgian or other Orthodox churches. Under the Ottoman Turks, prosperous Armenians gave money to church schools and community organizations, and the church became a focal point of religious, social, cultural, and community activities. Today, the Armenian diaspora is the source of church support.

GEORGIAN ORTHODOX CHURCH

Orthodox Christianity is the dominant religion in Georgia. Before Georgia adopted Christianity, many of its people followed Zoroastrianism, the ancient fire-worshipping religion as in Persia.[2] However, over thirty years, after the Armenian king accepted Christianity, the king of Georgia followed him. After baptism, Georgians kept close religious ties with the Roman Empire and later with the Byzantine Empire centered at Constantinople. The Christian religion was brought to Georgia by missionaries sent by the Roman Emperor Constantine in the fourth century. In the fifth century, the Bible was translated into Georgian. Tracing its foundation to the time of Constantine the Great, the Orthodox Church of Georgia is one of the oldest national churches in the world. It has a distinguished record of devotional and philosophical achievements, and of steadfastness in the face of persecution on the part of such overlords as Persian Zoroastrianism, the Mongols, and Bolshevik Russia. During all of the centuries, it was the bastion of Christianity in the Orient.

Although spiritual and devotional ideals of the Georgian Church differ little from Western Christian churches, Georgia and Armenia could not agree on theological controversies. The Georgian Church followed the doctrine formulated at Chalcedon for a while, but rejoined the Orthodox fold in 607 under Archbishop Kyrion I. The liturgy is celebrated in the national tongue. The church in Georgia was the center not only of religious faith but also of national life itself. It was in the lives of its saints that the aspirations of the Georgian nation found their earliest literary expressions.

Following Georgia's conversion by St. Nino, Archbishop John I (pontificated 335–363) was its first head. Since 1010, the title of the heads of the Georgian Orthodox Church is Catholicos patriarch. Originally, the patriarchs of Antioch consecrated them, but this ceased with John III (744–760). In the seventh and eighth centuries, Georgian patriarchs married from time to time. The church developed relationships with Zoroastrian Persia, the Arab caliphate, the imperial court of Constantinople, and the entire world of

A Georgian twelfth-century church in the region of Imereti. Courtesy of Mr. and Mrs. Mikhael Budagashvili.

medieval Christendom. Even under Islamic occupation, the Georgians kept their faith. In 1180, the Latin patriarch of Jerusalem, Jacques de Vitry, wrote about crusaders from a Christian country named *Georgia* who "revere and worship St. George, whom they make their patron and standard-bearer in their fight with the infidels, and they honor him above all other saints."[3]

Two separate catholicates of western and eastern Georgia existed between the thirteenth and nineteenth centuries. The situation reflected the division of the Georgian monarchy of the Bagratids after the Mongol invasion. The principal Georgian catholicate of Mtskheta remained in place until 1811, when the Russian imperial authorities arbitrarily abolished the autonomy of the Georgian Church. After Russia colonized Georgia, it introduced a strong Russification policy. The Russian Tsar Nicholas I ordered the Old Georgian language used in worship to be replaced with the Old Church Slavonic, of the Russian church. According to the tsar's edict, all Georgian church frescoes were to be whitewashed. Consequently, invaluable Byzantine wall paintings by outstanding medieval masters were destroyed or damaged. Russian icons painted in the Russian Italianate style of the nineteenth century replaced old Georgian icons.[4]

The Georgian orthodoxy had been autocephalous for eight hundred years prior to its subordination to the Moscow patriarchate between 1811 and 1943. This was taken as a serious assault upon Georgian nationhood and was strongly resisted. After the last autocephalous, Catholicos Antoni II was deposed in 1811, Russian-appointed archbishops headed the church until 1917. One of them, Archbishop Nikon Sofiiski was assassinated in Tbilisi in 1908. Following the abdication of the Russian emperor in February 1917, Georgian bishops proclaimed the reestablishment of the church's autocephaly, and elected, as Catholicos-patriarch Kyrion III, who was murdered in the following year. Before the Soviet annexation, the Georgian Church included 2,455 parishes. Catholicos Ambrose (1921–1927) protested against the Soviet annexation of Georgia and was imprisoned after a political show trial. After him, all other Catholicoses were subjected to vilification and abuse by Communist authorities, and churches were destroyed or converted into secular buildings. At Stalin's request, the Moscow patriarchate recognized the autocephaly of the Georgian Church in 1943.

Despite the fact that under the Communist regime Georgia retained its own Catholicos patriarch as a spiritual leader, and enjoyed autocephaly or independent status within the Orthodox community, the Georgian Orthodox Church appears to be weaker than the Armenian Church. That can be explained by more thorough secularization in the nineteenth century, when the Georgian elite preoccupied with socialist ideas did not pay attention to their traditional religious roots. Also, under Stalin the church was further weakened by rapid urbanization, mass education, and extreme repression, which continued during antireligious campaigns during the entire Soviet period. For many Georgians, the church's authority was weakened by corruption. Cases of embezzlement and the selling of church treasures were reported in the 1970s, and allegedly, Catholicos David V falsified his predecessor's will and bribed state officials to support his claim to the leadership of the church in 1972.

After World War II, new and severe restrictions were introduced against those who attended church services. For newly urbanized working Georgians, religious traditions were displaced but not entirely rejected. Antireligious propaganda was tolerated but not internalized. In the 1980s, the Communist ideology did not consider everyday experience, and the officially prescribed norms of behavior seemed less and less relevant.[5] Under these conditions, the remaining religious feelings provided a good grounding for the church's revival after the dissolution of the Soviet Union. In the newly independent Georgia, religious institutions are playing an unanticipated role in the social and political life. There has been a religious renaissance, and the church has been resurrected as a national symbol. In 1987, the Georgian Church was the first in the entire Soviet Union to canonize as a new saint an individual who had been murdered by the Bolsheviks. This honor was given to Ilia Chavchavadze the Just, a poet, writer, and politician.

Today the church is led by Patriarch Ilia II (b. 1933) who was elected in 1977 and claims family ties to the former Bagratid royal dynasty. Ilia II is a recognized theologian and church historian, and he holds an honorary doctorate of theology from Orthodox theological seminaries in New York and Pennsylvania.

ISLAM IN AZERBAIJAN

The most ancient religion of people living in the territory of Azerbaijan was Zoroastrianism. Because of the abundance of oil and gas reserves, flames of burning oil and methane gas were often seen on the surface. Native people believed in the mystical power of these fires and built stone temples where this everlasting fire, which on a windy day could reach up to eight feet high, had been worshipped by locals and traveling pilgrims, often Indians. Until the Soviet Union sealed the Azerbaijani borders, many pilgrims, mostly from India and Iran, traveled to Azerbaijan to visit and worship in sacred places, including the Surakhany Temple near Baku. This temple in the village of Surakhany, about thirty miles north of Baku, has been preserved. The temple was built in a dormitory style with a long hallway with monastic cells along it and a central altarlike structure in the middle, where the eternal flames of underground gas burned.

According to the ancient book Avesta, Azerbaijan is the birthplace of the prophet Zoroaster (or Zarathushtra) (seventh century b.c.), who established a religion focused on the cosmic struggle between a supreme god and an evil spirit. Until the Arab occupation of Azerbaijan in the seventh century, the Zoroastrian religion, the dominant ancient Persian belief system, was popular in what is today Azerbaijan. Local pagan cults and Zoroastrianism were substituted with Islam, which was brought to Azerbaijan by Arab invaders in the seventh century.

Islamization of Caucasian Albania, the state formation that existed on the territory of modern-day Azerbaijan, was slower than in other regions. Arabs were nomads, and their own religion was still new to them; they could not propagate it among other people. Although the Arab occupation was much shorter than those of the ancient Romans, Byzantines, or Persians, at the end of the eighth century, Islam, which was strongly resisted by neighboring Armenian and Georgian communities, became a leading religion among the people living on the slopes of the eastern Caucasus.

Turks, who substituted for the Arabs in medieval Azerbaijan, added centuries of Turkic influence, which was the basis for the future secular Azerbaijani culture. Today, the majority of the country's population professes the Shia version of Islam, which was established as the state religion in the sixteenth century. Although the Sunni population is minimal in Azerbaijan today, the authorities try to diminish antagonism between the two Muslim groups by emphasizing a common Turkic heritage and opposition to Iranian fundamentalist religious influence.

During the Soviet period, the authorities substantially suppressed Islam, and contacts with religious centers in Arab countries were almost nonexistent. The state closed mosques and destroyed shrines as soon as Azerbaijan was integrated into the Soviet Union. Because religion was tolerated again during World War II, the situation eased slightly.

After independence, the number of mosques built with support from Islamic countries rose dramatically. The headquarters of local Islamic authorities are at the Taza Pir mosque, built by a local merchant in 1905. It is the site of the Muslim Board of Transcaucasia, one of the governing bodies of Caucasian Muslims. As in other former Soviet republics, religious observances are not strict. Not many Azerbaijanis attend mosque regularly, women are rarely veiled or segregated, and drinking wine is permitted. However, the Azerbaijanis retain their Muslim names, and most turn to the imam or mullah when a relative dies. Most corpses are washed according to religious stipulations, and the influence of the Iranian fundamentalists who provide substantial financial support to Islamic organizations of Azerbaijan is growing.

A new mosque in a Baku suburb. Courtesy of Leila Alieva.

The most celebrated event among Azerbaijani Shiites is Ashura, the annual commemoration of Imam Husayn's and his companions' martyrdom in Karbala, a small town in present-day Iraq. Armed with the symbol of Husayn's sufferings, thousands of people participate on this day in the rituals of remembrance, which include memorial services and collective weeping, which allows believers to identify themselves with Husayn's cause and to express their regret of not being able to be with him in Karbala to help him win the battle. The celebrations begin on the eve of the holiday at the shrine of St. Khizir atop a mountain overlooking the Caspian Sea. On the morning of Ashura, crowds gather at the Taza Pir mosque—the headquarters of the religious directorate of Caucasian Muslims. The courtyard fills up with penitents at six in the morning, and by nine o'clock it is packed. The spiritual elite are joined by thousands of ordinary citizens, and male-only crowds spill out to the adjoining streets beating themselves up in religious excitement.[6]

Some commentators explain that, through weeping, believers can also protest emotionally against the injustice and oppression that they experience around themselves. In Azerbaijan, unlike in other Islamic countries, the commemoration ceremony is supplemented by the reenactment of the shedding of

Husain's blood. Theatrical and violent aspects of observances reinforce collective memories, form communal feelings, and allow followers to gain religious legitimacy in the process of pushing the secular state toward Islamic values.[7]

The second-largest denomination in Azerbaijan is Christianity, professed by Russians and Armenians. Non-Orthodox religions traditionally receive tolerant treatment in the Caucasus. Jewish communities existed throughout the centuries in Georgia, with major concentrations in the two largest cities, Tbilisi and Kutaisi. Azerbaijani groups have practiced Islam in Georgia for centuries, as have the Abkhazians and Ajarians. The Armenian Apostolic Church is independent in Georgia.

THE JEWS OF THE CAUCASUS

Presently, the Jewish population is almost nonexistent in the Caucasus. Following the fall of the iron curtain, almost the entire Jewish community, which was strong and influential, emigrated mostly to Israel, the United States, and Germany. Some moved to Russia and settled in and around Moscow. Only about 3,500 Jews still reside in Georgia,[8] and about 3,000 Jews live in one compact settlement in the village of Krasnaya Sloboda in Azerbaijan.[9] Traditionally, Jews did not settle in Armenia. Jews from this region were always divided into three major groups: Mountain Jews, Georgian Jews, and Ashkenazim, who came to the area after it was annexed by Russia and later during the general migration of people within the Soviet Union. These three communities were relatively closed and did not mix with the local population. Azerbaijan is home to 4,300 Ashkenazic and 700 Georgian Jews.[10]

The term *Mountain Jews* first appeared in documents of the colonial administration in the Caucasus around 1825, a period of active annexation of the Mountain Jews' territory. These people were living in the territory of present-day Azerbaijan since ancient times. According to some theories, they descended from Jewish military colonists, used in the sixth century B.C. by Parthian rulers as border guards against nomadic invaders. Because of constant invasions from the northern Caucasus, they resettled in the late eighteenth century to the lowlands along the Caspian coast, where unlike all other Jews in the Diaspora, they were allowed to own and develop land. Together with the neighbors, they produced grain, grapes, tobacco, and tea. Their houses did not differ from those of native people, but the ruins of synagogues destroyed at that time show that their persecutions continued. Before the mass emigration of the 1990s, Jews accounted for 35,000 people.[11]

Because of their traditionally negative attitude toward European learning, which was viewed as a threat that would lead Jewish children to assimilation, even twenty years ago, the majority of Mountain Jews were illiterate. Today, some Mountain Jewish men can read and write, which is an improvement, explained by necessities related to the extreme dislocation and the search for better lives after the fall of the Soviet Union. Trying to find their place among the Jews of Russia and the world, Mountain Jews were forced to go through a difficult process of self-understanding to be recognized by others.

Despite the fact that the community of Georgian Jews was even closer, their language was Gruzinic, a variation of Georgian with Hebrew inclusions, and written in the Georgian alphabet. The date of their arrival to the area is unknown, but researchers believe that it could not be later than the second century. Consisting of refugees, the community included those whose ancestors fled Babylonian armies in the sixth century B.C. and those who fled into refuge after the Romans destroyed the Second Temple in A.D. 70.[12]

Ashkenazic Jews started to arrive in 1804, after the Russian Empire annexed Georgia. They settled around Tbilisi, which was the administrative center of the Transcaucasus province and was included in the so-called Pale of Settlement, the area where Russian Jews were allowed to reside. As a rule, they were involved in crafts, as arriving Jews were mostly tailors, leather craftsmen, wood-carvers, carpenters, jewelers, and metalworkers. Despite the forceful assimilation conducted by Soviet authorities during the greater part of the

Central Jewish synagogue in Tbilisi. Courtesy of Mr. and Mrs. Omari Budagashvili.

twentieth century, the community managed to preserve its traditions and even language among younger members. In the 1980s, the community numbered about 1,000 members, but only 3,500 Jews reside in Georgia according to the 2002 national census.

RELIGIONS OF THE ASSYRIANS

Throughout their history the Assyrians, who reside in all three Caucasus republics, professed two religions. The earlier religion believed that Ashur was the highest god of the Assyrians, and this is reflected in the ethnic name of the people. In the third century A.D., however, most Assyrians became Christians. According to the Assyrian International News Agency, Assyrians belong to different churches: 45 percent to the Chaldean Catholic Church, 26 percent to the Syriac Orthodox Church, 19 percent to the Assyrian Church of the East, 4 percent to the Syriac Catholic Church, and the remainder to other churches.[13]

In the past, when the Assyrians came to Georgia, nearly all of them were Catholics; however, during the Soviet era, the Assyrians found it hard to freely profess their religions. Under Soviet power, there were no Catholic churches in the Caucasian republics, so the Christian Orthodox Church took the Assyrians under its wing. As a result, nearly all Assyrians became Orthodox Christians and now attend Assyrian Chaldean liturgies in the Catholic church. The first such service was held in Tbilisi in 1995, in a Catholic Church. Father Benny Bethyadgar, head of the Assyrian Chaldean Church in the South Caucasus led the ceremony. The church runs a Sunday school that teaches the Assyrian language and the history of the religion. Today there is no church in the region with a structure and architecture suited to the Assyrian Chaldean canons. Liturgies in the Catholic Church are conducted in Modern Aramaic.

VIEWS OF THE NINETEENTH CENTURY INTELLECTUALS

Modern political thinking originated in the southern Caucasus in the early nineteenth century and coincided with Russian colonization. Russian involvement in Caucasian affairs opened the area to external influences, allowed local intellectuals to learn about European cultural achievements of the romantic age, and provoked further growth of the nationalist movement. The first members of the Georgian intellectual elite, known later as the "fathers," were a small group of aristocratic writers who enjoyed the benefits of Russian state service. They met occasionally in literary salons to read their works and discuss current events. Leading literary figures were Alexander Chavchavadze (1786–1846) and Grigol Orbeliani (1800–1883). They were among the activists of the 1832 plot to replace the tsarist power with a Bagratid monarch by assassinating top Russian officials, but they later accepted Russia's presence and were elevated to leading administrative positions. The poetry of Chavchavadze lamented the lost past of Georgia. He favorably contrasted Georgia's golden age with its mundane present. Orbeliani, who eventually became governor-general of Tbilisi Province, was a contradictory figure who served loyally as a tsarist officer but in his poems called for the restoration of Georgia's past glory.[14]

With the expansion of education, the new generation of Georgians emerged, known as the "sons," who graduated from Russian universities. Together the two groups, the fathers and the sons, made up what later would be referred to as the first generation of the Georgian intellectual elite. The most intensive development of legal and political thought occurred during the second half of the nineteenth century, when the Russian democratic movement strongly influenced the national schools of thought. Many literary works of Caucasian authors contain a thorough description of ongoing political processes and express the writers' social views. Until the 1860s, when the emancipation of serfs occurred, the main concern of the Georgian nobility had been the protection, preservation, and recognition of their privileges by the Russian authorities, who steadily eroded the political powers of the Georgian elite. Later, their attention switched to the threat that came from the increased wealth and influence of the Armenian middle class.

One of the most radical thinkers was Ilia Chavchavadze (1837–1907), who attended St. Petersburg University Law School. There he became familiar with the major ideas in European philosophy and established contacts with the revolutionary student movement. In 1861, he was expelled from the university for his revolutionary activities and returned to Georgia, where he started the publication of the newspaper *Iveria* (the ancient name for the country of Georgia) and continued this work for the next twenty-five years. His ideological development can be divided into two periods. During the first, he was close to the revolutionary democrats and supported the cause of the oppressed peasants. He believed that peasants' reprisals over landlords were justified by the landlords' cruelty, but he stopped short of calling for a revolution. During the second period, he expressed the views of the Georgian nobility and suggested the reconciliation of all social groups in his book *Life and Law*.

Another Georgian political scholar was Nikoloz Nikoladze (1843–1928). After studying in Paris and Geneva, he worked as a law professor at the University of Zurich, where he published his books *On Economic and Social Consequences of Disarmament* and *Government and Young Generation*. Regarding the organization of political life in Georgia, Nikoladze believed that communal organization was the best form of state government. He proposed the distribution of all national property among the communities of peasants, including land ownership. He favored the abolition of class privileges, the prohibition of corporal punishments, and freedom of the press. Upon his return to Georgia in the 1890s, he rejected utopian socialism and turned to the ideas of liberal democracy.

An important place in the history of Georgian political thought belongs to Egnate Ninoshvili (1859–1894). In his book *Uprising in Guria*, Ninoshvili described social contradictions among those who took part in the uprising and explained why Georgia could not achieve full separation from Russia, as tsarist policies contributed to further exploitation of the country. He rejected the tactics of individual terrorist acts and advocated policies of enlightenment.

Another strong follower of the enlightenment policy was the Armenian writer and national public figure Khachatur Abovian (1805–1848). Fighting for the emancipation of peasants, Abovian actively protested the policies of the Russian government in regard to Armenia, but he never doubted the importance of Armenian inclusion in Russia, which saved thousands of Armenian lives. He believed that the friendship between the Russian and Armenian people would guarantee further national, political, and cultural developments of his native country. Another proponent of Armenian–Russian friendship was Mikael Nalbandian (1829–1866). As did his contemporaries, Nalbandian supported the socialist revolution if conducted by and on behalf of peasants. He believed that agriculture was the key to prosperity and independence. According to Kevork Bardarkjian, the words from his poem *Song of the Italian Girl* were adopted with some minor changes as the current national anthem of Armenia.[15]

Gasanbek Melikov (1837–1907) published the first Azerbaijani newspaper that appeared in Azerbaijani, which is also called Azeri. Throughout his life he advocated secularism and education among the Muslim population in the South Caucasus. Although he advocated peaceful resistance to Russian authorities, Melikov did not reject the violent methods of public disobedience to ensure the progress and social development of his fellow countrymen. Initially he supported Russian rule, but he later reevaluated his views and the benefits of imperial rule and came to the conclusion that Azerbaijan could not reject its own cultural heritage.

NATIONALISM AS A POLITICAL IDEA

In Armenia, all political and social thinking was associated with nationalism, an idea that had been discussed for centuries. The manner in which Armenian nationalism was expressed varied from one social class to another. Clergy, nobility, peasants, merchants, and intellectuals adhered to nationalistic ideas according to their cultural characteristics (education, political views, understanding of group's historical role, and patterns of social behavior), but in most cases it was nothing more than nostalgia for their home country.[16] Until the beginning of the twentieth century, Armenian nationalism weighed the negative aspects of Russian annexation, which were autocracy and colonialism, against such positive aspects as physical security and economic and cultural developments. At the end of the nineteenth century, the sporadic nationalist movement gave birth to several pan-Armenian organizations that aimed to create the Armenian state. The largest organization was Dashnaktsutiun (Armenian Revolutionary Federation), established in 1890 and devoted to the liberation of western Armenia. Later, this organization transformed into a socialist political party.

Although the nationalist idea was always popular in Georgia, political and social resistance to Russian rule was an extremely differentiated process. The specifically nationalist movement, while shaping a sense of Georgia's nationality and alienation from dominant Russian and Armenian nationalities, was not at the forefront of the liberation movement at the end of nineteenth century. Marxism, brought to Georgia in the 1890s by a small group of Russian-educated intellectuals, had a much bigger impact on public opinion. In 1892, Noe Zhordania (1868–1953) and Filipp Makharadze (1868–1941) organized the first conference of Georgian Marxists, which provided an intellectual critique of Georgia's embryonic capitalist society. They proposed overthrowing the monarchy and developing a democratic society, which would lead eventually to socialism. By 1895, the Marxists became the most powerful intellectual movement among the Georgians. Armenians made socialism and Marxism a part of their national movement. But Marxism, which spread rapidly among the Georgians, made only slow progress among the Armenians and imposed itself as the official ideology after the incorporation of Armenia into the Soviet Union.

In Azerbaijan, the bourgeoisie became the enlightening force in the city of Baku. Members of the elite were involved in various Russian Muslim organizations and revolutionary movements in Iran and Turkey. Their social and political views were complex and included those of French democracy, European socialism, Russian and German federalism, pan-Turkism, Young Turk radicalism, and Iranian constitutionalism. All these ideological components were incorporated into ideas of local nationalism. The result of their activities was the education of the Muslim masses and the formulation of some nationalistic ideas, which were important to the future emergence of the Azerbaijani nation.

Regardless of the official policy to promote Marxism during the seventy-year period of Soviet rule, local intellectuals did not accept Marxism and never gave up the nationalist ideas. In the late 1960s, nationalism became the dominant political idea of Caucasian society. Literature, cinema, art, poetry, and theater commonly exalted the nation and the vernacular languages. All three state universities in the capitals of Armenia, Azerbaijan, and Georgia became thoroughly national institutions with restrictive admission policies against nonnative people; as a result, intellectual elites had the ability to actively promote nationalist themes.

During the late Soviet era, there was a religious revival among Armenian and Georgian intellectuals. In the 1980s, for example, a series of prayers for the Georgian nation was created that used text and music by contemporary Georgian authors. The modern Georgian version of the Bible was widely distributed, and the Russified icons were replaced by icons and frescoes painted by contemporary native artists.

The leading figure of Georgian religious and nationalist subculture was Zviad Gamsakhurdia (1939–1993), nationalist, human rights activist, and eventually president of the republic. He was instrumental in spearheading the national religious revival among youths, and he led campaigns against corruption within the Georgian church, sought the preservation of churches and religious monuments, fought the deportation of Georgian Muslims, and organized a Helsinki Watch Group.

LATE-TWENTIETH-CENTURY PHILOSOPHY

In the second half of the twentieth century, social scientists of the Caucasus developed a number of interpretive concepts that soon pervaded academic circles. However, they were forced to add some ideological biases to such concepts as totalitarianism, modernization, nationalism, nation building, and political integration to demonstrate political loyalty.[17]

While it was an unwavering requirement to follow the Marxist ideology, two major philosophers born in the southern Caucasus departed most radically from Marxism. They brought political, legal, and scholarly thought of the region and of the Soviet Union into European contexts. These scholars were the Georgian Merab Mamardashvili (1930–1990) and Vladik Nersesiants from Mountainous Karabakh (1938–2005).

Merab Mamardashvili had worked in both Moscow and Prague, and he returned to Tbilisi in 1980, where he lectured on phenomenology and its role in contemporary philosophy. Mamardashvili taught forms and contents of thinking, as well as the philosophical principles of Marcel Proust, at Tbilisi State University. He was even called the "Georgian Socrates" for his masterful lecturing. Most of his works originated as notes taken by students during his lectures. Mamardashvili was influenced by classical German philosophy, especially Immanuel Kant, and contributed to the rationalist theory of perception. His main research interest was the origin of consciousness, which, according to him, was not a natural human capability or a natural feature of environment, but rather a subject in a metaphysical space of language and human cooperation. He viewed consciousness as an act of human existence, stating that the "act of thinking is correlated with being at a transcendental level of human existence,"[18] the ultimate goal of which was to find and keep the unity of the past, present, and future.

Vladik Nersesiants worked at the Institute of State and Law in Moscow, one of the most reputable think tanks in the former Soviet Union and then Russia. A researcher of Georg Hegel and a famous professor of jurisprudence, he was the author of the only theory that attempted to meet the challenges caused by the failure of the actual equality theory, which was cornerstone of the socialist legal theory. He found an answer to the question of what could bring post-Soviet societies to the advantages of legal equality and all associated freedoms, the only plausible alternative to socialism. According to Nersesiants, countries that survived Communist rule should have entered the next phase of social development, which he called "civilism" or "a civilitarian society." He stated that instead of distributing wealth so that everybody has more or less the same amount, society needed to reshape ownership relations in regard to the former state property of all and create a social contract among owners, nonowners, and the state as an owner. The key was a fund comprising property and property rights still in state ownership that had returned from the private sector on an agreed contractual basis. Nersesiants believed that, if implemented, all people in the newly independent states would have had a minimum participatory share in the civil ownership of their nation's property and the revenues generated by that property granted for life to every citizen. While people would be guaranteed a minimum, there would be no maximum on the wealth they could earn or otherwise accumulate.[19] His ideas could have become a national ideal for the three Caucasian republics and for all post-Soviet states.

MODERN POLITICAL THOUGHT

Contemporary political development of all Caucasian republics is concentrated around the ideas of regional cooperation, especially in the fields of military, economic, and energy security; the preservation of sovereignty; and the further democratization of society.

In regard to security, discussions about potential cooperation were initiated in 1999, when the presidents of the three Caucasian republics called for the creation of a South Caucasus security system. Prior to that, all security problems in the region had been resolved with Moscow's active participation, which aimed to preserve Russia's strategic influence in geopolitical affairs in the Caucasus. The countries in the Caucasus are members of the Commonwealth of Independent States (CIS), a loose community of former Soviet republics, and are supposed to follow the CIS policies. Since the idea of the South Caucasus security system was announced, Azerbaijan and Georgia withdrew from the CIS Collective Security Pact, a treaty that imposed obligations on military and law enforcement activities, and the former Armenian president Robert Kocharian introduced his Roundtable on Stability, a regional system facilitated by the European Union and the United States.

In recent years, all countries of the region have attempted to develop their relations with the United States, including military ties. This policy is condemned by Iran because of fears that U.S. military assets in the South Caucasus could be used in an attack against Iran. The Iranian president emphasizes the need to have "brotherly borders" between his country and Azerbaijan,[20] while blocking all multinational efforts to delimit state borders in the Caspian Sea.

Another major pertinent political concept is the idea of resisting Russian domination and securing energy transport and supply outside of Russian control. This idea is promoted in another framework of regional cooperation, GUAM (based on the initials of the member states: Georgia, Ukraine, Azerbaijan, and Moldova). Formed in 1997, this organization conducted its first joint military exercises aimed to protect Georgia's oil pipeline in 1999. In 2002, GUAM countries signed the Agreement on Cooperation in Fighting Terrorism, Organized Crime, and Other Dangerous Types of Crime, and military coordinators were appointed to work out security cooperation among the member states and to prepare countries for future NATO membership. It is expected that by the end of 2008, Georgia's admission to NATO will be resolved. The rose revolution in Georgia in 2003, the orange revolution in Ukraine in 2004, and political reforms in Moldova and Azerbaijan gave GUAM a democratic orientation. At the organization's 2005 summit, it declared a major task to be the consolidation of democracies in the Black Sea region and beyond. In May 2006, the organization changed its name to GUAM: The Organization for Democracy and Economic Development, indicating that it seeks economic and security integration with the West, and highlighting the fight against crime, terrorism, and separatism as its main goals.

Further democratization depends on overcoming the elements of totalitarian culture, which are still alive among the political elite in every republic. Realizing that the principles of division of power are unacceptable for preserving their dominant position in government structures, former state bureaucrats transferred the most important powers to the executive bodies. Since the late 1990s, presidential administrations in all three countries have manifested signs of the administrative-command system and totalitarian ideology. Even today, elements of authoritarian culture play a decisive role in the political life of the Caucasian republics, where power and the political regime are closely associated with the president. All three republics have recently passed constitutional changes that strengthened the authority of the chief executive.

The unique combination of patriarchal views and a modern political culture shapes the historically based trust in a charismatic leader by the majority of people in all three Caucasian states. The small size of the countries, their weak economies, and constant mass media reminders to retain independence and stability push people to choose a "strong leader" whom large states will support. After the Caucasian states obtained independence, each of their leaders embodied a specific ideal. For example in Georgia, ideas of national independence were associated with Zviad Gamsakhurdia, stabilization with Eduard Shevardnadze, and improved social conditions with Mikheil Saakashvili. The same ideas were attributed, respectively, to Abulfaz Elchibey, Aliyev Senior, and incumbent Ilhom Aliyev in Azerbaijan. A similar process occurred in Armenia, where each leader met expectations and received support from certain social strata.

NOTES

1. Hank Johnston, "Religio-Nationalist Subcultures under the Communists: Comparisons from the Baltics, Transcaucasia, and Ukraine," *Sociology of Religion* 54, no. 3 (1993): 241.

2. Thomas Streissguth, *The Ttranscaucasus* (San Diego: Lucent Books, 2001), 24.

3. Cited by David Lang, *Lives and Legends of the Georgian Saints* (London: Mowbrays, 1976), 4.

4. Fairy Von Lilienfeld, "Reflections on the Current State of the Georgian Church and Nation," in *Seeking God: The Recovery of Religious Identity in Orthodox Russia, Ukraine, and Georgia*, ed. Stephen Vatalden (De Kalb: Northern Illinois University Press, 1993), 223.

5. Juliet Johnson, "Religion after Communism: Belief, Identity, and the Soviet Legacy," in Juliet Johnson, Marietta Stepaniants, and Benjamin Foster, *Religion and Identity in Modern Russia: The Revival of Orthodoxy and Islam* (London: Ashgate, 2005), 18.

6. Thomas Goltz, *Azerbaijan Diary* (Armonk, NY: M. E. Sharpe, 1998), 441.

7. Yitzhak Nakash, "An Attempt to Trace the Origin of the Rituals of Ashura," *Die Welt des Islams* 33, no. 2 (1993): 168.

8. Zvi Gitelman, *A Century of Ambivalence: The Jews of Russia and the Soviet Union, 1881 to the Present* (Bloomington: Indiana University Press, 2001), 236.

9. Sascha Goluboff, "Are They Jews or Asians? A Cautionary Tale about Mountain Jewish Ethnography," *Slavic Review* 63, no. 1 (2004): 115.

10. Ibid., 117.

11. Itzhak David, *History of the Jews in the Caucasus* (Tel Aviv: Cavasioni, 1989), 1:96.

12. Ibid., 99.

13. http://www.aina.org/index.shtml.

14. Ronald Suny, *The Emergence of Political Society in Georgia*, in Ronald Suny, ed. *Transcaucasia: Nationalism and Social Change* (Ann Arbor: University of Michigan Press, 1996), 121.

15. Kevork Bardarkjan, *A Reference Guide to Modern Armenian Literature* (Detroit: Wayne State University Press, 2000), 27.

16. Anahide Ter Minosian, *Nationalism and Socialism in the Armenian Revolutionary Movement (1887–1912)*, in Ronald Suny, ed. *Transcaucasia: Nationalism and Social Change* (Ann Arbor: University of Michigan Press, 1996), 141.

17. See Johnston, "Religio-Nationalist Subcultures," 270.

18. Merab Mamardashvili, *Strela Poznaniia* [Arrow of Cognition, in Russian] (Moscow: Shkola, 1996), 23.

19. William Buler, preface to V. S. Nersesiants, *The Civilism Manifesto* (London: Simmonds and Hill Publishing, 2000), 3.

20. Ibid., 5.

5

Languages, Folklore, and Literature

A LOCAL PROVERB says that there are more poets than mountains among the Caucasian people,[1] reflecting on the fact that local people have very strong poetic feelings and appreciate literature. Education, literacy, and the culture of writing were always among the most treasured social values in the Caucasus. Literature is the most developed art in the Caucasus, having served for more than 1,500 years as a method of reflecting on the political aspirations of the people who have fought against persecutions and suppression. Because professional writers were always put at the top of social hierarchy by public opinion, local kings attempted to demonstrate their own literary abilities or tried to gain the support of writers. The creators of local alphabets were recognized as saints, and the Armenian Church celebrates the festival of the translator-saints to honor those who, in the fifth century, translated the Bible into Armenian.

All of the region's national literature began as folklore. The performers of folkloric literature were expected to safeguard the wise words of the nations' ancestors and to pass on high moral values from one generation to another, all while reflecting the diversity of the people and languages in the area. All languages spoken by the people of the South Caucasus are dissimilar. Even those who generally consider themselves Georgians, Kartvelians, Mingrelians, and Svans speak dissimilar languages. The Armenian, Azerbaijani, and Georgian languages grew in different directions. Armenian developed from a combination of Indo-European and non–Indo-European language groups; Azerbaijani is a Turkish language. Although Azerbaijani originated in Central Asia, it uses the Latin script now; however, there were periods in which it was written using Arabic and Cyrillic alphabets. Georgian, on the other hand, is unrelated to any major world language. It uses a Greek-based alphabet that is different from that of Armenian. All three nations managed to preserve their languages as a central element of their national survival and preservation of ethnic identity, despite being ruled by invaders for centuries. Nationalist movements and fights for national independence were concentrated around the idea of linguistic survival. Demands for political changes traditionally started in these republics with attempts to reform the legal status of the native language.

The relative independence of these states and their early cultural developments allowed the three civilizations to individualize their forms of art and literature and to preserve their unique characteristics. During the periods of Turkish, Persian, and Russian occupations, books were written in languages of the local people, leading to a literary heritage based on ethnic identity, religion, and history. During Communist control, the writers of the region sought greater freedoms of expression, writing in the vernacular languages and realistically reflecting the surrounding social problems, as they understood their role as the nation's educators. The circulation of books and literary magazines was significant during the twentieth century, books and book reviews were publicly debated, libraries were popular places, and bookstores thrived. Writers were initiators of social changes in the 1980s, and they organized the democratic movement, which brought basic democratic values and freedoms to the republics.

After the breakup of the Soviet Union, the writers were not prepared for the ongoing reforms and did not know what to write about. The publication of previously prohibited books was the center of public attention at the beginning of the independence period, when interest in contemporary books decreased. Writers started to earn money in the newspapers and busied themselves with attempts to respond to public taste by writing screenplays for soap operas in order to survive. Some writers associate themselves closely with the government to receive government payments for their service, but the majority of writers avoid the topics of political and social problems. Because book publishing became economically difficult and people could not afford to buy books, many authors switched to Internet publications and daily newspapers that publish literary works.

This chapter concentrates on works of twentieth-century authors and contemporary literary trends, such as change in the subjects of authors' interest, the use of slang in books, and the reprinting of domestic and foreign classics. However, the works of previous generations are not disregarded because they are the pillars and traditions of cultural heritage.

LANGUAGE

Languages of the Christian Nations

In the first century B.C., Strabo noted that 300 languages were spoken on the Black Sea coast of Georgia, a comment echoed later by Pliny the Elder.[2] The explanation for this diversity is that the impassable terrain and harsh climate kept small communities free from external influence. Because mighty empires rarely bothered with the mountaintops, no centralizing cultural influence forced the fragments together. Elsewhere, archaic languages evolved into simple and widely spoken languages, but in the Caucasus they remained in their pristine stage—unwritten, unread, and helpfully uncontested.[3] The expansion of Christianity in the region and the conversion of local people to the Christian religion contributed to the "invention of a script for the native language, the rapid translation of Christian texts, and the consequent development of original literature."[4] Armenian and Georgian people created their own scripts at the end of the fourth century to conduct religious services in the vernacular language and to access liturgical and biblical texts in their own language, not in Greek or Syriac, which were used before.

As an Indo-European language, Armenian shares some phonetic and grammatical features with other Caucasian languages. Some words were borrowed from Iranian languages. The thirty-eight-letter Armenian alphabet is unique because it is completely different from Roman, Cyrillic, or Arabic letterings, but it unexplainably has many characters almost identical to the Amharic language of Ethiopia. The creation of the Armenian alphabet is attributed to St. Mesrop Mashtots, a monk who lived at the end of the fourth century. His first effort was to adopt a Semitic script, but its twenty-two letters were inadequate to reflect Armenian phonology. After further trials, he prepared a script of thirty-six letters based on the order of the Greek alphabet, but with additional letters. Many original forms, which are still used today for uppercase letters, reflect the form of a corresponding Greek letter.[5]

The ancient original form of language, known as Grabar, remained in use until the thirteenth century. During the Middle Ages, when connections between Armenia and Europe intensified, Grabar was modernized to reflect modern writing styles and usage, and it was replaced by Middle Armenian, which evolved into the present-day eastern and western dialects of modern Armenian, which differs largely in pronunciation and spelling and has some differences in vocabulary, grammar, and orthography. Classical Armenian Grabar is used today only in the Armenian Apostolic Church as a liturgical language.

The alphabet played an important role in the development of the Armenian culture and the formation of the nation's ethnic consciousness. Later, the alphabet was the most important tool to keep ties between the Armenians

Monument to Mesrop Mashtots, creator of the
Armenian alphabet, in Yerevan. Courtesy of
Wikipedia.

dispersed around different parts of the world.[6] Even during times of war and
persecution, the Armenians tried to rescue manuscripts. People believed that
even if everything else was lost, the manuscripts preserved their connection
with Armenia and gave them the hope of return. More than 25,000 Armenian manuscripts dated from the fifth through the seventeenth centuries are
preserved and known today. These writings encompass history, mathematics,
astronomy, geography, medicine, law, philosophy, theology, and various genres of folk and professional creativity. The decoration of the books equals and
often exceeds the best examples of book design culture.

    The Georgian alphabet is one of fourteen existing alphabets in the world. It
consists of thirty-three letters (five vowels and twenty-eight consonants), and
its creation is not attributed to anyone. The majority of scholars believe that it
was derived from a Semitic alphabet between the sixth and fifth centuries B.C.
The alphabet has been modernized during the centuries but has never lost its
original roots. The language is very conservative and has not changed much

over the centuries. Modern Georgians can easily read books from the classic period. The mosaic inscription in the Judean Desert in Israel is known as the oldest Georgian inscription ever found, dating back to A.D. 433. The oldest Georgian manuscript (A.D. 864) is kept in St. Catherine's Monastery on the Sinai Peninsula.

The Georgian language is linguistically distant from Turkic and Indo-European languages. It forms the independent Kartvelian language family, deriving its name from the word *Kartveli*, used by Georgians to name their country. While the literacy rate in Georgia is almost 100 percent, and all citizens know the literary Georgian language, such groups as the Mingrelians, Laz, and Svan speak their own languages at home, which differ from mainstream Georgian but belong to the same language family. The Meskhetians, Kartlians, Pshav, Kakhetians, and Khevsur speak dialects of the official Georgian language. Regardless of Turkish influence and the acceptance of Islam, Ajarians preserved their Georgian ethnic roots and continue to speak a dialect of the Georgian language. Different pronunciations distinguish these dialects from one another.

The Georgian language played an important role as the common language of scholarship, culture, religion, law, and interethnic communications. But with Russia's colonization of Georgia, Russian replaced Georgian as the official language of the administration and the church. A policy of Russification was carried out throughout the nineteenth and twentieth centuries. Attempts were also made to undermine Georgian through the development of minority languages and their alphabets textbooks in Mingrelian, Abkhaz, and Svan. During a brief period of independence from 1918 to 1921, a policy of Georgianization was introduced. Georgian was defined as the only official language of the republic, and Tbilisi State University was founded as a higher learning institution in the Georgian language. Under Stalin, an ethnic Georgian, policies of Georgianization were preserved, and Georgian-based scripts were introduced for the Abkhazian and Ossetian languages.[7] The revival of minority languages, however, was secured by Soviet policies after Stalin's death.

The Georgians often expressed their nationalism through the fight aimed to preserve the language. In April 1978, thousands of Georgians took to the streets to protest the Soviet government's decision to remove Georgian as the official state language of the republic. Facing escalating demands, the government decided against removing the disputed clause and effectively acknowledged its defeat. Currently, Article 8 of the Constitution declares Georgian as the state language of Georgia, and the Georgian and Abkhaz languages as the official languages of the territory of Abkhazia.

In 1989, the Georgian government adopted the State Program for the Georgian Language, aimed to develop linguistic history and defend the purity of the written language. The program contained a large number of measures designed specifically to enhance the position of Georgian, such as furthering the teaching of Georgian to nonnative residents in the country, introducing compulsory examinations in Georgian for university students, creating special courses in Georgian stylistics and the history of Georgian literature for non-native students, and establishing a Georgian Language Day. These policies increased tensions among minorities toward one another and further polarized society. From time to time, different public forces lament that this program was never fully implemented and call for its revival.

Significant language problems are experienced by Greek and Assyrian minorities who reside in rural Georgia. During the Soviet period, they did not study Georgian and attended Russian schools, as knowledge of Russian was needed to enter colleges and universities and to become employable across the country. With the Soviet Union out of the picture, the Georgian language became the main language of the country, while the Greeks and Assyrians living in isolated groups did not know Georgian at all. The Greeks living in Tbilisi have a more or less adequate command of Georgian, yet Russian is still their main spoken language. Because of that, they are virtually unemployable; they survive in an information vacuum and are excluded from the country's sociopolitical life. The only Greek deputy who served two terms in the Georgian parliament (of the 1995 and 1999 convocations) was practically excluded from lawmaking because of the language barrier. The younger generation sees no prospects for itself and, therefore, sees no reason to study Georgian, preferring emigration. The state attempted to organize programs to teach Georgian in the areas of minorities, but only modest results have been achieved so far and little hope exists of a breakthrough.[8]

Azerbaijani Language

The official language of Azerbaijan, Azerbaijani, is a variation of a western Turkic language spoken earlier by the tribes of Oghuz. The language belongs to the southern branch of Altaic languages. Almost 90 percent of the population speaks Azerbaijani and about half speak fluent Russian, reflecting Russian domination over the region. Since the nineteenth century, Russian loanwords, especially technical terms, entered the Azerbaijani language in Russian-controlled Azerbaijan, as did Persian words in Iranian Azerbaijan. Mirza Muhammad Ali Kazembek is considered the father of the modern Azerbaijani language. In the 1830s, he wrote a series of grammar textbooks and promoted language reform that established a set of simplified uniform rules. A model of the language usage was set in plays written by Mirza Akhundzade (1812–1878) in the 1840s.

Before the admission of Azerbaijan to the Soviet Union, Arabic was used for writing. In 1924, under pressure from Soviet officials, a modified Latin alphabet was introduced to isolate Muslim people from their Islamic culture and reduce the threat of nationalism. The Cyrillic alphabet, common with Russian and other Slavic languages, became official in 1940, following Stalin's intention to secure the further isolation of Azerbaijan, after Turkey switched to the Latin script in 1928. After the disintegration of the Soviet Union, the alphabet question arose again, and the Latin alphabet returned in 1991. It was supplemented with some new symbols for unique Azerbaijani phonology. The idea to introduce Arabic from Iran was not accepted by Azerbaijani intellectuals.

Because of the people's common knowledge and tradition, a language controversy exists in contemporary Azerbaijan. Cyrillic letters are still used in private correspondence, street signs, and some newspaper articles, although headlines always appear in the Latin alphabet. According to Thomas Streissguth, this has created a "curious cultural phenomenon" where younger Azerbaijanis read only newspaper headlines and older generations that grew up in the Soviet Union read only the main text of the articles.[9] Fluency in Azerbaijani is required by law for all government officials and is a requirement for high school graduation.

Conservative forces fight for the return of Arabic scripts, which would connect local and other Islamic people. The tradition of calligraphy associated with the Arabic alphabet is preserved in Azerbaijan and can be seen in elaborate letterings on pottery, metalwork, and sculpture. This move is opposed by the government, which aims to preserve the secular character of the country and avoid religious radicalization. Small groups of Kurds, Tats, and Talyshin, whose languages are close to Farsi, reside in Azerbaijan and use Azerbaijani in daily life.

CAUCASUS FOLKLORE

Historical roots of literature and other arts lie in folklore. The best-preserved forms of folklore are fairy tales, songs, and poems delivered by wandering performers. Local literature began with heroic ballads and ancient epics peformed orally over the centuries. The oldest surviving folk poems date as far back as the fifth century. With minor local variations, the fairy tales of the South Caucasus follow similar trends that make all objects magical. Almost all fairy tales feature animals and objects made from wool, for example, carpets and caps, and equipment used on animals, such as whips, reflecting the role of animals in the life of local people in ancient times. In the fairy tales, animals always share their supernatural powers with the main protagonist, giving him omnipotence, invincibility, and fantastic success.[10]

Armenian fairy tales have an interesting particularity. They usually close with the phrase "three apples fell from heaven." Although the distribution of the apples varies, one always goes to the storyteller, one to the listener, and the third may be divided between the master of the house, a child who reads the story in a book, the world, or may be taken back by God. It appears that the distribution is not related to characters in the tales, but reflects the Armenian's view of the apple as a simple gift of friendship. This view is supported by a custom in the region of Van. On a moonlit night, young girls and brides used to climb apple trees and paste parsley leaves on apples that were on the verge of coloring. When the apples reached full maturity, they were picked, the parsley leaves were removed, and the lovely pale leaf designs stood out against the red color of the apples. Such an apple accompanied an invitation to a loved one or a friend who was to be honored or offered congratulations for a special event.[11]

Wandering poets and singers used violins and mandolins to perform folk songs and poems. In addition to simple performances, they often created their own verses to sing during the festivals and markets. These poets and singers were called *ashugi*, which in Turkish means "somebody with a great love." The *ashugi* were not just mere entertainers but educators who developed people's tastes and taught the legendary past of the country. In the Middle Ages, they created a guild with special rules and initiation rites. The most famous Armenian epic sung by the *ashugi* in the tenth century was *David of Sassoon*,

A folkloric performance in a Georgian village. Photograph by Badri Vadachkoria provided by the Embassy of Georgia to the United States.

reported by Portuguese travelers in the sixteenth century and recorded in 1873 as a hefty volume. The epic describes four generations of the house of Sassoon, a mountainous enclave in the Armenian highlands. The epic consists of several cycles, each devoted to a particular fight against oppressors. The story begins with two brothers born to the Armenian princess Dzovinar, who was taken from Armenia to Baghdad by the caliph when most of Armenia was under Arab domination. The caliph decided to kill her sons, but they were able to escape to Armenia, where they slew dragons, built cities, and restored Armenia to prosperity, and then returned to Baghdad to rescue their mother. The next cycle is the story of David's father, who symbolizes a fair, wise, noble, and self-sacrificing father-king. Centuries later, kings claimed their relations with David of Sassoon.

Azerbaijani folklore is represented by poems, *dastans*, which were authored in the form of a heroic ballad and performed by *ashugi*. *Dastans* were read as poetry or prose with heavy poetic additions, often with musical accompaniment. Many *dastans* were based on romantic plots. The best-known *dastan* is *Kior-ogly*, a heroic poem created in the seventeenth century and dedicated to the fight against Turkish enslavement. Other genres of Azerbaijani folklore are legends, fairy tales, proverbs, riddles, jokes, and songs, which vary depending on the performance occasion, such as labor songs, songs associated with particular rites or customs, and songs performed during festive dinners. Since the sixteenth century, the *ashugi* preserved their works in written forms. Today, performances of amateur folkloric ensembles, which show folk dances and read classical poems with the accompaniment of traditional folk music, are popular during public festivities.

LITERATURE

Early Writings

Literary traditions were developed by the Armenians and Georgians, who shared Eastern Christian culture and adopted themes already described in Greek writings. Medieval Armenian literature was created by monks. St. Mesrop Mashtots (362–440), considered the founder of the Armenian alphabet, was also one of the first Armenian poets. Monks' poetry consisted of short chants, *sharakans*, which were read during religious services. The *sharakans'* structure and rhythm were continuously used by many poets in the following centuries. Information about literary activities before the fifth century is fragmented. There is evidence of the existence of official monastery books and official annals that originated in pagan Armenia. The first monument of written Armenian literature is the translation of the Holy Scriptures from Syriac into Armenian in 411. Foreign historical works translated into

Armenian between the fifth and thirteenth centuries, including the ecclesiastical histories of Eusebius of Caesarea and Socrates and the *Jewish War* of Josephus, influenced Armenian literary traditions.

After Christianity was establishd in Georgia, local writers began to produce religious works, such as biographies of the saints and translations of the Bible dated to the fifth and sixth centuries. In Georgia, the most popular genre of historical writings became the biography. The first original book was the *Life of St. Shushanik*, a daughter of an Armenian hero who married a Georgian prince and whose beliefs in Zoroastrianism led to her harsh treatment and eventual death. The date of this book is attributed to the fifth century. Later, kings of Kartli attempted to write their biographies, which combined local oral traditions with written materials extracted from Greek and Syrian chronographers. The Gospels were among the first works translated into Georgian from ancient Armenian following the invention and introduction of the Georgian alphabet. One of the first original books was the *Passion of St. Eustace of Mtskheta*, a document from the second half of the sixth century that explains Christian doctrine. The first manuscripts originating in the monasteries in southwestern Georgia were associated with the career and personality of St. Gregory of Khandzta (759–861), a militant and energetic religious leader. The chronicles were known for their truthfulness and objectivity, and they continue to serve as a major source on the nation's history.

In tenth-century Armenia, literature moved away from purely religious subjects. Mystical interpretations of the Song of Songs by the Armenian Krikor Naregatsi (951–1003), titled *The Book of Lamentations*, combined sacred images with intimate personal feelings. The further development of Armenian poetry was strongly influenced by about 1,000 songs, supposedly written by the first folk-song writer and performer, Harutyun Sayatian (1712–1795), known as Sayat Nova, which means "King of Song," though only 220 songs are definitely attributed to him. While performing at the court of the Georgian King Irakli II, he was able to secure an alliance between Georgia and Armenia against the Persian Empire. His songs remain popular even today, and Armenian theater companies regularly perform his works. Competitions among touring groups performing Sayat Nova's works can be seen on weekends in public squares of many Armenian towns. The audience is often engaged in these performances. Today, the largest American Armenian dance company in Boston is named after Sayat Nova.

In Georgia, a cycle of stories titled *Georgia's Appeal* appeared in the tenth century. The book provided a new explanation of the acceptance of Christianity, in which the author denied the arrival of Christianity from Armenia and told a new theory of Georgian national consciousness that traced the origins of Christianity in Georgia to a young native woman named Nino. Secular literature appeard in the twelfth century with Mose Khoneli's chivalrous adventures *Amiran-Darejaniani*, and then in the twelfth century Iovane Shavteli and Grigol Chakhrukhadze wrote odes glorifying King David the Builder and Queen Tamar. In these odes, the Old and New Testaments were viewed as prologues to Tamar's rule, which symbolized the establishment of the Georgian national statehood.

The best-known Georgian lyrics are *The Knight in the Panther's Skin*, authored by Shota Rustaveli, a poet and official in Queen Tamar's court at the end of the twelfth century. This lyrical poem describes adventures of three heroes who defend their country and queen. The poem is a hymn to love, friendship, freedom, and bravery, as well as a serious philosophical tractate on life, duty, patriotism, and friendship between different nations. Georgians say that the soul of their people is expressed in this poem. The book remains so popular, and respect for the written word is so high among Georgians, that even today an old, well-adorned copy is often included in a bride's dowry. The book is essential to the learning of educated Georgians, and each girl must memorize large parts of the book before her marriage.

Early Azerbaijani literature includes the Zoroastrian sacred text *Avesta*, Turkish poetry, and oral recitations of history. The classical medieval books are the *Khamseh*, a collection of five long romantic poems written in Persian by Nezami Ganjavi (1141–1209) and sixteen works of Muhammed Fizuli (1500–1563), who used the language of ordinary people.

In the seventeenth century, Georgian King Teymuraz I (1589–1663) was known as a writer. He imitated Rustaveli and authored several philosophical poems, such as "Dispute between Spring and Autumn" and "Dialogues of a Candle and a Butterfly," in which he attempted to explain basic moral principles. The first printed book in the Georgian language appeared in Rome in 1629. Book printing developed in Geogia in the eighteenth century; 14,000 copies of books, mostly of religious content, were published in Tbilisi in the 1780s. The texts were not related to particular church services and covered general subjects of religion. Georgian literature of that time also included popular plays and comedies, often written with musical scores to entertain the audience. By the mid–eighteenth century, Georgian books, mostly with liturgical and biblical texts, were printed in Rome, Moscow, Tbilisi, and St. Petersburg. At the same time, the revival of the Georgian national literature was reflected with the first edition of Rustaveli's epic poem *The Knight in the Panther's Skin*. Scientific and educational books, such as a Persian astronomical treatise or the Russian manual of elementary education, were translated into Georgian. From a bibliographical point of view, all of these books are rarities because, in some cases, only one or two copies survived.

Armenian book printing began in Amsterdam with the publication of the Bible (1666), History, a general tractate on the nation's past by Arakel Davrizhetsi (1669), The History of Armenia by Movses Khorenatsi (1695), and others. In 1695, the first geographic map of Armenia, considered among the first artistically designed maps in the history of cartography, was produced. The publication of the first Armenian periodical Azdarar (Herald) began in Madras, India, in 1794. The first weekly newspaper Arevelian Azanutsmunks (Oriental News), appeared in 1815, although the first printing house in Armenia was established in 1772.

Throughout their history, Armenians revered books. They washed their hands before handling them, spent their money to buy back books stolen from them, and—believing that books possess divine qualities—placed books under sick people's heads to cure them. Even though many people never read books, they bought them because they were a symbol of prestige and people wanted to display fashionable books on their bookshelves.

The turning point for Caucasian literature was the Russian occupation in the beginning of the nineteenth century. On one hand, it had a discouraging effect on the production of books because the area was under martial law and strong censorship, and most printing houses were closed. On the other hand, Russian poets of the period and Russian translations of European literature influenced local authors. The first literary movement in which both the Georgians and the Russians engaged was romanticism. At the same time, the creation of written literature began in Azerbaijan. The modern literary Azerbaijani language formed from local oral tradition, and substituted for Persian, which had been used as a means of writing before. The most outstanding among the first Azerbaijani writers was Mirza Fatali Akhundov (1812–1878), who created national drama.

In the 1870s, Ilya Chavchavadze (1837–1907) initiated the language reform in Georgia, which changed the orthography, expanded the vocabulary, and transformed the old Georgian language into the one that is in use today. Similar language reform was initiated in Armenia by Mikael Nalbandian (1829–1866), who strived for the introduction of the new Armenian literary language, Ashkharabar, instead of the dead bookish language, Grabar, for which he was ostracized by the clerics. Mikael Nalbandian was the first Armenian poet who combined political issues with literature. His most famous poem is "Liberty," which promotes the idea of freedom. Vazha-Pshavela (1861–1915) dedicated his works to the mountainous Georgians, the Khevsurs. He described their culture, tribal relations, and national consciousness, as well as the beautiful Caucasian nature. The poet was upset that progress and civilization had destroyed the traditional way of life.

In the nineteenth century, the church lost power and literature became secular. Through translations published in newly initiated literary magazines, the public learned about Russian and European contemporary writers who focused on social themes, introduced elements of psychological analysis, and developed Western European traditions of intimate lyrics. Aleksander Movsesian, also known as Shirvanzade (1858–1935), promoted these traditions in Armenia. Western culture and European influence were also reflected in the works of many Azerbaijanis, who at the end of the nineteenth century studied abroad. Gasanbek Zardabi (1837–1907) started to publish the nation's first newspaper *Ekinchi* (Peasant). This newspaper was closed by the Russian authorities in 1877, and the literary magazine *Ziia Kavkasia* (Caucasus Dawn) was published until 1905.

Literature of the Twentieth Century

At the beginning of the twentieth century, Armenian literature was characterized by different styles, including realism, romanticism, symbolism, and avant-gardism. Of special success was the development of lyrical poems. Vahan Teryan (1885–1920) and Avetik Isahakian (1875–1957) connected the vision of people's philosophy with European thoughts, and showed the conflict between the society and an individual to reflect the tragic lives of the Armenian people. The ties between new ideas of the early twentieth century and classical art were shown in Armenian literature by Eghishe Charents (1897–1937). Charents initiated the tradition of symbolic poetry in Armenian literature. Paolo Iashvili (1894–1937) was one of the cofounders of the Georgian symbolism movement. His devotion to mysticism and "pure art" faded under Soviet ideological pressure, when the classics of Georgian literature were effectively banned and the Georgian literary establishment was pressured into the submission of socialist dogmas. At the beginning of the century, Baku became the center of Muslim journalism and literature in the Russian Empire. Sixty-three newspapers and magazines of varied periodicity were published in Baku between 1905 and 1917. Gasanbek Melikov (1837–1907) was a popular writer, who became a reporter for the progressive *Hayat* newspaper in 1905. In his articles, Melikov called for cultural unification of Muslims in Russia and the establishment of a unified Turkic language that would ensure the progress and social development of Russia's Muslims. The hopes of a national revival were expressed in poems of Alekper Sabir (1862–1911), who promoted the idea of linguistic independence and called for the further distancing of Azerbaijani from the Turkish.

During the Soviet era, Armenian writers attempted to stay out of politics, and their works were devoted mostly to national history and personal lyrics. However, to be published, writers had to create works about people's excitement about the Bolshevik revolution, such as Nairi Zarian's (1900–1969) *November Days* and Stepan Zorian's (1890–1967) description of the lives of local activists. Writers who were not able to adjust their works to party requirements were prohibited from publishing. Many were prosecuted. Aksel

Bakunts (1899–1937) was arrested because he had written a story in which an old man complained about a lack of land in Armenia and sadly pointed toward Turkey, noting that there was a lot of land there. Eghishe Charents, who strongly supported Soviet power in Armenia, was accused of being a nationalist because of his poem "Message." The poem appeared to be a standard verse in praise of Stalin, but when one red the second letter in each line vertically, a secret message read: "Oh, Armenian people, your only salvation lies in your collective powers." Both Bakunts and Charents died in prison.[12] Patriotic ballads were created during World War II by Hovhannes Shiraz (1915–1984). Poetry and historical novels, which were the favorite genres of Armenian writers, allowed the authors to distance themselves from the realities of Soviet life.

In the late 1950s, Armenian writers were among the first to denounce the years of Stalin's rule, creating literary works that raised questions of social significance. These works appeared in the *Armenian Writers' Journal* and in the Armenian weekly *Literary Journal*. The first to react to new policies after Stalin's death was Derenik Demirjian (1877–1957). For many years Demirjian was in Stalin's service, but he continued to write respected historical novels. Three weeks after the cult of Stalin was denounced by the Soviet leadership in spring 1956, Demirjian came out with a poem scorning flattery. The poem, titled "The One and the Other," was directed ironically at all writers who had practiced adulation during the Stalin era. Later this theme was elaborated on by other Armenian writers.[13]

Georgian twentieth-century literature survived many changes and influences. At the beginning of the twentieth century, the influence of symbolism, which was popular in European and Russian poetry, was especially strong in Georgia. Georgian poets dreamed about the transformation of Georgia into a shining country of sun and poetry, and they established parallels between Paris and Tbilisi. Later, they were forced to subordinate their talents to the Communist Party's requests to serve the party's goals. Many became victims of Stalin's purges and repressions. Mikhail Dzhavakhishvili (1880–1937) was one of them. The plot of his series of stories *Kvachi Kvachantiradze* is set around the events of the Bolshevik revolution.[14] Because of social problems, a former prince goes into exile and asks for refuge at the house of a rich but illiterate peasant who humiliates the prince and uses the prince's wife as a servant. His historical novel *Arcen from Marabda* shows Georgia in the early nineteenth century after Russian annexation and social injustices survived by poor Georgian peasants, who were forced into serfdom. The leading Georgian poet who influenced all following generations of writers was Galaktion Tabidze (1891–1959). He authored more than 1,000 poems, most of which reflected the theme of isolation, lovelessness, and nightmarish visions. He shared the tragic fate of a majority of Georgian writers, who never experienced a happy life. Tabidze survived the purges but went into a depression and became an alcoholic, jumping out the window of the psychiatric ward where he was forced to live.

The most enigmatic Georgian prose writer of the twentieth century, Konstantine Gamsakhurdia (1893–1975), whose works were influenced by the German philosopher Friedrich Nietzsche, wrote several outstanding novels, including the autobiography *Dionysus' Smile*, dedicated to the search of humans' place in the contemporary world. The book *Kidnapping of the Moon* tells the story of agricultural reform in Soviet Georgia. Konstantine Gamsakhurdia was forced to glorify the Soviet reality and wrote books describing Stalin's childhood. He became extremely popular after publishing historical novels about the construction of the Svetitskhoveli Cathedral in Mtskheta, and the tetralogy *David the Builder* that compared the presence of Soviet institutions with the eleventh-century Turkish occupation, which Soviet authorities criticized for promoting Georgian patriotism and making parallels between historic events and contemporary situations in Georgia. Gamsakhurdia was not persecuted because he did not touch on acute social problems and denounced his views regarding Georgian independence; however, his son, who later became the first president of Georgia in 1990, was imprisoned.

Irakli Abashidze (1911–1995) belonged to the senior generation of Georgian writers. Abashidze created dictionaries of many Georgian dialects and introduced the local lexicon in literary works. His book of poems *The Palestinian Cycle* includes poems dedicated to Shota Rustaveli, written after the author's participation in an expedition to Jerusalem, where Rustaveli's frescoes in a local monastery were discovered. The second half of the twentieth century produced a new generation of writers. Anna Kalandadze (b. 1924) was recognized in the middle of the 1950s immediately after her first book was published. Unlike other writers, she did not touch on social or political problems and described in her works the beauty of Georgian landscapes and nature. Critics compare her poems and stories with still-life paintings because her main characters are mountains, flowers, and trees.

The Soviet period was relatively beneficial to the development of literature in Azerbaijan. During this time, the number of readers grew tremendously and illiteracy was eliminated. Because socialist realism was extensively promoted as the only style allowed to writers by Soviet authorities, the general level of writers' creativity substantially decreased, though such talented authors as Samed Vurgun (1906–1956), Jafar Jabarly (1899–1934), and Ilias Efendiev (b. 1914) were hard at work during that time. After 1945, the subject of the national unity of all Azerbaijani people, regardless of their place of residence, became especially popular. Mamed Ordubady (1872–1950), Suleiman Rustam (1906–1989), and Mirza Ibragimov (b. 1911) wrote extensively on the subject. Their works described the bravery of Azerbaijani people in World War II battles and reflected local life, placing the characters of their books in mountainous villages or small towns. The life of oil explorers moved into the center of writers' attention in the 1970s. Chinghis Guseinov (b. 1929) studied the psychology of Baku workers in his novel *Magomed, Mamed, Mamish*. His later books were based on historical research of Russian policies in the Caucasus and on nineteenth-century Muslim freedom movements.

The best-known Abkhazian writer is Fazil Iskander (b. 1918). He became popular in the 1960s and 1970s, publishing books full of stories about the rapid erosion of traditional values. The elders in his idyllic Abkhazia still remember the traditional society in which they lived and the customs and traditions they held dear. The writer is convinced that the attachment to traditions makes human beings stronger, while a loss of this attachment makes them weak and cynical. A distinctive feature of Iskander's prose is the use of folktales, as well as the multilingual, colorful, variously accented chatter of mid-twentieth-century Abkhazia. Iskander appears to be the first author to break with the prescribed Soviet stereotype of depicting a person from the Caucasus as one who is expected to speak in incomplete sentences, and use the vocabulary of a newspaper article with slight grammatical inaccuracies.[15] In Iskander's books, language situations are described with a wide range of comic effects, from light jokes to scathing satire. An illustration of this is found in *The Beginning*: during a university admission interview a student adjusts his Abkhazian accent to the degree of the professor's expectations.

Because during Communist rule adherence to the tenets of the Communist Party was required for any literary work, and writings in native languages were expected to be within the Soviet framework, literature of great value was not produced in large quantities. The result was the accumulation of novels, plays, and short stories designed to indoctrinate politically rather than to ennoble spiritually. Refuge was found in the older classical writers and in translations of available Western writers. Among the most popular were the Americans James Fennimore Cooper, Jack London, F. Scott Fitzgerald, and Theodore Dreiser. But most of all, the people on all levels and of all ethnicities seized on Shakespeare, whose translations were published extensively throughout the Caucasus.[16]

Modern Caucasus Authors

Since the late 1980s, when writers received relative freedom, a new generation of authors has appeared. They search for untraditional methods to express their views and attempt to reflect the life around them with documentary realism, evaluating hidden motives behind human behavior and paying attention to the internal world of an individual. For many years, the Karabakh conflict remained the most popular subject for writers in Armenia and Azerbaijan. Azerbaijani authors focused on such issues as the return of lands annexed by Armenia during the war, the securing of a place for Azerbaijan among the developed nations of the world, the patriotic education of the young generation of readers, and the development of friendly relations with neighboring countries. Armenian writers portray the ongoing war as a unromantic event and analyze varied features of human life. After achieving independence, Armenia wanted to become more open to the West and made the translation of classical Armenian literature into English and other Western European languages a top priority, financed usually by the diaspora.

The economic difficulties of the first years of independence had a devastating impact on literature. Book publishing and bookstores became unprofitable because people had no money to spend on books; literary magazines ceased to exist; young writers moved their works to the Internet, disassociating from the government-supported literary establishment; and ties with authors in neighboring republics were lost. Today, the situation has slightly improved, but the books are printed in very low quantities. According to local standards, a best seller is a book with 1,000 sold copies. The number of published copies decreased about one hundred times compared to the number in 1995. According to the Armenian National Statistics Agency, 1,070 titles were published in 2006. That is more than in 2005, when 991 titles were published, but the circulation of all books in 2006 decreased to 726,000 copies, compared with 796,000 copies sold in 2005.[17] Readers' preferences and literary tastes have changed too. Professional literature is much more popular than fiction, and fantasy books and detective stories and texts on soap operas are among the most purchased books.

Understanding the importance of intellectual support, the Azerbaijani government finances literary magazines and newspapers, and it heavily subsidizes the publishing industry. In recent years, the government initiated worldwide celebrations of Fizuli's 500-year birthday and the *Kior-ogly* anniversary. In 2004, the president of Azerbaijan ordered that the most important books of Azerbaijani literary heritage be republished in the Latin alphabet; work on the preparation of the Azerbaijani National Encyclopedia was initiated as well.

Azerbaijan is probably the only former Soviet republic in which writers are still respected. The Writers' Union, a professional organization for writers created in 1932 by Soviet authorities to exercise control over writers' activities and monitor their behavior, was preserved by the Azerbaijani government. State financing of the Writers' Union was ordered by President Heydar Aliyev in 2002, and good working conditions were created for those authors who did not oppose government policies. Many obedient writers were elected to the state's legislature or appointed to high offices.

The best-selling Azerbaijani author is Chingis Abdullaev (b. 1959), who has authored about seventy books, publishing a book every two months for four consecutive years. All of his books are thrillers in which a private detective, Drongo, discloses mafia plots or fights international terrorists. Famous domestic and foreign political figures are characters in his books too. A writer who became a translator and an essayist, Malkhaz Kharbedia (b. 1974), promotes the idea that there are no cultural problems among the people of the South Caucasus but that existing political problems do not allow the people to cooperate, including in culturally. Azerbaijani writers initiated the democratic changes in their republic. Sabir Rustamhanly (b. 1946) was the leader of the democratic opposition. He argues against chauvinism and nationalism, and he defends the ideology of the national freedom movement. In 2008, he ran for president of Azerbaijan.

In the twenty-first century, Armenian writers are discussing the Karabakh war less and addressing issues of general interest. Their works are more social, with moods of despair and discomfort caused by the controversies of independent Armenia. Sometimes they express themselves with humor. Gurgen Khanjyan (b. 1950) represents this generation. With nine books published since 1987, many Internet publications, and translations in foreign languages, he is recognized as a modern author whose work is destined to become part of the classics. Difficulties of present-day life are told in his books with humor, and typical national features are revealed through descriptions of small events or items, like a metro station escalator. Krikor Beledian (b. 1948) is a leading novelist, poet, and critic. His works revolve around questions of Armenian identity in the diaspora and follow traces, themes, and allegories of catastrophe in modern Armenian literature. A contemporary playwright is Karine Khodikian (b. 1957). People in her dramas do not fight, but rather follow the circumstances and do not listen to their emotions; the only disobedience they allow themselves is a free choice of death. All women characters in her plays remain true to their obligations and sacrifice their love for children, family, parents, or work. Vagram Martirosian (b. 1969) is the only modern Armenian writer who has been translated into Azerbaijani; his novel *Landslide* was published in the Azerbaijani newspaper *Senet* (Art). The book describes present-day events and is written in slangy language. The main character is not an intellectual searching his internal world to identify himself, as has been common in Armenian literature, but a cynical pseudo-intellectual, pseudo-businessman, semi-illiterate with a higher education who drifts between banquets and clubs and is surrounded by personal and national stereotypes. He seems to be a real product of the Soviet society and adjusts to his new life.

Modern Georgian literature and journalism emerged as part of a broad movement of ideological renewal aimed to restore Georgian self-consciousness and national identity. The distinctive feature of this new literature is formalistic experimentation. Even though the ideas are original, their implementation does not always show the high level of mastery established by earlier generations of Georgian writers.

The most popular young prose writer is Aka Morchiladze (b. 1966), who already has published twelve novels. He writes two types of books: stylizations of the Georgian customs and language of early twentieth century, in which he re-creates myths of the old Tbilisi, and contemporary novels that reflect the life of Tbilisi teenagers. Some of the novels are detective stories that involve personages from other classical Georgian books or Georgian historical and artistic figures. Zurab Kuramidze (b. 1957) is another master of stylization. His book *Dark Wine Sea* (2000) is called "a Georgian Ulysses." Readers who are familiar with the Tbilisi artistic elite may recognize many people in his books. David Kartvelishvili (b. 1976) describes the events that occurred more than a hundred years ago but places them in modern setting. Recently, he has begun to write stories based on Orthodox Christian ethics. The novel *Nata, or New Julia* authored by Diana Vachnadze (b. 1966) is the first example of Georgian nonlinear prose. This novel was written in the form of a letter exchange. It includes essays, diaries, and dream interpretations, which make the text multidimensional. The publication of this novel started in 1999, in a literary magazine, though it was not completely finished at that time. During the course of publication, the same magazine published six reviews of the novel. Later, these reviews were incorporated in the text, and reviewers became the novel's characters. *Butterfly's Honeymoon*, written by Marsiani (b. 1953) in 1982, was published in 2003. The ironic story mixes different genres and manipulates writing techniques. It starts as a detective story, which then becomes erotic, then a fantasy, and then a detective story again.

The old generation of Georgian writers is represented by the recognized masters. Otar Chkheidze (b. 1920) is one of them. All of his more than twenty books are dedicated to specific events in twentieth-century Georgian history. The most recent books combine fiction and documentary descriptions of modern events, allowing the author to set the literary plot in real Georgian present-day life. Famous politicians and public figures are described in Chkheidze's works of fiction. The author does not limit himself to just a description of the events. Using different literary styles, he expresses his own political position and his evaluations of politicians' activities. All of his books were accompanied by scandals when people who recognized themselves in the book expressed their disagreements. The last book was titled *The Year 2001*, with main character Mikheil Saakashvili, the current president of Georgia.

Data Tutashkhia, by Chabua Amirejibi (b. 1921) published in 1975, is a must-read Georgian book about a Robin Hood–like outlaw who, at the end of the nineteenth century, was hiding in the mountains of Georgia from his cousin, the head of the Caucasian gendarmerie. The book is a tale of many episodes told from different points of view and stretching over almost thirty years. Each part has a clever, often humorous character and provides interesting portraits of Georgian society in those long-gone days. Amirejibi's next book, *Gora Mborgali*, appeared in 1995. The protagonist of the book is a sixty-year old man who escapes from Siberian confinement, where he had been sentenced to life in prison. He runs 2,000 miles through ice and snowstorms of the Russian taiga. During his five months of travel, he remembers his life, stories he has heard from his relatives, and two centuries of Georgian history. This book reflects the difficult life of the author, who spent many years in Soviet imprisonment for his political views.

NOTES

1. Graham Smith, Vivien Law, and Andrew Wilson, *Nation-Building in the Post-Soviet Borderlands: The Politics of National Identities* (Cambridge: Cambridge University Press, 1998), 168.

2. Ibid., 170.

3. Yo'av Karny, *Highlanders: A Journey to the Caucasus in Quest of Memory* (New York: Farrar, Straus and Giroux, 2000), 231.

4. Robert Thomson, *Rewriting Caucasian History* (Oxford: Clarendon Press, 1996), 19.

5. Ibid., 22.

6. Even during the period of forceful Russification conducted by Soviet authorities between 1920 and 1990, more than 95 percent of Armenians residing in the Soviet Union declared Armenian as their native language.

7. The Ossetians are the only surviving people to speak the language of the ancient Scythians.

8. Mamuka Komakhia, "The Greeks of Georgia: Migration and Socioeconomic Problems," *Central Asia and the Caucasus*, no. 6 (2005): 158.

9. Thomas Streissguth, *The Transcaucasus* (San Diego: Lucent Books, 2001), 78.

10. Rusudan Choloqashvili, "Magical Objects in Georgian Fairy Tales Featuring Animals," at http://www.caucasology.com/XIV-XV/Rusiko.pdf.

11. Anne Avakian, "Three Apples Fell from Heaven," *Folklore* 98, no. 1 (1987): 97–98.

12. Ronald Suny, *Looking toward Ararat: Armenia in Modern History* (Bloomington: Indiana University Press, 1993), 155.

13. Alexander Edward, "The Ferment in Soviet Armenian Literature," *American Slavic and East European Review* 17, no. 4 (1958): 503.

14. Most Georgian books are named after the main character, and thus are often personal names.

15. Marina Kanevskaya, "The Shortest Path to the Truth: Indirection in Fazil' Iskander," *Modern Language Review* 99, no. 1 (2004): 141.

16. Alexander Edward, "Shakespeare's Plays in Armenia," *Shakespeare Quarterly* 9, no. 3 (1958): 392.

17. See http://docs.armstat.am/nsdp/.

6

Food, Drinks, and Fashion

GENERALLY, PEOPLE OF the Caucasus follow a healthy diet, which is based on vegetable oil, nuts, whole grain, grilled lamb and poultry, greens, cheeses, and yogurt. The people also consume a lot of wine, which is produced commercially as well as individually in almost every private home, justifying the region's reputation as the cradle of wine making. While producing and consuming food, people of the Caucasus follow behavioral patterns that have existed since prehistoric times and have permitted them to survive. These include minimal cultivation as well as sharing instead of accumulating and hoarding, which result from long experiences of resisting invasions, during which cultivated fields and pastures full of livestock had served both as attraction and as sustenance for intruders.[1] Increasing globalization, new trends in food preparation, and general attitude toward food unite the republics of the Caucasus with the rest of the Western world. The same can be said about consumer habits and shopping patterns. Western European fashion brands have secured their positions in the Caucasus, moving traditional national costumes to the periphery of folk festivals and ethnographic research.

TRADITIONAL CUISINE

Food Traditions

Food is one of the few items of traditional material culture that has been preserved almost entirely. Cooking traditions are respected and passed from one generation to another. Because of historical influences, the region's cuisine is a modern mixture of Persian, Turkish, Greek, and Mediterranean dishes. The three Caucasian cultures have many similarities, though there are local differences. The usual components of each meal are soups, a variety of ground-meat specialties, stuffed vegetables and fruits, all kinds of flavorful vegetable preparations, rich sweets of nuts and honey, pastries, and fruit puddings. People of the Caucasus love aromatics and use spices heavily. Herbs, wild greens, onions, garlic, and hot pepper supplement each meal. Regional breads are produced in different styles and shapes and with various flours, such as corn, rye, or wheat depending on the region.

Kay Shaw Nelson describes a typical modern luncheon that favored typical Georgian dishes and began with a "splendid selection of appetizers, and an array of dishes placed along the center of the table." She tasted fresh and pickled vegetables, spinach puree, slices of air-dried beef called *basturma*, and *lobio*, which is made of highly seasoned red beans. After a bowl of spicy beef soup, she continued with a local version of beef Stroganoff cooked in a saffron-tomato sauce, cheese-stuffed bread known as *khachapuri*, and fresh fruits and a honey-walnut sweet, along with glasses of fruity white Tsinandali and robust red Mukuzani wines.[2] With this abundance of food, people do not overeat but enjoy food and wine leisurely with convivial companions and rarely dine alone.

People enjoy their meals not just because of the pleasures that food brings them, but mostly because of the companionship of family and friends. The tradition of hospitality demands that all guests be given the best that a host can provide. A good banquet with traditional dishes would include such appetizers as eggplant in walnut sauce, smoked sturgeon, red caviar with buttered bread, rice-stuffed peppers, cheeses, pickled garlic cloves, meat-filled dumplings, and spicy green and red peppers. The main dish is almost always made of lamb accompanied by a spicy *tkemali* (sour plum) sauce and bread baked in an outdoor round clay oven. Fruits are usually eaten for dessert, as homebaked cakes and pies are reserved for more festive occasions. And, of course, there is a lot of drinking. People drink, toasting to peace, political leaders, families, ancestors, the arts, holidays, beautiful women, September's harvest, and a happy future. They drink from small clay bowls and from ornate ibex horns, and almost no one is excused from drinking bottoms up.

The ceremonial dinner, a frequent occurrence in Caucasian homes, is a highly ritualized event that itself forms a direct link to the nation's past. On such occasions, rounds of standardized and improvised toasts typically extend long into the night, and the cuisine, which includes a traditional and almost obligatory variety of dishes, sauces, and spices, links generations together. Formal dinners are led by a *tamada*, usually the host or an honored guest, whose responsibilities are to "pace the drinking and entertain the company with his

eloquent words; though not in a single speech, but in a rich and variegated series of discourses."[3] Subjects of the *tamada*'s verbal virtuosity include the holy
places of Georgia, the visitor from afar, the parents who gave us birth, our
revered teachers, the state of the nation, and so on. After the *tamada* makes
a toast to honor somebody, he takes a drink and then anyone present can
continue the toast to honor the person or to elaborate on the subject. When
everyone who wanted to make a speech has spoken, the person in whose honor
a toast was pronounced may respond and thank all people present or each person individually. Because of this procedure, which looks like a relay, it is not
unusual for one toast to continue for more than an hour.

Fairy tales and legends are also told during toasts. Sometimes, toasts can
be paradoxical. It is not rare for somebody to make a speech like this: "Dear
Friend, I want to drink to your coffin." Then, after a pause and embarrass-
ment, the speaker continues: "I wish that this coffin will be made out of a
hundred-year old oak that we will plant when you retire." This toast is an in-
direct wish of long and healthy life, which should continue at least a hundred
years after retirement. Besides long toasts, there are very short one-sentence
toasts, like "Let's not be ashamed to look at each other's eyes," or "Let's hope
that God would never think that we don't deserve what he gave to us."

Only after finishing to speak does a person drink from his or her glass. After
a while, the *tamada* proposes a new toast, thus renewing a cycle of dialogue
around the table. Sometimes, raising his toast, the *tamada* alerts one of the
guests with the word *Alaverdy* ("to you"), indicating that the guest is expected
to pick up and develop the proposed subject.[4] Because of long intervals between drinks, it is almost impossible to lose control and get drunk. Always,
before thanking the master of the house for his hospitality, the guests will toast
to the parents, regardless of whether they are alive or already deceased. It is a
shame to miss this toast, which is drunk while standing up, which is another
thing that helps people monitor their behavior and volume of consumption.

Children are regular participants at feasts, even little ones. They are usually
seated together with the grown-ups and listen to the general conversation,
learning how to behave and speak. When the feast continues late into the
night, children fall asleep right at the table. Manners at the table reflect those
of Western Europe, and as everywhere, they reveal social relationships, though
certain regional aspects stand out. Among the major rules are the requirements
to exercise control at the table. People must not appear hungry even if they
want to eat, and gestures should be slow and measured as food is brought to
the mouth. Gulping or stuffing the mouth is not acceptable. The use of uten-
sils is regulated by local rules and traditions. In many situations, fingers are
used to scoop the food, as with drumsticks or chicken wings, which are almost
always eaten with fingers. Roasted meat is also picked up with the hand.

An Azerbaijani street vendor. Courtesy of Leila Alieva.

People usually have a full breakfast together with children before they leave home for work. During the day, another family member who is at home will accompany the children to regular meals after school. At work, employees receive time to eat in the early afternoon, though many wait until later in the day. Cafeterias used to exist in schools, but presently the state school systems have no funds to feed children, and many parents prefer for their children to eat a sandwich, cake, or fruit brought from home. Because the business day usually starts at nine in the morning, by five or six o'clock at night, people arrive home for the family meal, which is the principal meal of the day. Because people stay late, they often have a snack just before bedtime around midnight. The regular meal is almost never consumed alone, and the eating schedule is organized so that family members are able to stay connected with one another. For example, a grandmother may feed the children after school but she waits to eat with adults later in the evening. Regular dinners in a family usually consist of three dishes: soup, meat and gravy, and a sweet, often a fruit syrup. If a close friend or relative is present at a daily meal, the meal may take on more festive aspects. In such cases, toasts are offered by the master of the house or the guest, but drinking is looser and no formal toasting order is observed.[5]

The new lifestyle, increased Western influences, and offers of new goods and techniques of food processing have affected traditional food consumption, though the main principles remain and the urban–rural differences have not been eliminated. For example, snacking in the streets has increased noticeably. Earlier, food was eaten at the establishment where it was purchased, but now walking and eating an ice-cream cone, a doughnut, or drinking a Coke is common. Imported popcorn machines placed in front of shops appeal to passersby. The rise of sidewalk cafés, financed by foreign beer companies, has become significant in getting people to eat out. Many cafés cater especially to students and young people. Eating out has become more common, and a new trend is to sit in the new restaurants. Tables have begun to be placed in view of other customers, instead of in small private rooms, as had been the custom formerly. Another obvious novelty is the change in soft drinks' consumption. Local mineral water, which was traditionally sold in glass bottles for extremely cheap prices, is now produced in plastic bottles for triple the price. Meanwhile, the Coca-Cola Company has opened a bottling plant in the region and has become popular among people of all ages. People's tastes, and subsequently their food preferences, have changed because of the availability and affordability of newly arrived foreign food products, such as ham and bacon from Denmark and Germany, cheeses from France and Holland, and yogurts with added fruits from Turkey.

National Dishes

Armenian national cuisine combines vegetables and animal products. People consume lots of nutritious salads, and probably the world's best soups made with yogurt and stews of lamb and vegetables. Sometimes, apricots are added to soups. Rice or meat, stuffed grape leaves, cold white-bean appetizers, lamb patties, kebabs, fruit-stuffed trout, and pies are among the most popular dishes. Like most other people in the Caucasus, Armenians eat a lot of cookies and pastries for dessert.

Grain products make up the majority of the food. Wheat flour is used for baking thin wheat bread called *lavash*, cookies, and other sweets. Grains are added to make soups richer, and all types of milk products are part of Armenian meals. Milk is often used to prepare refreshing beverages and soups. Many religious rites require eating meat. According to traditions, cooked meat is eaten during religious holidays and fried meat is prepared for secular festivities. Many dishes require the simultaneous preparation of vegetables, meat, and grain. Traditionally, to preserve meat for a long winter, smoked sausages were made or fried pieces of meat were put in bowls full of liquid fat.

The usual improvised Armenian meal that anyone entering a house will receive consists of bread, butter, sour milk, cheese, fresh and pickled vegetables, and radishes. There are many types of bread, but lavash is the most popular. A piece of lavash looks like a hand towel, because of its size and thickness. At a picnic, lavash may substitute for a tablecloth, a napkin, a spoon, or a fork. Fried meat and vegetables are placed on the lavash, and cheese and dill are wrapped inside it. Dried lavash can be stored for as long as needed, and it becomes soft and flexible again as soon as it is dampened with water.

A typical Armenian lunch consists of a vegetable or meat soup with meatballs and sour milk. Eggs and green beans are especially popular in the summer. Many complex meat and fish dishes are prepared for festivities, but the most popular are the *horovats* and the *hash*. *Horovats* is a kebab made from lamb or more often from pork. Eggplants, tomatoes, and green peppers are roasted together with meat. *Horovats* and *hash* are never made for just a family dinner. Cooking these dishes is always an event, and a large group of guests is almost always invited for such occasions. Unlike *horovats*, which is prepared during the day and eaten in the evening, beef legs and guts for *hash* are cooked all night long. After adding salt and garlic it is eaten in the morning, the stew is then used as a dip for lavash.

Armenian dinner is usually finished with tea or coffee, which require some desserts. Armenians are good at making pastries and sweets. The simplest sweets are dried peaches, plums, and apricots. Preserves and jams are made not only from fruits but also from unripe walnuts, pumpkins, eggplants, green tomatoes, and watermelon rind. Smoked peaches and nuts cooked in honey make a perfect desert too.

Cooking and food consumption among other Caucasian people is based mainly on the same principles. In Georgia, as in all other areas, culinary traditions are strictly preserved and followed today. Although Russian and other foreign dishes are prepared at home and in restaurants, the national cuisine still dominates. When guests are received at a home, they are fed almost exclusively traditional Georgian food. The eastern and western parts of Georgia have two different styles of cooking. Hot food with a variety of spices, walnuts, pomegranates, and herbs is preferred in western Georgia, influenced by Greece and Turkey. The food of eastern Georgia reflects the region's closeness to Iran and is based on grains, dairy products, fruits, and vegetables. The cuisine makes extensive use of walnuts, which are used to thicken soups and sauces flavored with herbs, garlic, walnuts, and eggs. Cafés, restaurants, and street-food traditions are better established in Georgia than in other republics, and the markets are full of locally grown fruit and vegetables. In Georgia, and all over the region, shopping is done by both men and women. Often men take pride in choosing cheeses, fruits, and vegetables. Men almost exclusively buy meat. In open bazaars and in food stores, men and women shop in equal numbers.

The culinary traditions of Azerbaijan are associated with those of Iran and Central Asia. The abundance of vegetables, fruits, fragrant herbs, and spices have inspired Azerbaijan's cooks to invent distinctive new dishes. Bread was always the basic food for Azerbaijanis, but in addition to the thin lavash popular all over the region, Azerbaijanis bake a thick bread called *churek*.

Azerbaijani appetizers are not as elaborate as they are in the two other republics. Usually they include dried fruits, nuts, vegetables and herbs, salads, bread, cheese, and sometimes yogurt. Lamb is the most popular meat. Tomatoes, potatoes, peas, and peppers are added to soups prepared from lamb. Soups are a very important part of Azerbaijani cuisine and are consumed daily. There are numerous variations of rice dishes made with many ingredients and served traditionally, with each person helping himself or herself. One of the most popular dishes is *plov*, rice with meat, fish, fruits, and other ingredients. Depending on the ingredients, there are more than forty plov varieties, for instance, lamb plov, chicken plov, dried fruit plov, and so on. Ground beef

Bread baking. Courtesy of Leila Alieva.

is an important component of main dishes, which are similar to Armenian dishes but differ in style of cooking. Many dishes are made from poultry. A very popular dish is *chygyrtma*, a boiled then fried chicken divided into pieces, mixed with fried onion, and glazed with eggs and grape or lemon juices.

An Azerbaijani meal consists of several courses prepared from a very concentrated meat stew. Heavily used spices give the courses a special aroma. Main dishes are prepared from ground or cubed meat, usually lamb, and are served with condiments. Some dishes are served as both the first and the second course. Among them are *piti* and *kyufta-bozbash*. In this case the meat stew is served separately from the other ingredients (meat, peas, potatoes), which are treated as a second course even though they were cooked in the stew. There are also many fish dishes. The most popular specialties are sturgeon kebab, sturgeon plov, and stuffed fish. After the second course, especially plov, Azerbaijanis often serve *dovga*, a meal prepared from sour milk and greens. It is believed that *dovga* improves digestion. Dinner ends with tea and sweet pastries served with jams and preserves.

Drinks

The most famous drinks of the Caucasus are mineral water, tea, brandy, and wine. The stony, treeless mountains of the South Caucasus, heated by the hot sun, provide ideal conditions for keeping water pure and fresh. Each republic has more than 200 mineral water springs with certified medicinal qualities. Azerbaijan is known for its table waters Badamly and Turshu. Georgian Borzhomi is widely recognized outside the republic, and for many years it was a major export. Water from the Armenian Bjni, Jermuk, and Arzni springs competes with water from the neighboring republics. No table is full without mineral water, particularly carbonated water. Recently, in Georgia, the right to lease the springs for twenty-five years was given to a group of young national entrepreneurs who increased the annual production of water to several million bottles from each spring, and began to produce and deliver mango, guava, and rosehip juices to the countries of the region. Another drink that has always been on the table is *matsun*, a kind of a kefir used to produce yogurt, or *tun*, a matsun diluted by cold water. Both drinks slake thirst and combine well with all the national dishes.

Tea leaves grow on the slopes of the Caucasus mountains, and tea is a very popular drink. Spices like cinnamon or mint are often added to a tea. Usually tea is served in small glasses with wide bottoms. Another popular drink, especially in Armenian cities, is coffee. Few Armenians can survive a day without having several cups of coffee in coffeehouses or street cafés. The cities of Sukhumi and Batumi in Georgia probably compete with Yerevan in terms of coffee consumption, but the coffee culture was brought there by the Armenians.[6]

Wine and brandy are produced in every republic of the Caucasus, but Armenia is best known for its brandy. The best wine is in Georgia, while Azerbaijan does not have a specialty but produces a variety of good-quality alcoholic drinks.

Wine Making

Georgia is the cradle of wine making. The contemporary Georgian language includes 1,200 words related to wine. A rich wine lexicon exists because wine making is an elaborate process.[7] There are thirty-two terms to explain the ripening of grapes, forty-one to describe the cultivation of a vine, and forty-nine to describe the harvesting of grapes—proving that the wine culture has long roots in Georgia. The antiquity of Georgian wine making is supported not only by archeological discoveries but also by modern interpretations of the Old Testament. It is believed that when Noah's ark arrived at Mount Ararat and he let all his companions go, he built a house at Ararat's foothills and planted vines. From the grapes he made wine and became the first wine producer. Armenian wines and their outstanding qualities were reported by Herodotus who described the passage of Armenian boats loaded with vessels of wine along the Euphrates River.[8]

Until the nineteenth century, almost all wine was produced in individual households. Wine making became an industry after a special agency was created in the Russian imperial court. The agency acquired numerous grape plantations in Georgia and created wineries that were a part of the emperor's property. A special school aimed to prepare wine-making specialists was created in Georgia in 1877. Several other distilleries were opened in Georgia in the 1870s. Each produced about 250,000 bottles of wine annually, including sparkling wine. In 1929, on the basis of the tsar's wineries, Samtrest, the institution of state management of the Georgian wine industry was created. In 2003, Samtrest was privatized and reorganized into the main national wine corporation, which occupies a leading position on the Georgian wine market.

Today, approximately ninety grape-processing plants and distilleries are working in the country. More than 500 original varieties of grapes are grown in Georgia, more than in any other country. Both red and white wine is produced there. The importance of this industry is revealed in the adoption of national laws on vineyards and wine, grapes, and trademarks by the Georgian legislature in 2003. Following the European Union's requirements, fifteen government regulations define the wine certification process. Georgian wine is well known outside of the republic too. The first prize that Georgian wine received was in 1889, at the World Exhibition in Paris. Later, Georgian wines received further international acclaim. In 1965, the Soviet Union began to participate in international wine competitions, and Georgian wines won 289 gold, 174 silver, and 43 bronze medals. The best known Georgian wines are the fruity, red Khvanchkara, reputed to have been Stalin's favorite drink, and the dry white Tsinandali.

Armenian wine making developed fairly successfully until the middle of the fifteenth century, when after the fall of Constantinople, all of western Armenia became dependent on the Ottoman Empire, and wine making was restricted because it violated Islamic religious norms. Armenians and Greeks were allowed to produce wine for their own needs only and industrial wine making was outlawed. This led to the exclusion of many sorts of grapes from the agricultural realm. At that time, grapes were grown in small gardens in the area of modern-day Yerevan. Only in the nineteenth century, after Russia annexed eastern Armenia, did the revival of wine making occur. In 1887, the first industrial winery was opened within the walls of the Yerevan fortress. Ten years later there were more than seventy wine production enterprises in the country.

Most of the 200 Armenian grapes are aboriginal, except two Georgian sorts, Saperavi and Rkatsiteli. During Soviet times, it was believed that sweet Armenian wines had medicinal qualities and they were sold in pharmacies. Armenian wines acquire special qualities because of the climate in which the grapes are grown. There are 300 sunny days in the Ararat Valley, while in Georgia, there are only 180–200 days with good weather. Humidity and sun radiation, which are more favorable in Armenia, also affect the taste of wine.

Armenian Brandy

Many sorts of grape wine are produced in Armenia, but world recognition was given to Armenian brandy (the Armenians call it cognac and say that brandy is made by another process). The industrialist Nerses Tairiants brought the technology from France and founded the Yerevan Cognac Factory in 1887. Twelve years later, his company was bought by Nikolai Shustov's trading house, a purveyor for the Russian imperial court. During the Soviet era, a network of separate Armenian distilleries produced 30 percent of all alcoholic beverages in the Soviet Union, and Armenian wineries were responsible for half of the entire national income in the food industry. In 1992, the National Cognac Consortium, Ararat, was established. It combined twenty distilleries in Armenia and many processing and distribution factories all over the former Soviet Union.

By 1998, old distilleries and wineries in the mountainous villages were restored, and the Armenian wine industry was divided between the French company Pernod Ricard, which purchased the Yerevan Cognac Factory and invests about US$5 million in the enterprise annually, and Great Valley, a joint Cypriot-Armenian company that started to produce new brands of old and very old, expensive brandies: King Tigran (aged thirty years), Arin Berd (twenty-five years), and Collection (eighteen years). Pernod Ricard redesigned the production process. Previously, cognac was aged in metal vessels with chips of oak bark thrown in. Now the cognac is properly aged in natural oak casks. For this purpose, the art of cooperage, lost in the nineteenth century, had to be revived in Armenia. The most famous brands of brandy are Ararat, Ani, Nairi, Akhtamar, and Vaspourakan. Armenian brandies received almost 500 medals in international exhibitions between 1998 and 2005. The tradition of supplying foreign dignitaries with Armenian brandy began in 1943, after Winston Churchill tried an Armenian brandy at the Tehran Conference. Brandy Dwyn, named after the ancient Armenian capital, became his favorite drink, and twenty cases of it were sent to him annually.[9]

In 2001, new national standards for brandy production were approved by the Armenian government. The standards introduced the name Armenian Cognac and state that this name can be given to products made from Armenian grapes according to established technology and bottled only in Armenia. In this matter, the Armenian legislation is even stricter than French laws, which allow for the export of cognac in barrels. Regardless of the legitimacy of applying the term *cognac*, the products of the Yerevan Cognac Factory are called "cognac" inside the country and in Russia, which is the main importer and consumer of alcoholic beverages produced in the Caucasus. The present-day annual output of the Yerevan Cognac Factory is 3.5 million bottles. Russia accounts for 75 percent of those, with 93 percent of production going to export, and another 10 percent goes to Ukraine and Belarus. Armenian brandy is sold in the United States, Japan, Canada, Austria, China, and even in France. The main feature of Armenian brandies is their sweetness and soft taste, with vanilla and chocolate flavors and a dark honey color that results from special oak barrels made from trees that grow in eastern Georgia. Traditional aboriginal sorts of white grapes are also used to produce brandy in Armenia. There are plans to increase exports to twenty-five more countries. However, the expansion of production is hampered by a shortage of grapes because the vineyards cannot satisfy market demands.

The drinking culture in Armenia is slightly different from that in Georgia. Unlike in the West, where cognac is a dessert drink or digestif, in Armenia brandy is drunk at major meals as a table drink. On a regular basis, it is consumed in much larger quantities than in other cultures. In Armenia, as everywhere in the Caucasus, many people make drinks at home. This is especially popular in rural areas; oftentimes villagers supply their relatives who live in cities with alcoholic beverages. The most popular homemade drink is peach vodka.

NATIONAL COSTUMES

John Steinbeck declared in his *Russian Journal*: "The Summer nights were wonderful in Tbilisi; the air soft, and light, and dry. Young men and girls walked aimlessly in the streets. . . . The costumes of the young men were rather nice: tunics, sometimes of heavy white silk, belted at the waist, and long narrow trousers, and soft black boots. They are a very handsome breed, the Georgian men."[10] This description can be justly applied to any of the Caucasian nations. Native people of the Caucasus are tall, lean, and stately; they usually have dark hair and black eyes. The cult of beauty evident in exterior appearances and the development of artistic expression is culturally ingrained and widely observed. While Western European clothes from the best stores are acquired regardless of price, national costumes reflect the features of local people better than anything else. Fur hats of different types are an essential element of men's costume. Chest pockets for bullets adorn the upper part of men's clothing and belts have metallic ornaments. With some local variations, women fame their faces with open-work tulle or an embroidered, light-colored scarf that beautifully contrasts with dark hair. Sleeves are the most expressive part of women's dress. Their decorative details and shapes differ depending on local customs.

A traditional adornment of all dresses in the Caucasus is lace made with a single needle by women who have learned the technique, which is passed on from generation to generation. Styles and stitches vary regionally. Usually, lace is an ornament for chalice covers and cross and Bible holders. Scarves and handkerchiefs were often fringed with a variety of miniature lace flowers. Many scholars believe that the origin of Venetian lace, one of the oldest and most developed lace-making centers, is in Armenia, which had contact with Italian merchants in the Middle Ages.[11]

Presently, regular European dress is common in the countries of the Caucasus. Branches of major European department stores have opened in the three capitals, and well-known designers sell goods in the boutique stores visited by local people. Native designers add traditional local themes to modern suites.

Georgian Dress

Georgian ethnic clothes have many features common throughout the Caucasus. However, there are some details specific to particular localities. Today, nobody wears the national dress, but the dress can be seen at folk concerts and festivals, and on some family occasions. Women usually wore shirts with

Georgian children in national clothes. Courtesy of Mr. and Mrs. Mikhael Budagashvili.

straight sleeves and put dresses made of silk or wool over the shirts. In the past, the dress worn by young women was of a light color, mostly pink or white; older women had darker-colored dresses. All dresses were long-necked with an embroidered breastplate. Sleeves had cuts for the entire length and buttons at the wrist. The belt and the breastplate were covered with beads and pearls ornamented as leaves or flowers. A warm velvet coat with fur lining was worn over the dress. The edge of the coat was adorned with numerous enamel or gold buttons. The coat went down to the knees. Long sleeves were typical for Georgian clothes. They freely hung down on women's dresses, and men threw them back at a jaunty angle. A dress with an airy hat, fitted at the waist, a wide skirt, and large sleeves created a graceful silhouette.

Men wore wide trousers tucked inside boots or woven socks and a long shirt with a small collar made from a dark sateen named *arkhaluk*. Above the *arkhaluk*, men usually wore pleated coats with many large pockets and decorative small pockets for bullets. Men's heads were covered with small felt gray or black hats stitched in a cross-like style at the top. In ancient times, these hats were worn under a metallic helmet. It is fashionable in Georgia to wear such a hat, and almost all men in cities and rural areas do so. The Khevsurs, who lived high in the mountains, often wore clothes made from a thick, blue wool fabric decorated with colorful geometric ornaments, usually in the form of crosses.

Armenian Dress

Armenian dress is complemented by a rich cultural tradition. Wool and fur were used, cotton was grown in the fertile valleys, and silk imported from China was used by royalty during the Urartian period. Later the Armenians cultivated silkworms and produced their own silk. National dress, which is used today for holiday celebrations and theatrical performances, reflects the differences between people of western and eastern Armenia. Men's suits in eastern Armenia are the same as suits throughout the Caucasus: a shirt with a small collar, a knee-length coat (*arkhaluk*) made of sateen or sackcloth, and a dark overcoat of heavy cloth or wool with buttons (*chukha*). Unlike overcoats of other Caucasus people, *chukhas* did not have breast pockets for bullets. Leather, silver, or silk belts were an important element of a suit. Low-income craftsmen and tradesmen paid special attention to their belts, viewing them as an investment and a way to save money for their own funerals. Broad pants were tucked into long ornamented stockings or wound around with a colorful band. Women wore pants of the same style too. Women wore an *arkhaluk* with a low cut on the front and cuts on both sides, and belted it with a silver belt or a colorful silk scarf. On holidays, women's dress was similar but with out being low cut.

Coats were not part of western Armenian dress. Instead of coats, a vest and short jacket were usually worn over shirts and tight pants. Except for the elderly, people decorated their clothing richly, especially with flower and leaf motifs. All parts of the suit, including jackets, vests, and pants were embroidered. Wide scarves were wound around men's waists, and knives, wallets, smoking pipes, tobacco bags, and other objects were put under the belt. The Western Armenian dress for women was similar to that of eastern Armenian but made from fabrics of lighter and brighter colors. Above the dress, the women wore an apron decorated with a velvet ribbon and gold embroidery.

Men wore fur caps called *papakha*, or knit or felt hats. Women's hats were more complex and different. The most common style was a small tower made from several layers of starched clothes; a headscarf on top of the layers covered the mouth and nose. Such "towers" were decorated with ribbons, small coins, and coral and silver pendants. The complicated headdress creations were intended to keep their shape for several days; as a result, women used to sleep on special cylindrical pillows.

Azerbaijani National Costume

Contrary to Georgia and Armenia, in Azerbaijani villages women still wear traditional ethnic clothes. The Azerbaijani national costume is the result of long and complicated processes of the development of the nation's culture, which is reflected in garments, embroidery, weaving, and knitting. Traditionally, the costume style was appropriate to family status and a person's age. The costume of a single woman differed noticeably from that of a married woman. Young women wore particularly colored and attractive garments. It appears that there was no difference in costume styles in the regions of Azerbaijan. Children's costumes were similar to those of adults, though there were some age-related differences.

Until the middle of the twentieth century, the traditional Azerbaijani female costume consisted of undergarments and outer garments. The outer garments were mainly robes with multicolored gussets, usually made of silk, lining, sleeves, and velvet jackets. Quilted waistcoats, *kyurdyu*, were made of velvet and decorated with fur and embroidery. The collar, skirt, and sleeves were trimmed with ferret fur. The outer clothes included a number of skirts, double skirts, and wide trousers, the edges of which were decorated with fabrics of another color. Pieces of jewelry were, for the most part, made by local craftsmen and enhanced the beauty of the female national costume. Multicolored socks and clogs complimented the dress. A small embroidered velvet cap and headscarf completed the look.

Today, most women wear just a tightly tied headscarf, which is becoming an element of city women's dress. City women follow Western European fashion, and if somebody sees a woman in the city in national dress, one can be sure that this woman came to the city from a village. In villages, women usually mix elements of European and traditional dress, adding to European clothes a wide, colorful skirt and long sleeves. Almost every village woman covers her head with a scarf, which indicates her age or religious affiliation with Islam.

Men's national costume used to consist of a shirt, single-and double-breasted coats, and wide trousers. A sheepskin overcoat with fur inside completed the national costume. Today, men all over Azerbaijan wear European-looking suits, although almost all year round they wear large fur hats, mostly made of lambskin, fur coats, and sometimes boots instead of regular shoes. Azerbaijani men prefer two-sided suit jackets, which probably dates back to ethnic coats like the *arkhaluk*, which were usually two-sided in Azerbaijan, unlike in other areas of Caucasus. Today, men's national dress can be seen only at wedding ceremonies and during performances.

Since 1995, a special museum in Baku has been dedicated to the history of Azerbaijani costumes. The museum was created by a local artist Elmira Abbasly, and is housed on the first floor of an old residence of Baku that has been renovated. The museum is one of the most charming presentations of Azerbaijan's past. Primarily, it features handmade dolls that reflect the life and times of personalities from the artist's childhood spent in the old city of

Baku. The costumes are based on the careful documentation of materials and styles of the periods they depict.

NOTES

1. Mary Chatwin, *Socio-Cultural Transformation and Foodways in the Republic of Georgia* (Commack, NY: Nova Science Publishers, 1997), 71.

2. Kay Nelson, *Cuisines of the Caucasus Mountains* (New York: Hippocrene Books, 2007), 13.

3. Graham Smith, Vivien Law, and Andrew Wilson, *Nation-Building in the Post-Soviet Borderlands: The Politics of National Identities* (Cambridge: Cambridge University Press, 1998), 168.

4. Marina Kanevskaya, "The Shortest Path to the Truth: Indirection in Fazil Iskander," *Modern Language Review* 99, no. 1 (2004): 139.

5. Chatwin, *Socio-Cultural Transformation*, 114–115.

6. Armenians were the first in the area to develop commercial food businesses such as shops and restaurants.

7. Lili Asatiani, *Wine Lexicon in Georgian Language* (Tbilisi: Academy of Science, 2003), 12.

8. Aristid Dovatur, *Narody Nashei Strany v Istorii Georodta* [Peoples of Our Country in Herodotus's *Histories*] (Moscow: Nauka, 1982), 154.

9. Brandy Dwyn, created in the 1930s, was the strongest drink of that time, with a 50-percent alcohol concentration, as it was intended to be used by Arctic explorers.

10. John Steinbeck, *A Russian Journal* (New York: Penguin Books, 1999), 174.

11. Dickran Koumjian, "Armenia Textiles: An Overview," http://armenianstudies. csufresno.edu/faculty/kouymjian/articles/armenia_textiles.htm.

7

Cinema and Performing Arts

ENTERTAINMENT PLAYS AN important role in the lives of Caucasian people. Market performers always attracted big crowds, and the first theaters were established in ancient times at the courts of local rulers. After the arrival of classical arts to the region in the beginning of the twentieth century, attendance at theaters and musical concerts became a part of social life. Today, the performing arts in the Caucasus include theater, opera, ballet, operetta, classical music, dance, and circus. Music and stage performances are among the most traditional Caucasian arts, and modern theater can often be understood only in connection with cultural traditions and foreign influences. Cinematography has always been more than just entertainment in the Caucasus, where it is considered a special form of artistic expression. It is difficult to evaluate the contributions of moviemakers from these republics to world cinema, but local filmmakers had influenced the development of this art in the Soviet Union since the beginning of its presence in the region. The evolution of the region's film industry reflects political and economic changes during the past century and magnifies the characteristics of each republic. In the Soviet era, Romantic comedies were made in Georgia, Azerbaijani films focused on industrial themes and criticized deficiencies of the Soviet system, and the State Film Studio in Armenia produced mostly documentaries and short features. No children's movies were produced in the Caucasus. Production value, special effects, and action were not the strong side of Caucasian movies, but they were known for psychological intrigue, emotional dramas of individuals in extreme situations, and reevaluation of traditional values.

During the Soviet era, all art forms were supported by the state and developed within the so-called socialist realism style. Because of Soviet centralization, national theaters were created in the capital cities of Caucasian republics, and a few theaters existed in other towns.[1] Most of them were housed in magnificent stately buildings. Today, the new generation of musicians, actors, and producers are independent from stereotypes of the past, new theaters have been established, and their repertoire reflects classical education and the public's social interests. Most performers are trained at state music academies and art universities established in capital cities.

FOLK PERFORMANCES

Folk art gives people of the Caucasus a chance to show the world that they have their own culture, traditions, and music.[2] The origins of theatrical performances are traced to ancient times, and performances are based on popular satire and sporting games and masquerades. In the seventeenth century, the Dutch sailor Yan Strace reported the arrival of six wandering wrestlers to the town of Shemakha in Azerbaijan, and he described how hundreds of people gathered to see their fights.[3] This art was formalized in the twentieth century with the formation of state folk theatrical groups and orchestras in every republic. A popular Azerbaijani folk performance is *kilim arasy*, which means "in the middle of a carpet." An actor hides under a carpet and plays positive roles with his hands and negative ones with his legs. Many theater pieces are performed in masks. Another popular play, *maral oyun* ("deer game"), involves a person wearing some elements of a deer and imitating the animal's movements.

Circuses are popular all over the Caucasus, but especially in Azerbaijan because its roots extend deeply into folk art, which includes performances of tightrope walkers, magicians, wrestlers, and snake charmers. The first permanent circus was built in Baku in 1904, and by 1945 the National Azerbaijani Circus had been founded. Many famous composers, artists, poets, and ballet dancers worked to produce the circus performances. In 1967, the present-day circus building was built in Baku; it was one of the largest circus buildings in Europe, with 2,400 seats. Stationary circuses were established in Tbilisi and Yerevan around the same time. Since 1991, these buildings have been used as places for plays, performers, and other circus groups.

The music performed by folk orchestras are tunes that were collected and harmonized by classically trained composers, who often were conductors too. The harmonization process is especially important in Armenian music, which is traditionally monophonic and must be richly harmonized for concert performances, unlike in neighboring Georgia, a country with a rich polyphonic

A Georgian man dancing. Photograph by Badri Vadachkoria provided by the Embassy of Georgia to the United States.

tradition. Georgian folk music is predominantly vocal and is founded on traditions of settled agricultural people, with specific songs for particular activities. Many agricultural songs are associated with festivals marking the conclusion of various farming activities. There are songs associated with religious ceremonies, cradle songs, love songs, and a whole series of songs for such occasions as weddings and funerals. Old social traditions are preserved in war, marching, and drinking songs. The texts and musical structure of Georgian songs illuminate the country's history. For example, traditional instrumentation with a collectively sung bass line supporting one or two higher solo lines is characteristic of a social model between the individual and the group, where everyone is able to participate and no one remains unengaged.[4]

There are three main groups of musical instruments in Georgia: strings, wind, and percussion. The strings often include the lute and the harp, probably the most common instrument in Georgia. To this day, historical ballads are sung to its accompaniment. Flutes and instruments resembling the oboe and the clarinet are among the wind instruments. The percussion instruments comprise tambourines and drums. The Rustavi Choir, formed in 1968, is the best known Georgian group, performing traditional repertoires.

Armenian folk music is close to the musical culture of other Near Eastern people. It was revived in the early twentieth century by the composer Komitas Vardapet (1869–1935), who collected, annotated, and published folk songs, mostly from western Armenia, which would have been otherwise lost after the genocide.

Original music performers in Azerbaijan were the *ashugi*, who sung two- and five-line poems in the villages without closing their lips. Often, they performed with closed eyes without taking the audience into consideration. Usually, three musicians who played a three-string violin, an eleven-string guitar, and a drum accompanied them. Popular were song dialogues among the ashugi, named *dyishme*, which often turned into folk music competitions. Choirs are not popular among Azerbaijanis, except singing a few songs together during hard work. Most songs are performed solo and reflect such themes as hard peasant labor, the difficulties of being a young woman in a strange family, and various love dialogues.

Azerbaijani music is closely connected with music written by Russian composers. For example, original Azerbaijani melodies can be heard in major Russian operas. The founder of the Azerbaijani opera, Uzeir Gajibekov (1885–1948), included songs from Russian operas by Ivan Glinka in his works. After classical music was introduced to Azerbaijan in the 1930s, local musicians created a new style that combined modern classical music with native traditions. Kara Karaev (1918–1982) led these efforts and added folkloric instruments to the symphonic orchestra.

Music

Classical music arrived to Transcaucasia at the end of the nineteenth century. Symphonic orchestras and a branch of the Russian Musical Society were established in Baku and Tbilisi. The opera theater in Tbilisi opened in 1852, and operas of Russian and Western European composers were performed. In 1897, Meliton Balanchivadze, father of the famous dancer and ballet producer George Balanchine, composed the first Georgian opera, *Daredzhan Insidious*, a Georgian variation of *Romeo and Juliet* that was staged in 1926. The excerpts from this opera were shown in St. Petersburg, and the first act was demonstrated as a concert performance in 1912. The first Azerbaijani opera, *Leila and Medzhun*, was directed in 1908. Uzeir Gajibekov wrote the libretto based on the sixteenth-century poem by Fizuli. In the first two or three years of Soviet rule, there was an attempt to remove funding for the opera completely and even forbid it on the grounds of it being a symbol of bourgeois culture, but this policy was soon reversed. The national opera theater was established in Azerbaijan in 1924 and in Yerevan in 1932.

The opera was the art that developed the new style of Azerbaijani music. The first operas combined classical music and folklore. The first completely classical national performance was created by Muslim Magomayev (1885–1937) in 1935. The first operettas on contemporary subjects were staged in 1939, and the first national ballet, *The Maiden Tower*, was performed in 1940.

Azerbaijani operas incorporated Islamic themes into their music and stories. The brothers Uzeir (1885–1948) and Jeyhun (1891–1962) Hajibeyli made significant contributions to Azerbaijani-language theater and opera. With their satire of traditional practices and cultural taboos, such as arranged marriages, they remain popular, and their pieces are still performed at the Baku Opera Theater. When first produced, the Hajibeylis' operas shocked the public because, for the first time in a Muslim society, they employed a female actress to play a woman.

The Armenian musical culture of the twentieth century cannot be separated from the names of such composers as Arno Babadjanian (1921–1983) and Aram Khachaturian (1903–1978). Both Babadjanian and Khachaturian connected the ongoing trend of Westernization of music in Armenia with folkloric traditions in their teachings, concerts, and compositions. The most celebrated of Babadjanian's work is the *Heroic Ballade*, for the piano and orchestra. Another popular work, *Armenian Rhapsody*, for two pianos, is a sign of Babadjanian's respect for his national roots. Aram Khachaturian opened Armenian music to the world. In addition, he wrote the Armenian state anthem. His ballets *Spartacus* and *Gayane* have been performed all over the world, and Stanley Kubrick used his music in the film *2001: A Space Odyssey*. The music from the *Spartacus* ballet was used as the theme for a popular BBC drama series *The Onedin Line* during the 1970s. Joel Coen's *The Hudsucker Proxy* also featured Khachaturian's music.

In Georgia, the most prolific composer was Vano Muradeli (1908–1970), who composed patriotic songs about his motherland. His opera *The Great Friendship* (1952) showcased traditional music and dance of Caucasian people but was criticized for ideological deficiencies.

In the present-day Caucasus, show business prevails over classical music, which is rarely heard on the radio. The music department at the Georgian national radio has been disbanded. The Georgian TV and Radio Orchestra, which existed for seventy-three years, and often first played Georgian composers' works, has been terminated. The national orchestra still exists but rarely performs. The only active orchestra is the State Symphonic Orchestra, but this orchestra does not perform works written by Georgian composers. Classical concerts of touring performers occur in small halls. Many young composers have moved out of the country to the West or to Russia, or they earn their living by teaching and composing music for movies. One such individual is Irakli Tsintsadze (b. 1964), a composer of mostly stage, orchestra, and chamber music that has been performed across Georgia and Russia. He is the son of the famous composer Sulkhan Tsintsadze (1925–1991), the longtime director of both the Tbilisi State Academy of Music and the Georgian Composers' Union. He currently teaches polyphony at Tbilisi Fine Arts Academy. One of his most recent works is music for the ballet *The King's Bride*, based on the work of E. T. A. Hoffman.

Recently, the situation has begun to improve. The Association of Georgian Composers has become more actively involved in the nation's cultural life. Since 2005, the association has published the bimonthly magazine *Musical Georgia*. The magazine reports on composers' new works, scholarly conferences, anniversaries, and music teaching methods. A special feature of the magazine is the publication of music scores, which had never been published before or have been completely forgotten and have become a bibliographic rarity. In Azerbaijan, Renara Akhundova (b. 1968?), a composer and piano player, is very popular. She writes and performs music of different styles from new age and pop classics to meditation music. As she says, she includes the philosophy of light and love in her unusual works, which have received international recognition. She also composes musical accompaniment for theater pieces and book recordings.

THEATER

The theatrical arts have been known in the Transcaucasus for many centuries. There are reports that, in the first century B.C., the Armenian king Artavazd II personally took part in performances. In Georgia, theater pieces were

Georgian dance performance. Photograph by Badri Vadachkoria provided by the Embassy of Georgia to the United States.

performed in 1649 during the festival dedicated to the visiting Russian delegation, but the real development of performing arts occurred in the eighteenth century. At that time, performances were an essential component of all feasts and festivals at the royal court. In Azerbaijan, theater was established in the middle of the nineteenth century as a consequence of literary developments. The founder of contemporary Azerbaijani literature, Mirza Fatali Akhundov (1812–1878), was the most prolific dramatist of that time. The national elite believed, in the nineteenth century, that theater was the best way to deliver ideas of enlightenment to the mostly illiterate masses. Azerbaijan became a theater pioneer in the entire Turkic world. Akhundov wrote comedies and satirized human sins. Tragedies were written by Nadzhaf Vezirov (1854–1926) and Abdurrahim Akhverdov (1870–1933). Professional theaters were established during the second decade of the twentieth century. Before, the plays had been performed by theater sections of different enlightenment groups and charitable societies.

When the Azerbaijani theater was established, it developed in a romantic way that had roots in the romanticism of folklore. Romantic traditions were implemented and developed by actors at the end of the twentieth century. Shakespearean plays and those of the local writer Jafar Jabarly, in which actors recognize general life contradictions through personal tragic events, are among the most popular. Armenian theater is based on the tradition of psychological realism. Armenian actors attempt to show the emotional environment of their personages. Even if a person in a play appears to be naive and funny, the actor shows how smart, honest, and polite the person may be. Such is the work of actor Giko Elbakian, who in the Armenian National Drama Theater plays the role of Pepo, a little guy who believes in honesty, the return of debt, and the fulfillment of obligations in a play written by Gabriel Sundukian (1825–1912). Many modern Armenian plays are based on folklore and have ethnographic precision. One of them is *60 Years and 3 Hours* by Alexander Araksmanian. Actor Mher Mkrtchian (b. 1930) plays a man who meets a person who slandered his father and wants to understand why people lose their clear consciousness. Despite some examples of interesting theatrical work, in general, Armenian theaters are in poor shape today. They are deprived of state funding, their buildings are falling apart, and the directors are looking with hope toward rich compatriots and expatriates.

The development of Georgian theater is connected to Kote Mardzhanishvili (1872–1933), a theater director, producer, and founder of the first national theater, which still exists and bears his name. Mardzhanishvili, who believed in the civil duty of the theater rather than its entertainment, pushed actors out of the genre framework. He called the theater a cathedral that can be transformed into a podium to announce the most progressive ideas.

His student Sandro Akhmeteli (1886–1937) condemned Mardzhanishvili's methods, saying that Georgian theater had to be softer, more temperamental, more fiery, emotional, stentorian, bold, and heroic. In 1924, Akhmeteli created a theater group that aimed to connect reality with performing arts, but he denounced realism in Georgian artistic traditions. Akhmeteli attempted to prove that the Stanislavski system was just a Russian event and not applicable to Georgian theater. He searched for exotic and effective forms that could be used in romantic theater. In his theater, several vertical scenes were built, and plays were performed around different groups of artists located at varied heights.

Modern theatrical directors try to find an answer to the same question about the relationship between art and reality by staging old classical plots, such as *Oedipus the King* by Sophocles. The ancient tragedy in which a man challenges the gods and meets his death for the sake of truth is performed presently at the Rustaveli Theater in Tbilisi. Shakespeare is one of the most popular playwrights in Georgia. Almost every theater company has such plays as *The Merchant of Venice*, *Richard III*, and *Othello* in their repertoires. Giga Lordkipanidze (b. 1927) represents the generation of Georgian actors that favors classical plays for their spirituality and warm humor, and uses them as an instrument to implement moral and ethical principles.

Several new theaters have opened in the past few decades in Georgia. In 1987, the famous actor Kote Makharadze (1926–2002), who re-created precisely documented real life in theatrical scenes, founded a theater for his wife, Sofiko Chiaureli (1937–2008), a national star and symbol of Georgian performing arts. The theater was on the first floor of the apartment complex where the couple lived, and Chiaureli played in solo dramas adapted for her.

The Youth Theater in Rustavi is also popular. The theater's performances link times described in ancient plays to modern days. Actors transform their personages into the audience's contemporaries to make statements as present-day people. For example, the drama *Stepmother Samanishvili* was performed not in the theater but in the memorial house where the playwright David Kldiashvili (1862–1931) lived. Actual objects from the museum, including the museum's furniture, were part of the decoration and actors behaved like visitors to the museum.

The Tbilisi Municipal Theater Studio founded by Rezo Gabriadze, a famous dramatist, movie director, and screenwriter, holds a special place among Georgian theaters. The studio is the only Georgian puppet-show theater. Gabriadze is a puppet maker, set designer, writer, and director. His marionettes, both human and animal, are exquisite and delicate; their heads are prominent and the limbs flexible. "They can look like rag dolls or skeletons, but all manage to carry the rich implications of real character. For example, a horse ridden by a puppet in military garb in *Autumn of My Springtime* has a body that looks to be fashioned from a gymnast's pommel horse, or maybe a car seat, and four legs that consist of short lengths of rope."[5] Controlled by one of the show's five black-clad puppeteers and accompanied by a recorded martial melody, the horse gallops with its rope legs sweeping the ground in rhythmic unison. In the imagery and movement, this horse, about the size of a cocker spaniel, looks remarkably real.

CINEMA

Filmmaking began in the Transcaucasus at the beginning of the twentieth century. A national film studio existed in each Caucasian capital city; their goals were to prove that, during Soviet rule, each nation was able to develop its own culture. In Georgia, filmmaking excelled much beyond Soviet cinema and developed an outstanding reputation. Many Georgian filmmakers achieved international recognition and received prestigious awards at international film festivals. In general, Georgian movies move slowly. They allow the viewer to see the personages in detail and understand their emotions; many are intentionally long, and panoramas are shot from the same spot with a still camera. A specific lyrical mood is created by not showing actors in the front but making them a part of the entire picture.

The first Georgian movie was released on May 15, 1908. In Yerevan, the first film was made in 1923, and the first Azerbaijani motion picture was produced in 1915: *Oil and Its Millions*, based on the short story written by the popular journalist Ibragim Musabekov. The film dramatized the story of a poor Muslim boy who by a combination of wit and good fortune exchanged his rags for the riches of an oil millionaire but lost his soul in the process. This was a timely production for oil-rich Baku, and one typical of other Russian productions of the day that moralized on the hopes and despairs of modern life.

After Soviet Russia annexed the Transcaucasus, the first productions of local film studios were factual documentaries showing chronicles of the Red Army's marches. During the short period of commercialization in the 1920s, national affiliates of the Soviet movie monopoly in Tbilisi, Baku, and Yerevan made their own popular films, mixing ideology with casual entertainment. Georgian moviemakers led the way. The public especially loved Ivan Perestiani's *Arsen Dzhordzhiashvili* (1921) for its passionate and brave revolutionary hero and his *Little Red Devils* (1923) for its action scenes of the civil war that featured rumors about the famous anarchist leader. A torrent of pseudo-nationalist films soon followed, from adaptations of Mikhail Lermontov's *Hero of Our Time* to lowbrow pieces like *Lost Treasure*, *Minaret of Death*, and *The Leper*

Woman. These films were usually shot on location with European directors and native actors. Sometimes these movies were loosely based on folk legends or historical events, and they were filled with realistic detail.

During the crackdown on foreign commercialism and the demands of ideological correctness in the 1930s, national cinema went into a state of disrepair and dysfunction. In all three republics, equipment was old; movie houses were plagued by electrical outages and materials shortages; projectionists were untrained and poorly paid, sometimes becoming itinerant salesmen to make a decent living. The movies were usually Russian productions in the Russian language. Because of the complexities and delays in the dubbing process, only a handful of native-language productions ever circulated among viewers.

During World War II, Moscow launched a campaign to promote patriotism, and movies made in the republics depicted Russians and non-Russians fighting fascism together. The serial *One Family*, filmed in Baku during 1943 and dedicated to one family's passage through the war, served as a broader metaphor for the big family of people in the Soviet Union. Other films resurrected patriotic military heroes from the Transcaucasus to stir national pride. From Georgia came *Georgii Saakadze* (1943); from Armenia, *David Bek* (1943); and from Azerbaijan, *Fatali Khan* (1947). These films covered the fabled exploits of the three early-modern warriors in defending their homelands against Persian hegemony, usually with the help of Russia's tsars and generals.[6]

After World War II, movie production was stopped in Baku for more than ten years, while Georgia achieved major artistic success in the field of cinema. After Stalin's death in 1953, Soviet art began to be revitalized, and many young artists entered cinematographic circles. Instead of state-requested impersonal, didactic, and glossy propaganda pieces, the new generation of young directors, actors, and screenwriters made less pretentious, sharper, and rather outspoken films about real people in modern settings. Georgian movies were especially truthful and free from official ideology. During the period from 1961 to 1991, approximately 1,200 movies were made in Georgia; more than 100 of them won awards at international festivals.

The Georgian movies were the first movies in the Soviet Union to introduce nudity,[7] first in the modern drama *Hello, It's Me* (1965) and then in Sergei Paradzhanov's (1924–1988) sensational historical picture *Shadows of Our Forgotten Ancestors.* Because he pioneered many artistic styles in Soviet cinematography, Paradzhanov was not allowed to work in his native Armenia or in Tbilisi, where he was born. He was assigned to a movie studio in Ukraine, where he made the fifteen-minute short movie *Kiev Frescoes* (1965), a fragmented mosaic of life in the Soviet city of Kiev during the tenth anniversary of its liberation from Nazi Germany. His movies received popular acclaim for their pictorial compositions, imaginative colors, ethnic visual and musical background details, and romanticized stories spiced up with nude scenes.[8] Paradzhanov's *Color of the Pomegranate*, a biography of the eighteenth-century Armenian poet Sayat Nova, reveals the poet's life more through his poetry than through conventional narration of the important events in his life. The movie shows the poet growing up, falling in love, entering a monastery, and dying; but these incidents are depicted with images from Paradzhanov's imagination. Sofiko Chiaureli played six roles, both male and female, in this nonnarrative film in which images remain imposed in the unconscious, making the film seem like a dreamlike experience.

When the policy of glasnost began in the Soviet Union in 1985, the Georgian movie *Repentance* by Tengiz Abuladze (1924–1994) became its symbol. The film's idea is that, to continue into the future with a clear conscience, each survivor of the old times who compromised with the regime must ask for and receive forgiveness. After receiving the first prize at the Cannes International Film Festival in 1956 for *Magdana's Little Donkey*, Abuladze directed *The Prayer* (1967) and *Tree of Desire* (1975), which carry the theme of maintaining responsibility for the past. The same theme is continued in *Repentance*, which opens with two typically Georgian scenes. The first presents a handsome, sad-eyed woman decorating cakes with tiny cathedrals and selling them. The second shows the local boss's funeral, with fresh flowers, an open casket, and obligatory visits to the deceased's family. Every detail, from the faces at the funeral to the envelope of money passed to the son of the deceased, now head of the family, to the song "Samshoblo," the anthem of free Georgia in the early 1920s, is clearly and typically Georgian. In the traditional Georgian culture, the past and its remains, including the dead, are holy. In *Repentance*, a Georgian woman, denies the main character proper treatment of a dead hero and violates his grave, proving that her actions have not violated the obligation of paying respect to the dead because the character deserves such treatment for all his previous actions.[9]

In the 1990s, independence brought with it the abolition of censorship and a new generation of filmmakers who focused on social problems and neglected the lyrical and poetical genres. More than twenty newly established private film studios marked the film boom in Armenia, which, with financial support from the new class of businesspeople, lasted until the late 1990s. The Georgian movie industry overcame the crisis of independence and, since 1993, new companies and studios have opened. Private sponsors and international organizations have financed the production of documentaries, as well as educational and short movies. For example, the U.S.-based Soros Foundation paid for production of documentaries about the role of women in the present-day Caucasus. Later, the movies were broadcast on PBS in the United States. After the independent television channels were established in the

Caucasian countries, they became interested in the production of local movies too. Since 1993, Tbilisi hosts the annual Golden Eagle Film Festival of the Black Sea Basin countries.

Modern Georgian movies are less romantic and pay more attention to those at the bottom of society. Often, they show the chaos and desperation of the present time. One of them is the documentary movie *Dignity Tested by War*, by Mamuka Kuparadze. The movie is based on a series of interviews and the memories of Georgians and Abkhazians about one another and their activities before, during, and after the war. Another example of a more realistic tone of new Georgian movies is *The Lake* (1998), by Kakha Kikabidze (b. 1961). The inspiration for the film is Thomas Mann's short story "Abdication." The main character Zura is very young when he witnesses the brutal murder of his father. Shortly after the murder, he and his mother move to another town, but the death of his father still haunts Zura. In his new school, he bullies all his classmates and orders them to perform different tasks as punishments. As a result, he is an extremely lonely boy. The only way to not be so alone is to become a slave, and Zura appoints the weakest and fattest boy to become the new leader.

The movie *Tbilisi-Tbilisi* (2005), by Levan Zakareyshvili, is evidence of the politicization of current Georgian cinema. Earlier, it was impossible to find a Georgian thief or prostitute in a Georgian movie; all Georgians were portrayed as noble and good. In this movie, however, viewers see a university professor who sells margarine to survive, street gangsters who steal from an old homeless woman, and a Georgian policeman who takes bribes. This makes for a scary but accurate illustration of modern life in the Georgian capital.

The realist documentary style about political turmoil in Azerbaijan is employed by director Rafigh Pooya in his film Broken Bridges (1999). Jeff, a filmmaker of American and Azerbaijani background, played by Peter Reckell, has devoted several years to his favorite project, a movie about the tragic death of his mother, who was relocated after her homeland was split between Iran and the Soviet Union. Jeff's obsession with his film has strained his marriage almost to the breaking point; when he travels to Azerbaijan for on-location filming, he meets Jayran, whom he first casts as his mother and then finds himself falling for, a turn of events that leads to dire consequences for both his marriage and his personal safety.

In Armenia, son of Armenian emigrants to France Rober Guédiguian follows the tradition of lyricism. In his *Armenia* (2007, distributed outside of Armenia as *Voyage en Armenie*), a Parisian woman comes to Yerevan to visit her father's birthplace. Additionally, she falls in love and decides to stay in the country, and the story is told from her point of view.

Today, the situation in the region's movie industry is not easy. Given the energy crisis of 1994–1995 and the very small government budget, all twenty Armenian private film studios were forced to close, and many filmmakers moved out of the region in search of work. Western and Russian films are predominant in local movie theaters because only a handful of movies are produced every year in each country's national studio, which are not equipped in accordance with international industry standards.

Great efforts and investments are required to support national cinemas. The government of each republic has developed national programs; however, they have not been fully implemented yet. State involvement with financing in Armenia and Georgia is much less than in Azerbaijan, but all three governments provide moral support to moviemakers. In response to requests from the nation's cinematographers, in 2005, the president of Georgia declared May 15 the Day of Georgian Film, which is celebrated annually and pays tribute to everyone who has worked in the nation's movie industry. Recently, Georgia decided to transform its movie industry in such a way that Western film companies would use the existing facilities to produce foreign movies because of the great scenery, cheap labor, and other low costs.

The former state and the major film studio in Armenia, Armenfilm, was privatized in 2005 for less than $800,000. An American businessman of Armenian decent purchased the enterprise and accepted the obligation to invest $70 million over the following ten years in the Armenian movie industry and to be involved in film productions for the following fifty years. No less than four full-feature movies, three animations, and five short movies will be made annually, according to the agreement. During the first two years, the studio was completely renovated, new equipment was purchased, and the digitization of old movies in the studio's archival collection began.

NOTES

1. Usually these were national theaters for opera, ballet, and operetta, and there were two drama theaters, one for the Russian language and another in which works were performed in the local language.

2. Andy Nersessian, "A Look at the Emergence of the Concept of National Culture in Armenia," *International Review of the Aesthetics and Sociology of Music* 31, no. 1 (January 2000): 89.

3. Cited by Audrey Altstadt, *The Azerbaijani Turks: Power and Identity under Russian Rule* (Palo Alto, CA: Hoover Institution Press, Stanford University, 1992), 39.

4. http://www.georgianholidays.com/georgia-folklore.php.

5. Bruce Weber, "String, Cloth, Twigs and Character," *New York Times*, June 29, 2002.

6. Michael Smith, "Cinema for the 'Soviet East': National Fact and Revolutionary Fiction in Early Azerbaijani Film," *Slavic Review* 56, no. 4 (Winter 1997): 648–649.

7. Steven Hill, "The Soviet Film Today," *Film Quarterly* 20, no. 4 (Summer 1967): 51.

8. James Steffen, Review of *Seven Visions*, by Sergey Paradjanov, *Film Quarterly* 54, no. 1 (Autumn 2000): 60.

9. Julie Christensen, "Tengiz Abuladze's Repentance and the Georgian Nationalist Cause," *Slavic Review* 50, no. 1 (Spring 1991): 170.

8

Visual Arts and Crafts

ARTS AND CRAFTS make up a major part of the rich and distinctive culture of the people of the Caucasus. Art traditions are old and range from rock paintings found in caves where prehistoric people lived to medieval folk art, to modern paintings and installations by contemporary artists. The scope of artists also varies from village craftspeople who create their works with great taste and skills to internationally recognized masters. Almost everything produced before the nineteenth century was a product of native cultural tradition rooted in antiquity. The tradition of decorative arts was represented by a wide range of handicrafts, such as chiseling; jewelry making; metal engraving; stone, wood, and bone carving; rug making; lace making; pattern weaving; knitting; and embroidery. After the region was incorporated into the Russian Empire, it became open to foreign cultural influence. In the twentieth century, the creativity of local artists mixed European art styles with local traditions, which widely varied within the region. The traditional isolation of individual artistic communities preserved the multiplicity of ornaments, patterns, methods, and schools. There is no common art in the region. Georgians are best known for their metalwork and pottery; Armenians are fond of stone carving, book illustrations, and leather processing; Azerbaijanis achieve more success in wood carving and rug making; and the production of jewelry is a local specialty marked by creativity and complexity everywhere in the South Caucasus.

Today, professional artists follow internationally recognized standards and principles. They apply ornaments used in ancient times and modern innovative forms. Many works are of museum quality and are displayed in the numerous local art galleries. Museums are an inalienable part of the Caucasus culture, especially museums of applied art. Almost every small town has a museum that proudly displays works of local masters. Art galleries can be found in any relatively large town, and the capital cities have state museums dedicated to specific fields of art, such as national galleries, national historical museums that display excavated ancient artifacts, and state museums of decorative arts that show the masterpieces of local craftspeople. Especially unique are rug museums in Azerbaijan, and the Golden Vault of the Georgian State Museum in Tbilisi, which contains thousands of incredible pieces, including ornamental jewelry and miniature animals made of gold. They were made with impressive quality and attention to detail. Even the arrowheads made from translucent smoky obsidian and kept in piles in showcases look like jewelry. In 2007, a large part of the Georgian State Museum's collection, which includes ancient golden treasures from Colchis, was transferred to the New York University museum for permanent exhibition.

TRADITIONAL CRAFTS

Applied and Decorative Arts

An Armenian craftsman is first a builder and a stone carver. Stone decorations are seen almost everywhere, in bridges built over deep canyons, in ancient monasteries and newly built chapels, in artistically decorated war memorials, in private gravestones in village cemeteries, in the ledges of residential buildings, and around water springs. Craftsmen consider the decoration of wells and water springs the most honorable assignment because the results of the work will serve many people and even many generations. Many artists view stone carving around water springs as an opportunity to express their love to the native place and to memorialize important events and people.

The most unique display of Armenian stone carving is *khachkar*, a traditional monument that looks like a flat vertical stone with an image of a cross in the middle. Literally, the word *khachkar* means "stone cross." During the past 1,500 years, *khachkars* were erected as gravestones, but most of the time they were used to commemorate a specific event or a person. *Khachkars* can be of different sizes, from small, two-foot plaques to upward of seven- or eight-foot-tall walls. Vegetative motifs were used in decorating *khachkars* to demonstrate that the monuments are stylized depictions of the tree of life. The edges of the stones were covered with intertwined geometric and vegetative ornaments. Some *khachkars* even contain dates, texts, and pictorial scenes. Modern sculptors and architects add new forms and motifs to *khachkars*.

Georgians are skilled smiths. Because of plentiful natural reserves of gold, silver, and bronze, Georgian craftsmen were able to forge, solder, stamp, and

emboss metal thousands of years ago. Metalwork was applied even to literature. In the medieval times, book covers were beautifully decorated in silver
and gold. Georgian medieval enamels are a specific form of art with an unresolved mystery: it is not clear how the compositions were created without
melting the thin golden wires, which served as small barriers between enamels of different colors. Except for Georgia, this art existed in very few other
places, mostly in China and Byzantium. Current Georgian artists apply old
traditions of craftsmanship in their work and restore almost forgotten styles
and techniques. The most popular methods of work among artists are metal
engravings and embossing, which allow ornately chisel weaponry and delicate
filigree jewelry. Traditional materials used by jewelers to create rings, bracelets,
and earrings are brass, silver, and black-colored mineral jet.

Another traditional Georgian craft is pottery. Georgian ceramics have many
variations. Usually, ceramic objects are red with white, dark red, or green
paintings or blue glaze. Professional masters make black lacquered ceramics,
having revitalized a 1,000-year-old technique. Very popular among tourists,

A Georgian pottery maker. Photo by Badri
Vadachkoria. Courtesy of the Georgian Embassy to the United States.

who browse galleries in Tbilisi, are wooden panels and cups that reproduce the ornaments on churches. It is impossible to count all the genres of Georgian art because almost every region has its own artistic specialty. The region of Tusheti, for example, in the northeastern part of the country is known for decorative strips of felt with brightly colored paintings. Dark blue scarves, shawls, and tablecloths with large white decorations are the most popular product of Tusheti.

Copper chiseling and jewelry making are two especially popular crafts in Azerbaijan. In ancient and medieval Azerbaijani cities, copperware was produced with great mastery from local ores. The most famous Caucasian center for the production of chased copperware was Lahich, with 180 copper shops at the beginning of the twentieth century. The items produced there were vessels, cooking pots, tableware, and bathing objects. Copper items were used for household purposes and usually plated with tin and decorated with engraved inscriptions in Arabic. Contemporary items are decorated with ornaments in the form of straight and broken lines with a multitude of dots, triangles, and rhombuses. Apart from geometric figures, the ornaments incorporate flowers, birds, animals, the sun, and people. Many items bear the master's mark, the date of completion, and sometimes the owner's name.

Azerbaijani jewelry makers employ such sophisticated techniques as stamping, chasing, granulation, wire drawing, and enamel work. The major centers of jewelry making have been Baku, Ganja, Shemaha, Shusha, Sheki, and Nakhichevan. In the nineteenth century, painted enamel held a prominent place among Azerbaijani jewelry. Gold jewelry was usually coated with red, blue, and green enamel, with a wide range of hues. The background was chiefly white enamel and the ornaments exclusively floral. This technique still remains popular. Silver jewelry is identical to that of gold in terms of form and technique. The silver items, depending on their purpose, are gilded or engraved.

Most of the jewelry produced is ornamentation for garments, bracelets, head and neck pieces, and sections of men's belts. Oval, hollow gold beads in combination with different stamped and engraved pendants are still popular in present-day Azerbaijan. Earlier, stamped plates with floral ornaments were sewn onto women's clothes, especially bridal clothes. The form of these plates varied from round, square, and rectangular to those stamped in the shape of petals, fish, or flowers. Such plates were also used to decorate different objects of everyday use, like watch covers, combs, tobacco bags, and book covers. Details were added in the form of medallions, flowers, fish, stars, leaves, and crescents. These elements of decoration, which had once served as charms, gradually lost their initial meaning and have reached our times as decorative elements of ornamental jewelry, often supplemented by diamonds, gems, and semiprecious stones set in a raised cast. The most popular gems are rubies, emeralds, and turquoise; colored minerals are also used.

Women's Crafts

There are a number of crafts specific to women, including silk and bead embroidery, lace making, and rug making. Even when manufactured production began in the nineteenth century, needlework remained competitive and attractive. This happened, for example, with the hand production of silk fabrics and ceramics in Azerbaijani settlements. The production of printed silk headscarves remains one of the most popular handicrafts. The print appears white on a colored background, then a wooden template with a picture on it is put in hot wax. After repeating this process several times, the scarf becomes multicolored. Gold embroidery on velvet, knitting silk, or wool socks are other popular crafts made by women. Embroidery is a part of national culture, especially in Azerbaijan. The simplest ornamental elements—straight and broken lines, zigzags, dots, circles, and triangles—found on excavated pottery can be traced to the early Bronze Age. Today, embroidery takes the form of flowers, animals, and geometric figures. Among favorite floral motifs are roses, daffodils, carnations, poppies, lilies, the blossoms of fruit trees, and leaves of various shapes. Geometrical ornaments consist of straight and broken lines, zigzags, triangles, rectangles, hexagonal and octagonal figures, stars, and depictions of the sun. The frequently occurring presentation of pairs of birds is the oldest and most favored image in applied decorative art. Birds are usually shown either loving each other or angry with each other. These two motifs symbolize love and parting. Among animals, turtles, dragons, snakes, and horses are the most common. Embroidery is used for covers of many household items, such as rose-water bottles, comb cases, cosmetic vials, and jugs. One of the most developed forms of embroidery is the stitching to embellish women's garments, large pillowcases, and bath rugs. Quilting is the method of decoration for prayer rugs and woolen garments. Pearling and beading are also old manners of decorating garments and household articles.

The most important women's craft is rug making. The largest centers of this industry are Mountainous Karabakh and the Ganja region in Azerbaijan. Since the fifteenth century, Armenians and Azerbaijanis have been expert rug makers. The rug-making process begins with the raising of tens of thousands of sheep, followed by shearing, combing, spinning, dyeing, and weaving of the wool. Typically, it takes four weavers three-and-a-half months to produce an eight-foot by ten-foot rug. Afterward, rugs are shipped to processing factories abroad, where they are washed, a process that reduces the colors but adds richness. The quality of the rugs is defined by the number of knots per square inch. Armenian rugs usually contain between 60 and 150 knots per square inch. The denser the weave is, the clearer and sharper the pattern is, and the higher the price.[1] The name of the master, dedication, and the date can be found on rugs as well.

Rugs are adorned with a variety of traditional ornaments. Usually, Armenian masters use images of plants, mountains, rivers, and animals. The most traditional ornament is pictures of snakes. In antiquity, snakes were worshipped as creatures connected with sources of water. Usually all surfaces of a rug are covered with highly stylized images of large and small snakes: figures with two small lines that symbolize the snake's eyes. Geometric ornaments, pictures of almonds, and other vegetative patterns decorate Azerbaijani rugs. Colors, pictures, and the length of the thread depend on the area where the rug was produced. Azerbaijani rugs are used not only as house decorations but also as covers for camels and horses, large bags, and artistic compositions of different shapes and sizes.

MONUMENTAL ARTS

The art of stone carving has been known in the Caucasus for centuries. Stone ornaments, often in the form of reliefs or medallions, many of which have been preserved since medieval times, always richly decorate building facades. Frescoes and mosaics cover the interior. In temples, icons painted and framed in different techniques cover the walls. The decoration of the churches varies significantly depending on local traditions, the church's patron saint, and the dedicatee of the church. The church sculptures reflect biblical themes, such as Adam and Eve, Abraham's sacrifice, and Samson and Goliath. Images of saints are sculpted also. Sometimes, the sculptures are placed high on the walls surrounding the church, which makes for a pleasant contrast with the bare surface below. In some cases, the original carvings are painted or gilded, though today this old tradition has become a rarity.

The interiors of churches, especially in Armenia, are decorated with images of various animals, real or fictional. The animals are depicted as independent figures and parts of larger scenes, such as saints on horseback, saints lancing dragons (or serpents in Armenia), or St. Serge, also on horseback in the same pose as St. George in the European churches, putting a panther to death. The busts of the saints and prophets are placed inside the churches, and their names are usually engraved nearby. The sculptures in Armenian churches are realistic, and their elegance shows strong Persian influence.[2]

Contemporary monumental art is very diverse. Mural paintings are not limited to the ornamentation of public buildings. It is now common to paint living rooms in private houses and apartments with murals. Many folk and amateur artists take such commissions. In the twentieth century, the streets of large and small cities were decorated with monuments and memorials dedicated to leading public personalities and historical events. Often, the monuments served as pieces of propaganda programs run by authorities. During the years of independence, some of the monuments were destroyed, and memorials were created to those whom the Communists had not recognized. Many public squares, especially in the capital cities, have been decorated with modern sculptures made by contemporary national artists.

PAINTINGS OF THE CAUCASUS

Historical Roots

Modern visual art of the Caucasus is based on centuries-old artistic traditions. The world's largest collection of more than 4,000 rock paintings on cave walls in the Gobustan area of Azerbaijan depicts scenes of hunting, harvesting, and ritual dancing. These rock paintings, dating approximately to the eighth and seventh millennia B.C., are the first examples of local pictorial arts. Between the ninth and seventeenth centuries, the roots of Armenian paintings formed, with the illumination of religious manuscripts, the most treasured rarities in Armenian museums. These illustrations, which were both realistic and romantic, and painted with bright colors, are the first examples of how Armenian masters combined Western ideals with Eastern colors and themes. The development of Armenian painting occurred in the nineteenth century. The portrait painter Hacop Hovnatanian (1806–1881) and the seascape artist Hovhannes Aivazovsky (1817–1900) were recognized internationally. Among twentieth-century figures, the most notable are Alexander Bazhbeuk-Melikian (1891–1966) and Archile Gorky (Vosdanik Adoian) (1904–1948), who influenced a generation of young American artists in New York.

Georgian painting takes its roots in icon making, which achieved its peak between the thirteenth and fifteenth centuries. Unlike in other Orthodox countries, Georgian icons of the time were painted as triptychs. The compositional structure of the triptychs varied from simple, with the central panel devoted to only one scene or holy image, and featuring traditional figures—apostles, archangels, warrior-saints, and gathering on the wings—to complex compositions of narrative scenes of equal importance on each panel.[3] Another form of Georgian art that was highly developed during the golden age of the twelfth and thirteenth centuries is murals. These monumental paintings featured both religious and secular themes. Many of them were destroyed by the Russians in the nineteenth century. Because in Azerbaijan invaders also destroyed many monumental objects, Azerbaijani masters focused at the end of the medieval period on illuminating manuscripts. In the seventeenth century, the art of book miniatures achieved its zenith. Especially well known

Georgian Table, one of the Pirosmani paintings. Photograph by Badri Vadachkoria provided by the Embassy of Georgia to the United States.

were masters from the Azerbaijani city of Tebriz who incorporated elaborate calligraphy and influenced this art all over the Middle East. A large collection of books decorated in the eighteenth and nineteenth centuries is exhibited in the Azerbaijani National Art Museum. Under European and Russian influence, traditional Azerbaijani romanticism was substituted with realistic trends. Mirza Kadym Irevani (1825–1875) added realistic images to the book illustrations. Later realism became the main style of other leading Azerbaijani artists of the early twentieth century.

Azim Azimzade (1880–1943) was a famous Azerbaijani satirical book illustrator. In his paintings, he often focused on society's injustices, women's rights, and educational opportunities. He made fun of religious traditions and superstitions. The most fruitful period of Azimzade's creative activity took place during the 1930s, when he dedicated works to old Azerbaijani traditions and customs. His well-known works include *Ram Fight, Tightrope Walker* (both were traditions in Novruz), and *Dog Fight*. In addition, he worked on the series *Old Baku*. He often developed contrasting scenes of wealth and poverty and societal attitudes toward men and women, such as in *Wealthy Wedding* and *Poor Wedding*. Featuring a wedding celebration in a rich home, he depicts a large bright room crowded with women dancing in elaborate dresses. One woman plays an accordion while everyone around her claps to the rhythm. The carpeted floor was laid with trays of candles and sugar cones, a traditional symbol of abundance. But at the poor people's celebration, the room was small and dark, and peasants were wearing their everyday clothes. Just a few men were present at the lively festivities.

To preserve the national cultural heritage through children's art education, special centers of aesthetic education were established in all large cities throughout the Caucasus during the 1950s and 1960s, and they still exist today. The centers were run as magnet schools for talented youths or as institutions for after-school activities. Artistically gifted children were supported there and taught to paint, make ornamental applications, and create whimsical dolls. The best works were demonstrated in galleries or permanent exhibition halls.

A unique institution was created in Armenia under the guidance of the nation's Children's Museum of Art. In cities, towns, and even villages of all administrative districts of the country, aesthetic education centers have been established. Their goal is to preserve the Armenian artistic agenda and encourage children's creativity. Believing that children provide the last vestige of hope for the survival of Armenian culture, the centers teach children traditional Armenian arts and crafts. Children learn to emulate the Armenian and Western masters, and they are encouraged to think independently, to create images based on experiences in their personal lives, and to develop their own interpretations of Armenian traditions and legends. The centers' curriculum includes studies of different media: drawing, sculpture, printmaking, ceramics, photography, and graphic design. Also, children learn the traditional crafts of Armenia: rug weaving, embroidery, and wood and stone carving. The centers use the human and material resources of the regional sites. For example, the center at Sevan, a region with a rich tradition of glasswork, began to teach the art of making stained glass. Art education at the centers is available to all Armenian youths at no expense to their families. They attend the classes at the centers in the afternoon after the end of their regular school activities.

Despite their separate functions, the Children's Museum of Art and the centers are organized to complement each other. The museum was established as an inspirational center for art education in Armenia. With a collection of 150,000 works by children from 110 nations, it testifies to Armenia's commitment to its children. Exhibitions at the museum reflect its international collection. The gallery contains permanent displays of children's art from all 110 nations. The exhibit of Armenian children's art changes periodically. Reflecting its international collection, the museum provides a forum for children to better understand national art in relation to cultures outside of Armenia.[4]

Fine Arts of the Twentieth Century

For the greater part of the twentieth century, the republics of the South Caucasus were part of the Soviet Union, and local artists were obligated to follow Communist ideological principles. They had to remain realistic in their works, because the only style allowed was realism. As a result, most artists created paintings on historical and modern subjects and developed the art of landscape painting. The leader of Armenian landscape painting was Martiros Sarian (1880–1972). Rich colors and simple natural forms were the main features of Sarian's paintings. As the most recognized Armenian artist, he was entrusted with designing the coat of arms for the Armenian Soviet Republic and the curtain for the first Armenian state theater.

Minas Avetisian (1928–1975) followed the Armenian national painting tradition by showing great freedom and originality in his usage of ancient techniques known to medieval miniaturists. His works are distinguished by bright colors, the coordination of pictorial tensions throughout the entire surface of the canvas, a rhythmic arrangement of lines, the static quality of representation, and the absence of perspective. Most of Avetisian's canvases are devoted to his people's past. One such painting, *The Road: A Recollection of My Parents* (1967), shows lonely people in a train car forced to go away from their native places.

Historical and modern themes served as a basis for Azerbaijani artists as well. Gazanfar Khalykov (1898–1981) followed the traditions of book miniatures, and Saltar Bahlulzade (1909–1974) created contemporary Azerbaijani landscape painting. Bahlulzade started to paint after he was convinced to do so by Marc Chagall, who had seen his early works. Although he experimented in various genres of art, his unique talent was landscape painting. He initially painted nature realistically as he had been taught, but soon developed his own style to express the emotional feelings it evoked in him. This new style was more surreal and cosmic. In fact, some of his paintings are reminiscent of photos of the earth from space. Using a combination of pastel colors and bold strokes, he made nature seem more colorful and lively, and sometimes even more surreal, than it was in reality.

Tahir Salahov (b. 1928) became a leading representative of the so-called severe style, a trend in Soviet art of the 1960s that aimed to set off a realist view against polished reality. Depiction of real life without any idealization was typical for Salahov's portraits of the Baku oil workers (*Repair Men*, 1961) and contemporary. Red, black, and gray were favorite colors of the Salahov's palette.[5] His later works are more peaceful and lyrically contemplative. Eastern influences are more apparent in *Portrait of Grandson Dan* (1983), in which the composition and colors follow rhythms of Eastern medieval miniature book illustrations.

Niko Pirosmani (1862–1918) occupies a special place in the history of Georgian culture. He was the first primitivist painter and created his own style. His works were based on his spontaneous, vivid, and sharp vision of the world around him and on a sincere interpretation of life. His paintings focused mostly on the streets of Tbilisi, village people, animals, and food. The main theme of works painted by Georgian artists during the Soviet era was the labor of the republic's citizens, the history of the nation, and the search for harmony between the ideal and the real. Paintings by Bagrat Shvelidze depict the strong patriotism of young Georgians. *Remembering the Fallen Sons* (1972) shows the aging men who gathered together to say good-bye to young military conscripts and to remember the fallen heroes of previous wars. Looking at the faces of these men, viewers can imagine the portraits of the fallen heroes. The static composition of the painting allows the artist to show the emotions of the people, who are depicted as dark figures on the light background. The people appear isolated from the surroundings and concentrated in thought, which reflects Georgia's national approach toward military service, destiny, and the dignity of a soldier. The painting is very nationalist because it shows a typical Georgian landscape and traditional food in still life.

A person in harmony with his or her surroundings was the subject of paintings by Radish Tordia (b. 1936). His painting *Feast* (1968) shows a traditional Georgian dinner. The importance of keeping tradition is emphasized by the details and the strong order around the table. The master did not paint people's individual features in his canvases, nor did he expose their personalities. However, he showed typical features of people's characters. Everyone in his paintings has a typical Georgian face and is a stereotype expressing the mood and feelings of the entire nation. The commonality of all people depicted in Tordia's paintings unites his works of different periods and genres into one epic cycle. Recently, the artist turned his attention to romantic female portraits. The works from this series are *Woman* (2004) and *Walk* (2005), each detailing a story of a person: her life, her mood, her feelings, and her expectations of love.

Contemporary Arts

Since the late 1980s when Communist ideological pressure became less intense under the policies of glasnost declared by Soviet leader Mikhail Gorbachev (b. 1931), artists all over the Soviet Union obtained almost unrestricted access to foreign art and established contacts with their colleagues abroad. State sovereignty and the involvement of the Caucasian republics in the general globalization process opened the region to international cultural exchanges, which froze for a while in the mid-1990s because of wars, self-imposed isolation, economic crises, and repressive government policies. Economic and political reforms conducted in the region in the twenty-first century had a positive impact on artistic life. The works of contemporary Caucasian artists nicely blend native traditions and foreign ideas, borrowed mostly from American and Western European artists, though the influence of the Russian school and Soviet traditions among artists of the older generation remains strong.

In Azerbaijan, which appears to be the most Westernized country of the Middle East, the artists preserve their Muslim heritage. The development of the arts in Azerbaijan is characterized today by an Islamic influence, which has led to the revitalization of the art of calligraphy and miniature book illustrations on the one side and strong government control on the other. The Azerbaijani government selects artists to support, provides them with salaries and other material benefits, patronizes the activities of the nation's Union of Artists, and promotes those whose works meet the government's demands. One of them is Farid Aliyev (b. 1985), who paints official portraits of historical and public figures. His best-known work is *God Bless Azerbaijan* (2004), a dual portrait of Heydar Aliyev, then the president of Azerbaijan, and Pope John Paul II made after the pope's visit to Azerbaijan. The portrait, which features two outstanding individuals who symbolize absolute power and absolute faith, is characterized by live expressions, which are unusual for official portraits. In painting the portraits, Aliyev applied different styles and techniques. Some look like romantic works, but others are more realistic or made in the Japanese graphic style, but everybody is shown alive with his own traits.

In 2001, the National Academy of Fine Arts was established in Azerbaijan. The academy is a state university that provides free undergraduate and graduate education to the most talented Azerbaijani artists. The dean of the Academy, Omar Eldarov (b. 1927), is the most prolific Azerbaijani sculptor, and his works featuring distinguished philosophers, poets, writers, musicians, composers, conductors, artists, and statesmen can be found in squares, parks, and museums in large and small cities across the republic. Although Eldarov's modern works are more individualistic and less heavy and bulky than most of the sculptures created during the Soviet period, his monuments still follow the tradition of socialist realism.[6]

In Armenia and Georgia, where state support for artists is insufficient and old artistic institutions did not survive the post-Soviet transformation, many artists began to work for tourists and the mass market, selling their works on the streets of Yerevan and Tbilisi. Since 1998, a widely popular biennial art show in the second-largest Armenian city of Gyumri is an artistic venue of regional significance. The show makes the city a center of artistic life in the entire South Caucasus. The artistic revitalization of Gyumri began in 1995, with the opening of the art exhibition *Metapolis*, featuring areas destroyed by the 1988 earthquake, and the project *Expedition 101*, which represented the distance in kilometers between Yerevan and Gyumri but symbolized the great economic and cultural divide between the two cities. These events became the prototypes for the first biennial in 1998, held ten years after the earthquake that destroyed the city. The exhibition was meant to be a cultural bridge not only within Armenia but also to the international community. Each time the exhibition, which involves contemporary artists from abroad, is structured around a particular theme, such as artists' responses to sacred places close to nature or the celebration of the 1,600th anniversary of the Armenian alphabet. The Gyumri Center of Contemporary Art receives sponsorship from the Ararat Cognac Company, the United Nations, and the British Council, and has established its presence in the region. The center publishes the biennial catalogue and *Art Now*, Armenia's only contemporary art magazine. An artist-in-residence program that partners Armenian and foreign artists has been established at the center too.

The Armenian alphabet exhibition, held in 2006, featured works of two major Armenian photographers, Garen Azizian and Vahram Mkhitaryan. These artists placed a giant portrait of the face of an Armenian man with the word *destiny* written in Armenian on his forehead on a staircase. *Destiny* is a word that is much used in the Armenian language and literally translates as "writing on the forehead." Their second piece was a collection of twenty photographs of tattoos taken in prisons and a collection of words and images that ranged from the religious to the ridiculous. *Sign Language*, a third piece, consisted of a long photograph with a series of hands making out Mesrop Mashtots's translation from the *Book of Proverbs*.

Modern Armenian and Georgian artists focus on styles traditional to Western culture and experiment with postmodernist forms. Armen Eloian (b. 1966) became popular in Armenia because of his comic-style paintings. His painting *The TV Room* (2006) is composed of rapid brushstrokes dragged over the canvas and depicts two dwarves sitting in front of a television set, staring silently into space and smoking joints. One of them is wearing a hat; the other has a protective peaked cap. Both have long noses, skinny legs, and oversized shoes. The composition of the work is based on variations of colors. At the edges of the painting, the white cube of the television screen, which brings light into the dark and empty scene, where something dramatic might occur, interrupts the chaos. The world of comics and toys is also depicted in the painting *Disaster* (2006), where Mickey Mouse stands exhausted in the yellow light of a battle scene in front of a charred body and next to a white bunny. The latter, pierced by an arrow, lies on the ground waiting to be collected by Cupid, in the form of a stylized paramedic.

Harutyun Simonian (b. 1972) deals with audio and visual installations that incorporate a variety of everyday items. According to the artist, the items symbolize the loneliness of a person and his or her alienation from the environment. A feeling of absence escalated by gruesome images of dismembered human beings dominates Simonian's installations. Koka Ramishvili (b. 1956) also presents different multimedia installations. Inspired by global changes in the political, social, and economic life in Tbilisi, which has become an open and intriguing city, Ramishvili initiated the project *Prognostic Eventuel*, which aims to make the architectural and political landscape visible from the outside and the inside for all Georgian citizens. The project began in 1997 and includes publications of four photographs from each foreign consular office or embassy in Tbilisi. They shows how architectural camouflage can express the real intentions of foreign missions and the degree of openness and tolerance.

The economic revival of the Caucasian republics in the early twenty-first century helped the artistic community fully enjoy the breakup of institutional boundaries. The community found itself involved in the international art world and able to react to the challenges of reality by freely selecting artistic means, whether original, post-Soviet, or Western-like.

NOTES

1. David Masello, "Floor Show," *Art and Antiques* 26, no. 2 (2003): 76.

2. Armenag Sarkisian, "Notes on the Sculpture of the Church of Akhtamar," *The Art Bulletin* 25, no. 4 (December 1943): 348.

3. Nina Chichinadze, "Some Compositional Characteristics of Georgian Triptychs of the Thirteenth through Fifteenth Centuries," *Gesta* 35, no. 1 (1996): 73.

4. Charles Garoian, "Teaching Art as a Matter of Cultural Survival: Esthetic Education in the Republic of Armenia," *Journal of Aesthetic Education* 28, no. 2 (Summer 1994): 92.

5. Mursal Nadzhaf, *Khudozhniki Azerbaijanu: Desiat' Tvorchikh Portretiv* [Artists of Azerbaijan: Ten Portraits] (Kyiv: Mystetstvo, 2002), 86.

6. Betty Blair, "Profiles in Transition," *Azerbaijan International* 2, no. 2 (Summer 1994): 36, available at http://www.azer.com/aiweb/categories/magazine/22_folder/22_articles/22_sculptor.html.

9

Sport, Leisure, and Festivals

PARTIES, FESTIVITIES, AND leisure are inseparable parts of life in the South Caucasus. People of the South Caucasus are known for their good mood and ability to celebrate any occasion. Hospitality is probably the most important trait of any native person, and long feasts occur on occasions of family, religious, and national holidays, which are celebrated in big groups at home and outside. The celebrations are accompanied by performances and competitions in sport, dance, and crafts. The number of nonworking holidays during the year varies from ten days in Armenia to fifteen days in Georgia. Because all three countries are secular states, weekends consist of Saturday and Sunday and are nonworking days for the majority of population, which follows the Gregorian calendar. The laws of all three republics provide for a forty-hour workweek, but this time often includes meetings with friends and consuming tea, coffee, and tasty sweets in sidewalk cafes. Such cafes have recently opened in large numbers in every city and town throughout the region. Art and sport play an important role in the lives of Caucasian people. Amateur music and theatrical performances are no less popular than concerts by professional artists, and it is a matter of dignity for people to be able to masterly perform folkloric songs and dances. It is typical for a family to spend time together at a museum or library. With the arrival of many popular Western brands in the republics, shopping has become much more popular than it was before. Sport is popular too. Almost every boy participates in one or another professional sport tryouts, famous athletes are national celebrities, and favorite teams receive unconditional popular support.

Lifestyle

Pastimes and Recreation

The social element of life is a very important component of daily activities in the South Caucasus. Personal connections, friendships, and close family ties are treasured more than anything else by the people of these three republics, which are known as nations of hospitality. Even though Caucasian hospitality may seem to be excessive sometimes, it is meant as a compliment and should be respected. Caucasians believe that being a guest is a duty and that being a host brings honor. It is not unusual when people who receive friends from out of town are joined by local friends or relatives who may not know the guests but want to be involved in the hosting and share their hospitable feelings with them. Many gifts are showered on guests and their friends, especially those who are visiting the home of a Georgian for the first time. Across the region, hospitality dominates all other duties and obligations, including work. Hospitality is a reciprocal act, and it is expected that guests provide similar kindness in return. It is a shame to be a bad guest and a bad host, and thus each party behaves according to centuries-old traditions. A ritualized part of social life is oral communication. Although this trait is common to all local people, it is more prevalent among Georgians. All generations of Georgians are expected to initiate and receive a large number of telephone calls and to maintain daily contact with a wide network of relatives, friends, and acquaintances. Visitors are expected to make an ever-increasing number of social visits, simply for the purpose of spending time together. Although this imposes difficulties on the hosts, they feel that they are duly fulfilling their social obligations.

Because the main activity when receiving guests and having parties is to eat, it is not necessary that these parties be hosted in homes. They are often conducted outdoors in country houses, forests, or city parks, where local kebab-like shashlik are grilled, or in restaurants and cafés, which have opened in large numbers recently. All three South Caucasian capital cities have an elaborate history of café life and an established café society. Although in Azerbaijan the drink of demand is tea, this does not change the atmosphere of establishments where people meet to read newspapers, discuss news, play chess, and even develop strategies for political campaigns.

Newspapers continue to be an important element of social and cultural life in these nations. National television is largely controlled by the governments and full of pro-government political coverage or Western-style entertainment, which is not well accepted by the mostly conservative population. Newspapers, because of their varied ownership and better-preserved journalistic independence, represent more opinions and often publish articles on historical or social issues. At the beginning of independence, the issue of the Georgian language was of constant interest to the public, and newspapers carried articles about the origin of the alphabet and stories about the purchase of Georgian typewriters by the independent government in 1918. Recent academic books and monographs are likely to be reviewed and summarized in popular newspaper articles, and the public favors translations from the Western press.

Although many modern media compete with traditional books, reading is among the traditional, though now less important, pastimes in the Caucasus. Each country has a wide network of libraries, starting with the national library in the capital city, university libraries, libraries at research institutions, and libraries for adults and youths in almost every administrative district. National libraries collect all books and periodicals published in the country and acquire many foreign publications through their participation in exchange programs with the libraries of foreign states. The national library of Azerbaijan was the first library in the region to establish a cooperative program with the National Library of France in 1962. Today, the supply of books to local libraries is inadequate because of the lack of financial resources, but the libraries' collection of national and foreign classics is fairly good; teachers often refer their students to local libraries in search of additional information. Attempts to promote reading and organize celebrations of books are periodically undertaken. National consortiums of major libraries aimed to digitize library resources have been created in each republic. Western-style bookstores were opened in Caucasian capital cities in the late 1990s and soon became popular places for families to visit. Sometimes local libraries are centers of local social life. They conduct public celebrations, host visiting lecturers, and organize movie screenings or local craftsmanship contests. People often enter their crafts in competitions. It is a tradition that during mass gatherings or public celebrations, girls are given hooks and different colored threads to crochet stockings. The winner is the girl who crochets the best stockings more quickly than the others do.

Each Caucasian republic has more than a hundred recognized museums and about twenty theaters. The theater season runs from October through June, and most performances nearly sell out. Many monuments and historical sights serve as open-air museums suitable for family time. Being outdoor people, Caucasians enjoy the opportunities that nature provides them. Because of the variety of landscapes and climates, there are many tourist attractions, ranging from snowcapped mountains for climbers and skiers to subtropical sea resorts and mineral spas near medicinal springs that offer possible health cures. The environment provides ample opportunities for bird-watchers, botanists, and fans of caving, hiking, horseback riding, and fishing. However, people of the Caucasus are not accustomed to domestic travel and tourism, partially because of the almost nonexistent tourist infrastructure in the region, wars, criminality, and general instability. Another reason is the widespread poverty

A hiking party in the Armenian mountains. Courtesy of Anushik Mazmanyan.

among the population, which prefers to visit relatives and stay with them during the holidays. Those who have means to travel prefer to go abroad.

The economic hardships of the 1990s had a strong impact on the lifestyles of people in all three republics. More work and less money decreased the expanse of festivities for a while and affected the mood of people who had lost their savings, retirement benefits, and other social support programs. In 1985, for example (the last year before Gorbachev's reforms), in Georgia, half the state budget was spent on food, housing assistance, health care, and education. New mothers were granted a year and a half of paid maternity leave, and all workers were guaranteed retirement benefits. This social support network allowed people to be selective in their pastimes and left them with more time for recreation instead of working second jobs to earn sustenance money for their families. In the 1990s, all social services ended abruptly. During this time, pensions averaged US$7 a month and were irregularly paid. In 2000, 42 percent of all Armenians, for example, earned less than $2 a day.[1] Retirees were spending all of their $6–$10 monthly pensions for electricity and heat. Usually they managed to get discounted bread from local bakeries, and for medicines they turned to a few relief organizations. The desperate situation led people to new avenues to make ends meet, such as gambling.

After the countries of the South Caucasus experienced a socioeconomic crisis, widespread poverty, mass unemployment, and a considerable influx of internally displaced people and refugees, the HIV/AIDS epidemic became a real danger for the small countries. However, the increased rates of drug use and HIV remain relatively low, compared to the rates in Russia, Ukraine, and other countries of the region. Official statistics show that the majority of HIV cases in the Caucasus republics resulted from intravenous drug use. However, there is no reliable data on drug use in these republics. Observers believe that each republic has approximately 25,000 drug users, the majority of whom reside in the capital cities.[2]

Laws in all three countries provide for a zero-tolerance policy and prohibit the sale, possession, and consumption of narcotics. In every republic drug-related crime is punishable by a fine and/or imprisonment, and regardless of each country's human rights obligations, all require HIV testing for every drug user apprehended or admitted to rehabilitation. Patient consent is not required, and there are no legal mechanisms that prevent the disclosure of information.

In 2003, Armenia was the last country to join the regional needle exchange program for intravenous drug users. Needle-exchange centers were established in all three capital cities of the region and in a few other large urban areas. The services provided by the centers include distribution of disposable syringes and dissemination of condoms and educational materials. The centers also offer voluntary HIV testing and counseling, symptomatic treatment for sexually transmitted diseases, and legal advice. Few, if any, people take advantage of the services provided by the needle-exchange centers because they distrust the staff and are afraid of being prosecuted for drug use. Existing legislative loopholes make such centers' activities questionable from a legal standpoint. Laws in each country prohibit the advertisement and propaganda of drugs. Armenian law is even stricter, making it a crime to disseminate information about the forms of use of narcotic drugs or to propagate the advantages of narcotic drugs over one another. Because the term *propaganda* is quite vague, any drug-related activity or literature seems to fall within it, the existence of these centers depends on the will of authorities.

People survived the turmoil of the first years of independence mostly because of strong family networks and unconditional support that family members provide one another. Even under harsh conditions, people of the Caucasus never lost their native optimism. Family and religious holidays were always celebrated with what was available, guests were received and fed, with the best food saved for such occasions, and traditional songs were sung regardless of the difficulties of daily life.

Celebratory Dancing and Singing

Most celebrations occur at the dinner table, and they often include songs and dances, which are an important part of public and family celebrations. Georgians traditionally have good voices and enjoy singing. Folk songs are usually sung around the table. The roots of Georgian songs can be found in religious song that accompanied church rites. Polyphony, which consists of complex three-part polyphonic harmonies, is the main feature of Georgian folk music. Men and women sing in separate ensembles with entirely different repertoires that reflect the individual regions of Georgia. Musical inspiration is often church, work in the fields, and special occasions. Folk music is still very much alive in Armenia too. Authentic Armenian music belongs to Middle Eastern traditions. It is monophonic and mainly accompanied by percussion instruments. The most commonly played folk instruments are the woodwind instruments *zurna* and *duduk*, the stringed instrument *gyamancha*, and the percussion instrument *dhol*.

Folk dancing is another local tradition. Dances in the Caucasus vary dramatically, including male, female, coed, solo, couple, group, and mass dances. The dances are solemnly flowing and charmingly graceful, but more often they are eccentric and acrobatic. Georgian male performers dance on their toes without the help of special shoes. Two dances, the *zemkrelo* and the *kartuli* are most popular among Georgians. In the *zemkrelo*, men dance in tight circles holding one another's hands, and sometimes a third tier of dancers is placed on the shoulders of the first or second tier of dancers. The speed of the dance constantly increases, and movements become more and more

Georgian children perform in a street concert. Photograph by Badri Vadachkoria provided by the Embassy of Georgia to the United States.

complicated, forcing the upper dancers to jump down. The *kartuli* begins with a man who slowly passes a line of young women and invites one of them to dance. The woman slowly dances in circles without removing her feet from the floor while the man follows her, protecting her and trying to attract her attention.

In Armenia, dances are an inseparable part of social life and have a long history. Dynamic and graceful on the one hand and passionate and expressive on the other, Armenian dance has been fascinating spectators for centuries. Many people feel that Armenian dances are special because of the passion, subtlety, and eloquence that they embody. At Armenian festivals, including weddings and funeral ceremonies, so-called war dances, which reveal the idea of combat and struggle, are often performed. About twenty such dances are known.[3] War dances are performed mostly by young and middle-aged men and are considered one of the main means of military training because of their complicated steps and the need for consistent training to master the dance. Those who cannot overcome performance difficulties were considered poor warriors, were not allowed to go into battle, and were deprived of being true members of the community. Usually such dances are performed in a line, in two lines one after another or facing each other, or in a circle or semicircle. The position of lines repeatedly changes during the dance. The lines step toward each other, bump against each other, and move back. Often they divide into pairs that chase and attack each other. The direction of the lines also changes, moving to the left and to the right, forward and backward. The tempo of the war dances is quick. The attacking and bellicose character of the movements represents the military content of these dances despite the absence of any weapon. When war dances are performed at weddings, on holidays at public squares, or in sporting contests, horsemen with large sticks called *makanasater* participate in the dance. These horsemen armed with rods symbolize the readiness of a dancer to combat actions.

HOLIDAYS AND FESTIVITIES

In the Caucasian republics, holidays are celebrated in memory of major historical or political events (see Table 9.1). Many are celebrated in all three states simultaneously because they are associated with events that had significance for all three countries and because of the common historical heritage—since the days when the three republics were constituent parts of the Soviet Union. The jointly celebrated holidays are New Year's Day; the day of victory over fascist Germany in World War II, a local combination of Veterans' and Memorial Day; and International Women's Day, which celebrates the equality of women and their rights. On this day, men give presents to women, and the streets are

Table 9.1
National Holidays

Holiday	Armenia	Azerbaijan	Georgia
New Year	January 1	January 1	January 1–2
Orthodox Christmas	January 7		January 7
Orthodox Epiphany			January 19
Mothers' Day	April 7		March 3
International Women's Day	March 8	March 8	March 8
Novruz Bayramy		March 20–21	
Orthodox Good Friday, Easter, and Easter Monday			March/April (movable)
Day of National Unity			April 9
Genocide Victims' Memorial Day	April 24		
Victory over Fascism Day	May 9	May 9	May 9
Feast Day of St. (Queen) Tamar			May 14
First Republic Day	May 28	May 28	
National Salvation Day		June 15	
National Army Day		June 26	
Constitution Day	July 5	November 12	
Independence Day	September 21	October 18	May 26
Feast Day of Mtsheta (Old Georgian capital)			October 14
National Revival Day		November 17	
Feast Day of St. George			November 23
Day of Remembrance of the 1988 Earthquake Victims	December 7		
Feast Day of St. Barbara			December 17
Solidarity Day of All Azeri People		December 31	

full of flowers. People usually celebrate the day with friends and have a good time in cafés, restaurants, or at home. Each republic has its own Constitution and Independence Day to celebrate the anniversaries of the adoption of the founding legal acts in the early 1990s.

Some holidays are specific to each republic. For example, in Azerbaijan, June 15 is a nonworking holiday that celebrates the return to power of Heydar Alieyv, a Communist ruler of Azerbaijan, whose election as president was a turning point in repressing the opposition, restricting political reforms, and creating a new regime that today runs the country under the leadership of Aliyev's son who succeeded him.

Because of strong ancient traditions in Azerbaijan, Novruz, a New Year celebrated in the spring during ancient times with ethnic performances, rites, ceremonies, and songs, was recognized as national holiday after independence. Mass festive gatherings are organized on this day too. For the people of the Soviet Union, the New Year's celebration on December 31 always had a special meaning because it was the only nonpolitical holiday, and people traditionally started advance preparations for New Year's Eve celebrations—taking December 31 off or just simply missing work. It appears that the authorities were looking for a good reason to declare this day officially nonworking. In Azerbaijan, this date coincided with the opening of the First World Congress of the Azeri People in Istanbul in 1992, and the day was declared Solidarity Day for Azeri People, although today almost no one in Azerbaijan knows what is officially celebrated on December 31 and most people believe that there is no work because of New Year's Eve and other necessary preparations for the holiday. All over the region, New Year's is celebrated a whole week, starting December 31, by baking New Year's cookies and loading up tables with food and different kinds of sweets. Although only the first two days of the year are officially off, people stay in the celebratory mood the entire week. During the week, people exchange gifts and congratulatory wishes, and keep their homes open to welcome everyone. Visitation begins on January 1 and lasts through Orthodox Christmas, which is celebrated on January 7.

Armenian Holidays

Armenian holidays commemorate both religious and historical events. Besides Christmas and Easter, the most important holidays are Vartanants, the day marking the fifth-century defense of Christianity against the Persians, and April 24, which commemorates the victims of the 1915 genocide of Armenians in Turkey. Of special importance is the remembrance of deceased ancestors. Cemeteries are often visited on the second day after an important religious holiday and on May 9, which is a national holiday often used for commemorations. A secular holiday is the First Republic Day. On this day in 1918, the Armenian people restored what was left of historical Armenia to statehood after half a millennium of lost sovereignty. The celebration of this day marks the beginning of the modern Armenian quest for independence. Short lived, the 1918 republic was swallowed by the Soviet Union for seventy more years, but it inspired a spirit of hope and self-determination for future generations. The restoration of the Republic of Armenia in 1991, after seventy years of Soviet rule and a national referendum on secession from the Soviet Union, is celebrated as Independence Day.

The celebration of Armenian holidays is always a festive and happy occasion, except for the one celebrated every year on April 24. This is the day of grief and mourning, when Armenians all over the world remember almost 2 million victims of the genocide committed by the Turks against Armenians in 1915. Thousands of people join in the annual procession to the eternal flame of the genocide victims' memorial on foot, on Tsitsernakaberd Hill, to pay their respect to those who perished in the massive attempt to exterminate the Armenian people and forcibly remove them from their ancestral lands. All day long a silent line of people passes the hill. They place flowers at the edge of the torch, bow their heads, and leave the hill. Another solemn remembering occurs every year on December 7. On this day in 1988, a devastating earthquake killed thousands of people and destroyed most of the republic's infrastructure. The earthquake was felt all over the republic, but it was the second and third most populous cities—Gyumri and Vanadzor—that were among the most devastated. Many events with local significance are commemorated also. Every year people in the village of Musaler, near Yerevan, celebrate the anniversary of a tragedy that occurred in August and September 1915 in southern Turkey at the top of Musadag Mountain (in Armenian, Musaler), where several thousand Armenian peasants were surrounded by invading Turkish troops and besieged in their village. Those who survived were evacuated by the French rescue force in Cairo and later relocated to Soviet Armenia. Thousands of people always attend this commemoration.

Armenia is a secular country and religious holidays, except for Orthodox Christmas, are not celebrated as official nonworking holidays. The Armenians celebrate the birth of Christ as a major Christian religious holiday, together with Epiphany, and attend church services in their neighborhoods. Part of the ritual is the blessing of water with the holy chrism symbolic of Christ's baptism. The most beautiful and meaningful parts of the holiday occur both at home and in the church. Many families go to church on Christmas Eve and Christmas morning. Then they sit down to enjoy a traditional Christmas dinner. According to tradition, the main dish is fish and rice prepared with butter. Wine is served with dinner. Armenian children believe that Dzmer Papik, the Armenian version of Santa Claus, brings gifts on Christmas Eve. Several days or weeks before the holiday, children write letters to Dzmer Papik telling him the toys they desire to have.

The favorite and most anticipated holiday is Easter (*Zatik*). During the Lenten fasting season forty days before Easter, Armenian families put lentils or other sprouting grains on a tray covered with a thin layer of cotton and keep them in a light place of the house until Easter, when sprouts appear. These green sprouts, symbolizing spring and the awakening of nature, are the "grass" on which people place colored eggs to decorate the Easter table. A day devoted to the Mother of God is celebrated on a Sunday that falls between August 12 and 18. The traditional ceremony of this holiday is the annual blessing of the grapes in the church, which coincides with the beginning of the harvest. February 21 is the Mother Language Day, a holiday dedicated to the creator of the Armenian alphabet Mesrop Mashtots and the translator and interpreter of the Bible Sahak Partev. St. Sargis is another beloved religious observance and is very popular among younger people. It is celebrated sixty-three days before Easter, on a Saturday that falls sometime between January 18 and February 23. On the night of the holiday, young people eat salty pies and do not drink water to encourage dreams at night. They believe that St. Sargis decides their fate, that the person who gives them water to drink in their dreams will become their future spouse. People also put a plate with flour outside their homes to have a record of St. Sargis's horse riding through the flour. They believe St. Sargis appears with lightning speed on his radiant horse, and that the traces in the flour are a good omen to bring the family luck. People imagine St. Sargis as handsome and appearing with a spear, a gold helmet, and gold armor.

In Armenia, many observed rites and holidays are connected with the change of the four seasons. For example, the holiday *Drndez*, which means "stack at the door," is celebrated in the middle of February. The holiday is dedicated to the rebirth of the sun's energy and the beginning of spring. This holiday is celebrated by burning bonfires and jumping over them, and youths and newlyweds dance around them. One of the most popular holidays is *Vardavar*, named after the ancient pagan god of water, Varda. In western Armenia, this holiday is celebrated in the end of August, but in eastern Armenia, the holiday is celebrated in the middle of July at the peak of the summer heat. It is common on Vardavar to walk high in the mountains to the places that were traditionally used for pasturing. On this day, people wash animals, sprinkle one another with water, and jokingly throw one another into rivers and ponds. An old tradition connects this holiday with legends about the biblical flood, but some ethnographers believe that it reflects pagan rituals of calling for a rain during the driest period of the year. Today, Vardavar is usually celebrated on the last Sunday of July. People go by car to the mountains, organize picnics, prepare food on grills, and perform and attend concerts by popular actors in the mountain meadows.

Azerbaijani Celebrations

Except for formal state holidays, most celebrations in Azerbaijan are based on old traditions and beliefs. Special respect is traditionally paid to many natural things, such as water, fire, mountaintops, stones, or trees. It is considered a good thing to visit a designated special place, often water springs, because Azerbaijanis believe in the purifying and curative features of water. According to many legends, good and evil spirits reside near the water springs, as do souls of deceased ancestors. A popular ritual is the celebration of water on the day *Su Dzheddim* in the middle of summer. On this day, people shower themselves

Many people of the Southern Caucasus spend their vacations at Black Sea resorts. Photograph by Badri Vadachkoria provided by the Embassy of Georgia to the United States.

with water from a spring under a quince tree that is believed to have special powers. Amulets made from quince wood are usually worn around the neck and attached to the cribs of small children or household animals.

Many former religious rites have transformed into games for youths. For instance, during summer droughts, children and teenagers make large dolls and carry them through the village streets making a lot of noise. As the procession passes by, the people step outside their houses and sprinkle the dolls and children with water; then the dolls are "drowned" in nearby rivers. It is believed that this may help bring rain. In early spring, a common entertainment that symbolizes the end of winter is jumping over a gigantic bonfire.

Because of the growing Islamic influence, Muslim religious celebrations have become more important, but they are celebrated with good food, concerts, sport tournaments, and competitions in traditional folk arts as nonreligious festivities because the country has no strong religious roots and fundamentalist ideas are not popular. The major holiday is Novruz, a celebration of spring and the New Year, which occurs between February 21 and March 21. On this day, people gather near a river or at a water mill, dance, ride horses, sing, and share specially prepared sweets with one another. It is believed that these activities will bring happiness and prosperity to the participants. Other widely celebrated religious holidays are the last day of the month of Ramadan, Ramazan Bayram, when after one month of fasting, Muslims bring gifts to the clergy and to one another, visit friends and relatives, and provide a lot of entertainment. Another important holiday celebrated by a great and festive dinner is Gurban Bayram, the holiday of sacrifices, which is commemorated by a ritual killing of a sheep.

Georgian Festivals

Georgian festivals derive from Orthodox religious holidays and major events in the country's history. A special day is April 9, an annual commemoration of the anniversary of a peaceful anti-Soviet public demonstration that was held in Tbilisi in 1989, when twenty young Georgians were killed and hundreds were wounded by Soviet soldiers in an attempt to disperse the rally. This event became a turning point in the democratization of Georgia and expedited the breakup of the Soviet Union.

Public holidays are mostly of a religious background and are associated with prayers and pilgrimages to holy places. One of them is Mtskhetoba, which for many centuries the church celebrated on October 14 of every year in the Svetitskhopveli Cathedral, located in the center of the ancient Georgian capital of Mtskheta. According to chronicles, the first Christian church in Georgia was established on this place in the fourth century when Georgia accepted Christianity. People from all corners of Georgia gather on this day in Mtskheta, and many come with their entire families. Many people go to the cathedral and others socialize on the streets. Some people meet old friends and others start conversations with those whom they have met for the first time. Young people compete in wrestling or folklore singing tournaments. Some young men take advantage of the occasion to meet girls or just to relax after the autumn harvest is collected.

There are many newer public holidays also. For example, Shotaoba, named after the famous writer Shota Rustaveli was established in the early 1960s by the people of the village of Ikalto. The ruins of the old Georgian academy where Shota Rustaveli was a student surround this village. The holiday is dedicated to the memory of this great writer. Famous Georgian scholars and writers born in Ikalto participated in the first Shotaoba celebration and told many interesting stories to the people who had come to celebrate. Famous sportsmen judged tournaments, and Nona Gaprindashvili, a world chess champion, played a game with the guests. People organized concerts and planted tress in memory of the fallen war veterans. Every year, more and more people from Georgia and abroad have arrived for these celebrations, and since 1965, Shota Rustaveli's birthday has been celebrated nationwide. Holidays dedicated to other famous Georgians are celebrated at their birthplaces. For example, on the birthday of the famous writer Ilia Chavchavadze, people gather under an old walnut tree in the front of his museum and read extracts from his works. One of the most popular holidays is Tbilisoba, a city holiday celebrated the last Sunday of October. Thousands of people attend theatrical performances, chorus performances, and dance concerts on the streets. Arts-and-craft shows are held all around the city, and many restaurants conduct tastings and cooking demonstrations. On such days, the entire city transforms into a carnival arena.

SPORT ACTIVITIES

Running, jumping, throwing, and climbing were the first physical exercises of the Caucasians. They became the basis for physical culture and sports in all areas of the Caucasus. For Caucasians, sport was part of celebrations devoted to pagan gods marking the new year, hospitality, awakening nature, flower decorations, love, fertility, and so on. Competitions in running, boxing, wrestling, archery, javelin throwing, equestrianism, and other games were held during the pagan celebrations too. These ancient sporting events had much in common with the Greek Olympic Games. It is known that the Armenian King Tiridates III was the winner in the chariot races of the 265th Olympic Games in 281 A.D. Armenian King Varazdat Arshakuni was the boxing champion at the 291st Olympic Games in 385 A.D.

Since the end of the eighteenth century, the subject of physical education was introduced into the curriculum of almost every Armenian school. Later, Pan-Armenian sports games, which involved ethnic Armenians from all over the world, were regularly organized. Some famous sportsmen first became known through their victories in the Pan-Armenian games: Mkrtich Mkrtchian and Vahram Papazian from Constantinople participated in the Stockholm Olympic Games in 1912. Mkrtchian placed fifth in the decathlon athletic competitions among fifty participants.

Physical training and sports are widespread in the Caucasus. There are physical education departments at all universities and colleges. Physical education classes are included in the curricula of secondary schools for the entire period of learning. All universities and schools have sports instructors and equipment. Various regional, national, and international sports competitions are held regularly. In rural areas the preference is given to national sports, such as wrestling, weightlifting, soccer, and *chovgan*, a local variety of polo.

Since 1996, national teams of all the three Caucasian republics have participated in the Olympic Games. Armenians won 26 Olympic medals, including 13 gold; six Azerbaijanis have won five gold, two silver, and five bronze Olympic medals; and Georgian athletes have brought 105 Olympic medals home, including 33 gold medals. Caucasian athletes have achieved the most success in historically popular sports, such as judo, wrestling, and weightlifting. However, they have made some successful developments recently in less traditional events, such as boxing, track-and-field, and gymnastics. Georgians are becoming active in winter sports too. At the Olympic Games in Nagano (1998), Salt Lake City (2002), and Turin (2006), the Georgian team competed in alpine skiing, ski jumping, luge, and figure skating.

Traditionally, Caucasian women have engaged in sports too. Along with the traditional women's sports, such as rhythmic gymnastics, synchronized swimming, or softball, women engage in such disciplines as sumo wrestling and shooting. Azerbaijani Zulfiya Hasanova became a world champion in sumo wrestling in 1995 and 1996, and Zemfira Meftaheddinova took the first place in team competitions in the European shooting championships in the 1990s.

Wrestling is probably the most popular sport all over the Caucasus. Every region has developed its own style of wrestling, and it is believed that Greco-Roman wrestling, which is an Olympic discipline, incorporates many Caucasian elements. Among other popular sports are soccer, basketball, and volleyball. The first Georgian rugby club was formed in 1959, and in 1961, the Tbilisi Championship, a three-team domestic tournament, had been conducted. Today, rugby is one of the most popular sports in the republic, with teams in almost every educational establishment. In 2001, the Georgian national rugby team won the European Nations Cup and became the seventh highest-ranked team in Europe. The team subsequently advanced through the qualifying stages for the next Rugby World Cup and made it to Australia for the 2003 Rugby World Cup. The team also qualified for the 2007 World Cup and won its first World Cup match. The national rugby team is nicknamed "The Lelos," which comes from *lelo*, an indigenous Georgian sport with strong similarities to rugby. In Georgian, the word *lelo* means "try," and the standard cheer of Georgian rugby fans is "Lelo, Lelo, Sakartvelo!" ("Try, Try, Georgia!").

Soccer is a widely popular sport that is played everywhere in the Caucasus. The national soccer federations govern soccer in each republic, organizing both men's and women's national soccer teams and competitions. It is said that soccer was introduced to the region by English sailors in the beginning of the twentieth century. In 1936, the Armenian Premiere League, a national soccer union, had been created to conduct regional tournaments within the Soviet Union. After Armenia became independent in 1991, the league, which currently consists of eight teams in two divisions, organizes top soccer competitions in the republic. Similar leagues were established in other republics. All of them are members of the Union of European Football Associations, and local teams are involved in all major European competitions. Local soccer seasons run from summer to spring. During the Soviet era, the teams Ararat from Yerevan, Neftchi from Baku, and Dynamo from Tbilisi were among the strongest. In 1973, Ararat Yerevan became the Soviet Union champion and played in European Cup tournaments. Dynamo Tbilisi was among the leading European soccer clubs for many years, and is one of the strongest regional teams today, together with Torpedo Kutaisi and Grand Tobacco FK from Yerevan. Today, the Georgian National Cup is named after David Kipiani (1951–2001), probably the best Georgian midfield player. After winning many Soviet and European soccer awards, and the bronze medal in the 1980 Olympic Games, he coached and managed the Dynamo Tbilisi team.

The game of chess is also among the most popular sports in the region. Brought from the east, this game has become a national pastime. It is common to see people playing chess in parks, and highly decorated handmade sets of chess are traditionally given by Georgian parents to their daughters as wedding gifts. There is a long history of great wins achieved by South Caucasians. This success was achieved because of a strong educational system, and the availability of chess training and exercises for almost all schoolchildren in each country. Georgia is specifically known for women chess players who have been very successful in international tournaments. Nona Gaprindashvili (b. 1941) became a women's world chess champion in 1962, at the age of twenty-one, and held the title for the next sixteen years, defending it against her fellow compatriot Nana Alexandria (b. 1949), who later became the chair of the World Chess Federation's (FIDE) Women's Committee. She also became the first female grandmaster and the strongest female chess player of her generation. In 1978, Gaprindashvili was bested by another Georgian, Maya Chiburdanidze (b. 1961), who started playing chess at the age of eight and kept the crown of women's world champion from 1978 to 1991. The team from Georgia had also won three Women's Chess Olympiads in 1992, 1994, and 1996.

Chess became even more popular when Garry Kasparov (b. 1963), a native of Baku, became the world's youngest chess champion in 1985 and held the title until 2000. From 1986 to his retirement in 2005, Kasparov was continuously rated the world's No. 1 chess player. His achievements include the all-time highest rating and records for consecutive tournament victories. Kasparov began his chess career at the chess school at the Baku Youth Palace, which has a good tradition of preparing young competitive players. Significant achievements have also been reached by Baku natives Aynur Sofiyeva, Firuza Velikhanli, and Ilaha Gadimova. In 1991, Ilaha Gadimova, who was twelve years old at the time, became a champion among sixteen-year-old chess players. In 1992, she won the silver medal in the European championship among juniors, and in 1994 she became the European champion among students. In 1996, she earned third place in the International Students Competition.

Sports that are beginning to develop in Georgia are skiing and snowboarding. Earlier these were considered elitist sports that were simply unaffordable for the public. Benefiting from steady snowfall, the Caucasus offers a great variety in terrain, plenty of natural snow powder, and an Old World feeling. The main ski areas are around the cities of Gudauri and Bakuriani. Several lifts have been built near each of them, and the ski season runs from November until late March. Sometimes it is possible to ski in April. During the Soviet era, the training center for the all-Soviet national ski team was located in Bakuriani. Heli-skiing, a new sport where a skier is brought to the top of a mountain by a helicopter and dropped off, is available too. All trails near Gudauri have different levels of difficulty, from beginner to advanced, and are up to several miles long. In Bakuriani, the mountains are not as high as in Gudauri and the snow melts sooner, but the area is great for cross-country skiing. On a good day, the full Caucasus range can be viewed from there.

Many games are popular leisure activities of Caucasians. The most popular national game, played by almost everybody, is *nardy* (similar to backgammon). The locals claim that *nardy*, which in the Persian language means "battle," is the oldest known recorded game in human history. It is widely believed that the game originated in Mesopotamia in the ancient Persian Empire. The game was played on wooden boards with stones as men and numbered dice made from bones, stones, wood, or pottery. Throughout the history of the game, backgammon has been associated with royals and nobles. Many recorded relics indicate the popularity of the game among the aristocrats of Persia, Greece, Rome, and the Far East.

During spring accession celebrations, such as Novruz, a game named Cock Fight is played. The game is played by two teams, "day" and "night," which consist of five to seven people in about a twenty-foot circle. Both teams keep their hands on their waist and stand on one leg. One of the teams stands on the left leg and the other stands on the right leg; then both teams try to push members of the other team out of the circle. During the fight, all participants must keep their hands on waist and one leg on air.

Notes

1. Thomas Streissguth, *The Transcaucasus* (San Diego: Lucent Books, 2001), 71.

2. Karine Markosyan, Aramayis Kocharyan, and Artur Potosyan, "Meeting the Challenge of Injection Drug Use and HIV in Armenia," *Health and Human Rights* 9, no. 1 (2006): 136.

3. Genya Khatchatryan, "War-Dancer among Armenians," *Studia Musicologica Academiae Scientiarum Hungaricae* 33, no. 1–4 (1991): 402.

Glossary

Alaverdy   Literally means "to you," indicating that the guest is expected to pick up and elaborate on the proposed toast.

Arkhaluk   A long-sleeved gray sateen shirt worn by men.

Ashugi   Folkloric poets and singers who fulfilled the enlightening mission during medieval times.

Atropatene   A Greek word to name the territory of the South Caucasus that is present-day Azerbaijan.

Autocephaly   Independent status of churches in Armenia and Georgia.

Basturma   Air-dried beef.

Bolsheviks   A Communist faction within the Russian Social Democratic Party that usurped power in Russia in 1917 and expanded into the Caucasus. Bolsheviks ruled the Soviet Union until 1991.

Borzhomi   The most popular Georgian mineral water with medicinal properties.

Catholicos   Head of the Armenian Apostolic Church.

Chacha   Extremely potent, homemade mulberry brew.

Chovgan   A local variety of polo.

Cuneiform   The earliest known form of writing, which began as a system of pictographs ca. 3000 B.C. and later became more abstract.

Dastan   A folkloric poem in the genre of a heroic ballad authored and performed by Azerbaijani bards.

Diaspora   Exile—refers to Armenians who reside outside Armenia.

Dyishme   Song competitions among the performers of folk music.

Garadam   Azerbaijani log residence.

Gazan   Cauldron for cooking meals in Azerbaijan, usually made of copper.

Glkhatun   Square buildings with earth-covered roofs used for storage in rural Armenia.

Gobustan   A cave complex in Azerbaijan with the world's largest (more than 4,000) collection of prehistoric rock paintings, dating back 5,000 to 20,000 years.

Grabar   First version of the written Armenian language introduced by the church to educate people.

Hash   A festive Armenian stew that is cooked all night long and eaten early morning on the day after festivities.

Horovats   A kind of kebab made from lamb or more often pork, popular in Armenia.

Icheri Sheher   Original name of the Baku fortress.

Jigit   A horse rider or warrior in present-day Caucasus, referred to as a strong, brave man.

Karawan-sarai   Traditional guesthouse along trade routes in the Middle Ages.

Khachkar   A traditional Armenian stone-carved monument in the form of a cross built to preserve the memory of historic events and people.

Khan   A feudal ruler in medieval state established in the territory of Azerbaijan.

Kinzhal   A long knife; a traditional local weapon and an element of an male dress.

Lavash   The most popular form of thin wheat bread, baked in an outdoor round clay oven; varies regionally.

Lelo   Indigenous Georgian sport with strong similarities to rugby.

Lobio   An appetizer made of highly seasoned red beans.

Makanasater   Large sticks used by horsemen at war dances or war game contests.

Milli Majlis   The unicameral Azerbaijani legislature.

Mugama   A classical poem read accompanied by traditional folk music.

Nardy   A popular table game similar to backgammon, played by men as a pastime.

Navruz   A spring festival that celebrates the ancient New Year in Azerbaijan.

Papakha   A fur hat used as men's adornment.

Perestroika   A policy of economic and political reforms initiated by Mikhail Gorbachev from 1985 to 1991.

Post-Soviet   Period of transition to independence after the collapse of the Soviet Union in 1991.

Red Army   Pro-Bolshevik military units that occupied the region in 1921 and served as a foundation for the Soviet armed forces.

Rootenization   Bolshevik policy in the 1920s and 1930s aimed to promote native Caucasus people to highest administrative positions.

Russification   Policy of tsarist and Bolshevik Russian governments aimed to eliminate national cultures and assimilation of the native people.

Saklia   Traditional house in rural mountainous areas.

Samtrest   The institution of state management of Georgian wine industry; major producer of alcoholic beverages in the Caucasus.

Shamaness   Abkhazian women who, according to popular belief, are able to treat illnesses through prayer and meditation.

Sharakans   Short poems written by Armenian monks from the fifth to the tenth century and meant to be chanted during religious services.

Shashlyk   Caucasian version of kebab, the most popular traditional dish.

Shirvanshah   A fortress and palace complex in downtown Baku that belonged to medieval Azerbaijani rulers.

Socialist realism   The only artistic style permitted by the Soviet regime.

Soviet Union   State that existed between 1922 and 1991, comprising Russia and fourteen other colonized republics.

Tamada   A toastmaster whose job is to pace drinking and entertain company with eloquent words in a series of discourses at a formal dinner.

Tkemali   Spicy sour-plum sauce.

Tsar   A medieval ruler of a Georgian or Armenian state during the period of independence.

Urartu   Armenian prototype state in the ancient South Caucasus.

Vartanants   Armenian holiday marking the fifth-century defense of Christianity against the Persians.

Zurna   A commonly played woodwind instrument in folk music.

Bibliography

BOOKS AND JOURNALS

Abrahamian, Levon. *Armenian Identity in a Changing World.* Costa Mesa, CA: Mazda Publishers, 2006.

Adalian, Rouben. *From Humanism to Rationalism: Armenian Scholarship in the Nineteenth Century.* Atlanta: Scholars Press, 1992.

Adalian, Rouben. *Historical Dictionary of Armenia.* Lanham, MD: Scarecrow Press, 2002.

Adalian, Rouben, and Joseph Masih. *Armenia and Karabagh Factbook.* Washington, DC: Office of Research and Analysis, Armenian Assembly of America, 1996.

Aghai-Diba, Bahman. *The Law and Politics of the Caspian Sea.* Charleston, SC: BookSerge, 2006.

Allen, William. *A History of the Georgian People: From the Beginning Down to the Russian Conquest in the Nineteenth Century.* New York: Barnes and Noble, 1971.

Altstadt, Audrey. *The Azerbaijani Turks: Power and Identity under Russian Rule.* Palo Alto, CA: Hoover Institution Press, Stanford University, 1992.

Avakian, Arra. *Armenia: A Journey through History.* Fresno, CA: Electric Press, 2003.

Aves, Jonathan. *Post-Soviet Transcaucasia.* London: Royal Institute of International Affairs, 1993.

Baliozian, Ara, ed. *Armenian Wisdom: A Treasury of Quotations and Proverbs.* Glendale, CA: Armenian Reference Books, 1993.

Bardarkjian, Kevork. *A Reference Guide to Modern Armenian Literature.* Detroit: Wayne State University Press, 2000.

Bournoutian, George. *A Concise History of the Armenian People: From Ancient Times to the Present.* Costa Mesa, CA: Mazda Publishers, 2002.

Braund, David. *Georgia in Antiquity: A History of Colchis and Transcaucasian Iberia, 550 B.C.–A.D. 562*. Oxford: Oxford University Press, 1994.

Brook, Stephen. *Claws of the Crab: Georgia and Armenia in Crisis*. London: Pan, 1993.

Brook, Stephen. *Wine People*. New York: Vendome Press, 2001.

Buckley, Mary, ed. *Post-Soviet Women: From the Baltic to Central Asia*. Cambridge: Cambridge University Press, 1997.

Burney, Charles. *The Peoples of the Hills: Ancient Ararat and Caucasus*. London: Phoenix, 2001.

Burns, James. *The Caucasus: Traditions in Weaving*. Seattle: Court Street Press, 1987.

Chalabian, Antranig. *Armenia after the Coming of Islam*. Southfield, MI: A. Chalabian, 2002.

Chatwin, Mary. *Socio-Cultural Transformation and Foodways in the Republic of Georgia*. Commack, NY: Nova Science Publishers, 1997.

Cherry, Ashur. *Armenian Churches*. Toronto: Ashur Cherry, 2001.

Chorbaijian, Levon, Patrick Donabedian, and Claude Mutafian, eds. *The Caucasian Knot: The History and Geopolitics of Nagorno-Karabakh*. London: Zed Books, 1994.

Cornell, Svante. *Small Nations and Great Powers: A Study of Ethnopolitical Conflict in the Caucasus*. Richmond, UK: Curzon, 2001.

Croissant, Michael. *The Armenia-Azerbaijan Conflict: Causes and Implications*. Westport, CT: Praeger, 1998.

Curtis, Glenn, ed. *Armenia, Azerbaijan, and Georgia: Country Studies*. Washington, DC: Federal Research Division, Library of Congress, 1995.

Curzon, Robert. *Armenia: A Year at Erzeroom, and on the Frontiers of Russia, Turkey and Persia*, new ed. London: Cambridge Scholars, 2002.

David, Itzhac. *History of the Jews in the Caucasus*. Tel Aviv: Cavcasioni, 1989.

De Waal, Thomas. *Black Garden: Armenia and Azerbaijan through Peace and War*. New York: New York University Press, 2003.

Dhilawala, Sakina. *Armenia*. New York: Marshall Cavendish Benchmark, 2007.

Dickinson, Sara. *Breaking Ground: Travel and National Culture in Russia from Peter I to the Era of Pushkin; Studies in Literature and Poetics*. Amsterdam: Rodopi, 2006.

Diuk, Nadia, and Adrian Karatnycky, eds. *New Nations Rising: The Fall of the Soviets and the Challenge of Independence*. New York: John Wiley & Sons, 1993.

Draitser, Emil. *Taking Penguins to the Movies*. Detroit: Wayne State University Press, 1998.

Dudwick, Nora. "Out of the Kitchen into the Crossfire: Women in Independent Armenia." In *Commonwealth or Empire? Russia, Central Asia, and the Transcaucasus*, ed. William Odom, 241–263. Washington, DC: Hudson Institute, 1995.

Ekedahl, Carolyn, and Melvin Goodman. *The Wars of Eduard Shevardnadze*. University Park, PA: Penn State University Press, 1987.

Gammer, Moshe. *The Caspian: A Re-emerging Region*. Portland, OR: Frank Cass, 2004.

Gink, Károly, and Ilona Turánszky. *Azerbaijan: Mosques, Turrets, Palaces.* Budapest: Corvina Press, 1979.

Gitelman, Zvi. *A Century of Ambivalence: The Jews of Russia and the Soviet Union, 1881 to the Present,* 2nd ed. Bloomington: Indiana University Press, 2001.

Goldenberg, Suzanne. *Pride of Small Nations: The Caucasus and Post-Soviet Disorder.* London: Zed Books, 1994.

Goldstein, Darra, and Niko Pirosmani., *The Georgian Feast: The Vibrant Culture and Savory Food of the Republic of Georgia.* Berkley: University of California Press, 1999.

Goltz, Thomas. *Azerbaijan Diary: A Rogue Reporter's Adventures in an Oil-Rich, War-Torn, Post-Soviet Republic,* rev. ed. Armonk, NY: M. E. Sharpe, 1998.

Goluboff, Sascha. "Are They Jews or Asians? A Cautionary Tale about Mountain Jew-ish Ethnography." *Slavic Review* 63, no. 1 (2004): 112–137.

Gombos, Károly, and Károly Gink. *Armenia: Landscape and Architecture.* New York: Corvina Press, 1974.

Griffin, Nicholas. *Caucasus: A Journey to the Land between Christianity and Islam.* Chicago: University of Chicago Press, 2004.

Hasratian, Murad, and Zaven Sargsian. *Armenia: 1,700 Years of Christian Architecture.* Yerevan: Moughni Publishers, 2001.

Herzig, Edmund. *The New Caucasus: Armenia, Azerbaijan, and Georgia.* London: RIIA, 1999.

Hewitt, George. *The Abkhazians: A Handbook.* New York: St. Martin's Press, 1998.

Hunter, Shireen. *Transcaucasus in Transition: Nation-Building and Conflict.* Washington, DC: CSIS, 1994.

Kaeter, Margaret. *Nations in Transition: The Caucasian Republics.* New York: Facts on File, 2004.

Kaiser, Robert. *The Geography of Nationalism in Russia and the USSR.* Princeton, NJ: Princeton University Press, 1994.

Kanevskaya, Marina. "The Shortest Path to the Truth: Indirection in Fazil Iskander." *Modern Language Review* 99, no. 1 (January, 2004): 126–149.

Kapidze, Aleksandro. *Caucasus Region: Geopolitical Nexus?* New York: Nova Science Publishers, 2007.

King, David. *Azerbaijan.* New York: Marshall Cavendish Benchmark, 2006.

Komitas, Vardapet. *Armenian Sacred and Folk Music.* Richmond, UK: Curzon Press, 1998.

Lang, David. *Armenia, Cradle of Civilization.* Boston: Allen & Unwin, 1980.

Lang, David. *The Last Years of the Georgian Monarchy, 1658–1832.* New York: Columbia University Press, 1957.

Lang, David. *Lives and Legends of the Georgian Saints.* London: Mowbrays, 1976.

MacPhee, Craig. "Economic Education and Government Reform in the Republic of Georgia." *Journal of Economic Education* 32, no. 1 (Winter 2001): 68–77.

Maranci, Christina. "The Architect Trdat: Building Practices and Cross-Cultural Exchange in Byzantium and Armenia." *Journal of the Society of Architectural Historians* 62, no. 3 (September 2003): 294–305.

Markosyan, Karine, Aramayis Kocharyan, and Artur Potosyan. "Meeting the Challenge of Injection Drug Use and HIV in Armenia." *Health and Human Rights* 9, no. 1 (2006): 134–142.

Marsden, Philip. *The Crossing Place: A Journey among the Armenians*. New York: Kondasha International, 1995.

Menteshashvili, Avtandil, ed. *Trouble in the Caucasus*. New York: Nova Science Publishers, 1995.

Mgaloblishvili, Tamila. *Ancient Christianity in the Caucasus*. Richmond, UK: Curzon Press, 1998.

Mikaberidze, Alexander. *Historical Dictionary of Georgia*. Lanham, MD: Scarecrow Press, 2007.

Najafizadeh, Mehrangiz. "Women's Empowering Carework in Post-Soviet Azerbaijan." *Gender and Society* 17, no. 2 (April 2003): 282–297.

Nasmyth, Peter. *Georgia: In the Mountains of Poetry*. New York: Routledge, 2006.

Nersesiants, Vladik. *The Civilism Manifesto*. London: Simmonds & Hill, 2000.

Pavlović, Zoran, and Charles Gritzner. *Republic of Georgia*. Philadelphia: Chelsea House Publishers, 2002.

Pejić, Bozana, and David Elliott, eds. *After the Wall: Art and Culture in Post-Communist Europe*. Stockholm: Moderna Museet, 1999.

Piddock, Charles. *Republic of Georgia*. Milwaukee, WI: World Almanac Library, 2007.

Rayfield, Donald. *The Literature of Georgia: A History*. Richmond, UK: Curzon Press, 2000.

Ro'I, Yaacov. *Islam in the Soviet Union: From the Second World War to Gorbachev*. New York: Columbia University Press, 2000.

Rumiantsev, Sergei. "The Influence of Urbanization on Forming the Social Structure of Azerbaijan Society" *Central Asia and Caucasus*, no. 30 (June 2004): 105–109.

Shirinian, Lorne, and Alan Whitehorn. *The Armenian Genocide: Resisting the Inertia of Indifference*. Kingston, ON: Blue Heron Press, 2001.

Smith, Graham, Vivien Law, Andrew Wilson, Annette Bohr, and Edward Allworth, eds. *Nation-Building in the Post-Soviet Borderlands: The Politics of National Identities*. Cambridge: Cambridge University Press, 1998.

Smith, Michael. "Cinema for the 'Soviet East': National Fact and Revolutionary Fiction in Early Azerbaijani Film." *Slavic Review* 56, no. 4 (Winter 1997): 645–678.

Steffen, James. "Review of Seven Visions by Sergey Paradjanov." *Film Quarterly* 54, no. 1 (Autumn 2000): 59–60.

Streissguth, Thomas. *The Transcaucasus*. San Diego: Lucent Books, 2001.

Suny, Ronald. *The Baku Commune, 1917–1918*. Princeton, NJ: Princeton University Press, 1972.

Suny, Ronald. *Looking toward Ararat: Armenia in Modern History*. Bloomington: Indiana University Press, 1993.